Employment Guarantee Programme and Pro-Poor Growth

Published by Academic Foundation
in association with

I • D • F

CFDA
CENTRE FOR
DEVELOPMENT
ALTERNATIVES

Indira Hirway has a Masters degree in Economics from Delhi School of Economics and PhD from Bombay University. She is Director, Centre for Development Alternatives, Ahmedabad. Her areas of interest include: development alternatives, employment and labour, poverty and human development, environment and development, time-use studies etc., on which she has published several books and articles in national and international journals. She has been a visiting faculty/fellow to several universities in Europe and USA, and has been associated with several national and international expert groups, advisory committees, and policymaking bodies.

M.R. Saluja has a Masters degree in Mathematics from Delhi University and a Masters in Statistics from the Indian Statistical Institute. He has published widely in reputed journals, a number of them relating to database, input-output techniques, social accounting matrices (SAM), tourist satellite accounts and poverty. The titles of two of his books are Indian Official Statistical System and Input-Output Tables for India: Concepts, Construction and Applications. His third book, Social Accounting Matrix for India: Concepts, Construction and Applications relates to the construction and applications of SAM for the Indian economy for the years 1994-95, 1997-98 and 2002-03. Recently, he led the technical team that helped the working group that revised the methodology for estimating state level poverty incidence carried by the Planning Commission. He has been an advisor to both the national and various state governments. He is a Fellow of India Development Foundation and has been there since its inception.

Bhupesh Yadav graduated in Commerce from Andhra University. He then completed a postgraduate diploma in Finance and Marketing from SIES College of Management Studies, Mumbai. He has work experience of eight years, having worked with Centre for Monitoring Indian Economy (CMIE) before joining IDF. His areas of interest are construction of SAM, input-output tables for India and states and working with large datasets such as Census, NSS (National Sample Survey), and ASI (Annual survey of Industries). He has been an important member of the team that has constructed the latest all-India SAM and the latest input-output tables for the Planning Commission, Government of India and the Central Statistical Office. He is currently working as a Fellow at IDF.

Employment Guarantee Programme and Pro-Poor Growth

The Study of a Village in Gujarat

INDIRA HIRWAY
M.R. SALUJA
BHUPESH YADAV

ACADEMIC FOUNDATION
NEW DELHI

First published in 2010
by

ACADEMIC FOUNDATION
4772-73 / 23 Bharat Ram Road, (23 Ansari Road),
Darya Ganj, New Delhi - 110 002 (India).
Phones : 23245001 / 02 / 03 / 04.
Fax : +91-11-23245005.
E-mail : books@academicfoundation.com
www. academicfoundation.com

in association with

India Development Foundation
&
Centre for Development Alternatives

Cataloging in Publication Data--DK
Courtesy: D.K. Agencies (P) Ltd. <docinfo@dkagencies.com>

Hirway, Indira.
Employment guarantee programme and pro-poor growth : the study of a village in Gujarat / Indira Hirway, M.R. Saluja, Bhupesh Yadav.
p. cm
Includes bibliographical references (p.).
ISBN 13: 9788171888481
ISBN 10: 8171888480

1. India. National Rural Employment Guarantee Act, 2005. 2. National Rural Employment Guarantee Scheme (India). 3. Guaranteed annual income--India--Nana Kotda. 4. Rural poor--Government policy--India--Nana Kotda. I. Saluja, M. R., joint author. II. Yadav, Bhupesh, joint author. III. Title.

DDC 331.11095475 22

Typeset and cover design: Italics India, New Delhi.

Printed and bound in India.

Contents

List of Tables, Figures and Appendices

Tables

Figures

Appendices

Preface

This study is a part of the project entitled *From Unpaid Work to Public Service Job creation: Towards a Strategy for Pro-Poor Economic Development and Gender Equity*. The aim of the project was to examine the economic and gender equality implications of public job creation in economic activities currently served by unpaid work, including unpaid care work. This book, an outcome of the Indian part of the study, has been undertaken with a view to assess the impact of substituting portions of unpaid work by employment guarantee programmes in a village economy.

The study was commissioned by the Levy Economics Institute of Bard College, New York (US) to Centre for Development Alternatives, Ahmedabad (India). We would like to express our thanks to Dr. Dimitri Papadimitriou and Dr. Rania Antonopoulos of Levy Institute for giving us this opportunity to undertake this study. We are also thankful to Dr. Marzia Fontana of Levy Institute for her expert comments and suggestions on the draft report.

We are thankful to Dr. Shubhashis Gangopadhyay, Research Director of India Development Foundation, for his comments and suggestions at different points of time.

We are also thankful to Mr. Jagdishbhai, the village *sarpanch* and Mr. Kantibhai Patel, the *talati* (revenue incharge) of Nana Kotda village for taking interest and sparing time for discussions related to our study. The BDO (block development officer) of Idar block and Mr. S.M. Ninama, the project officer (NREGA), helped us in understanding the functioning of NREGS in Idar block and in Nana Kotda village. Their help is much appreciated.

We would also like to express our thanks to Jyotika Shah, Kanubhai Lakum and Raghubhai Desai from CFDA for providing research support to this study and to Yogesh Ringwala and Roja Nair for their valuable administrative support.

And finally, and perhaps most importantly, we are grateful to all the villagers, men and women, of Nana Kotda for sparing hours and days for us to discuss the different aspects of the village economy, the NREGS and innumerable other matters, all of which helped us to understand the ground realities better.

Indira Hirway

M.R. Saluja

Bhupesh Yadav

1 Employment Guarantee

A Critical Component of Full Employment Strategy in Developing Countries

> There is plenty of evidence that unemployment has many far reaching effects other than loss of income, including psychological harm, loss of work motivation, skill and self confidence; increase in ailment and morbidity (and even mortality); disruption is family relations and social life; hardening of social exclusion and accentuation of racial tensions and gender asymmetries (Amartya Sen, 2000).

It is now recognised that ensuring employment to all those who are willing and ready to work is an important goal for any economy. It is accepted that benefits of employment are microeconomic as well as macroeconomic, and there is an important mutually reinforcing relationship between economic and social benefits of employment. At the individual level, employment increases financial security and promotes higher living standards; improves physical and mental health; raises self-esteem and self-confidence; and enables a person to become a responsible citizen. At the macro level, full employment ensures financial and macroeconomic stability; ensures social and political stability by reducing social tensions, crime and conflicts; and promotes economic and social multiplier effects (Fullwiler, 2005).

The goal of ensuring employment to all is very much in line with Article 23 of the UN Declaration of Human Rights that states that "Every one has a right to work, to free choice of employment, to just and favourable conditions of work and to protection against unemployment (Universal Declaration of Human Rights, UN, 1948). The ILO Convention 122 also reiterates this goal. The Convention declares, "With a view to stimulating economic growth and development, raising levels of living, meeting manpower requirements and overcoming unemployment and under-employment, each Member shall declare and pursue, as a major goal, an active policy designed to promote full, productive and freely chosen employment." It is further declared that the said policy shall aim at ensuring that: (1) there is work for all who are available for and seeking work, (2) such work is as productive as possible, and (3) there is freedom of choice of employment and the fullest possible opportunity for each worker...select work irrespective of race, colour, sex, religion, political opinion, national extraction or social origin. (*www.ilo.org*)

Legal guarantee of work therefore, can be considered as a part of global commitment to full employment by nations. Apart from having the intrinsic value of guarantee of work, an employment guarantee programme (EGP), to a considerable extent, answers the employment crisis in the developing world that has become increasingly acute over the past few decades.

The Employment Challenge in Developing Countries

The recent trends in the global labour market are highly unfavourable in several ways. Between 1995-2005, open unemployment has grown by 22 per cent, putting the global unemployment rate at 6.3 per cent. The output growth during this period has been higher than the employment growth, which has not been matching with the growth of the global labour force. The annual average output growth has been 1 per cent as against 0.3 per cent rate of growth of employment. The employment elasticity of growth at the global level is low and is observed to be declining during the past decades (Rodgers, 2007; ILO, 2009).

In the case of most developing countries, the situation is much worse. The rate of growth of employment in these countries has been much lower than the rate of growth of labour force, adding to the already existing large stock of unemployment. Most new jobs are created in the informal economy, with the result that the size of the working poor has been increasing in these economies. In 2005, 48 per cent of workers were observed to be poor on $2 a day criterion in these economies, and 18 per cent workers were poor on $1 a day criterion in these economies.

The gaps between winner and loser (developing) countries as well as between winners and losers within countries seem to have widened over the years. These gaps refer to rural-urban gaps, regional gaps as well as gaps within different socioeconomic groups. Along with rising inequalities, there are rising vulnerabilities and insecurities emanating from increased incidence of shocks and uncertainties (Devereux and Solomon, 2006; Standing, 2004). Several country level studies, have shown that the overall employment situation is fast deteriorating in developing countries under the policies of liberalisation and globalisation (Epstein and Heintz, 2006; Altman, 2007; Devereux and Soloman, 2006). One common observation of most country studies in Africa, Asia and Latin America is that irrespective of the weak or strong growth performance, unemployment is increasing, as economic growth has not been able to generate adequate employment for the labour force; the employment elasticity is declining; and the quality of employment is also deteriorating. Another observation is that many of these countries have suffered heavily from the recent financial crisis leading to loss of employment and incomes, on a large scale.

In short, the neoliberal policies have treated employment very indifferently, creating severe shortages of decent work opportunities in most developing countries. How to reverse these trends is a major challenge faced by policymakers.

Neoliberal Policies and Deteriorating Employment Scene

The neoliberal policies have impacted on the employment scene in developing countries in multiple ways: Firstly, under neoliberal policies, a high rate of growth is achieved through a jump in technical progress, leading to increasingly capital-intensive technologies, which is accompanied by declining labour intensity.

When developing countries under neoliberal policies open up to the global economy, they import high capital intensive technology from industrialised countries, (which are on the frontiers of technology). Many developing countries have achieved a high rate of growth through taking a jump in technology and in labour productivity. The higher the technical progress, the higher has been the labour productivity and the higher has been the rate of growth of the economy. However, this is accompanied by a sharp decline in employment elasticity, i.e. lower rate of growth of employment per unit of output. Creating massive employment outside agriculture, to transfer bulk of surplus labour from agriculture to the non-primary modern sectors, therefore, still remains a formidable task in these economies. The present industrialised countries could achieve a substantial shift in the workforce from agriculture to non-agriculture during the period of their rapid growth in the past in spite of the use of capital-intensive technology, because they had highly favourable global conditions.[1] Since these conditions are not available to the developing countries today, they are not likely to enjoy high technical progress along with rapid employment growth.

Though improved labour productivity is welcome in these economies, where masses (of poor) are employed at a very low productivity, it is necessary that this jump in productivity is made accessible, at least in the medium term, to all the sectors and all the sections of the population, so that it does not create a wide/wider gap between the productivities of workers, resulting in dualistic growth of these economies. That is, economic growth should not create a situation where a small modern sector enjoys high tech and high incomes and the majority is left in low productivity low income sectors. Unfortunately, under neoliberal policies there is no built-in mechanism that ensures generation of adequate employment at high productivity. In the absence of this mechanism, most developing countries have fallen in the trap of dualistic growth leading to large inequalities in the economy on the one hand and an army of unemployed on the other. This lopsided growth has also created aggregate demand deficiency in these economies, restricting the sustainability of its growth process.

Secondly, growth of labour-intensive exports has increased employment opportunities in many developing economies, but with

1. The industrialised countries had four favourable conditions: (1) massive emigration from Europe to the "new world", (2) the production of machinery for consumer goods itself was labour-intensive, (3) markets available in colonies and (4) export of "the unemployed" from Europe to outside (Patnaik, 2007).

poor quality of work. This is because, the producers of these goods are subjected to several pressures from the global production networks, which are usually in the hands of large multinational corporations (MNCs). The global production networks, which control the global market, keep a few core activities with themselves and distribute labour-intensive production activities among developing countries, depending on the comparative advantages in the value chains. Developing countries, which are in cut-throat competition with each other to acquire orders from global production networks, are at the receiving end under this lopsided structure in the global market. They are forced to restructure their production, to meet: (1) the need for technological up-gradation to compete in the global market, (2) the need to expand the size of the units to increase the control over the value chains for better bargaining in the global market, (3) the need to acquire flexibility in production to address the fluctuating demand in the volatile global market, and (4) the need to minimise cost of production to compete in the global market. The restructuring of production leads to subcontracting of production to acquire flexibility and reduction in cost of labour, both leading to creation of sub-standard employment for workers. In short, developing countries are pressurised to lower the quality of employment under neoliberal policies (Hirway, 2008). How to ensure quality employment to workers under the new environment is another major challenge faced by policymakers.

Thirdly, opening of the economies has frequently led to import of cheap products from outside, as developed countries produce cheaper goods with their superior technologies. These imports have been observed to have led to closure of domestic units in some cases, leading to loss of jobs. In addition, opening of the economies to the global market has also exposed these economies to increased global competition, leading to uncertainties and vulnerability, and to increased economic insecurity. It is observed by ILO, for example, that the recent economic and technological developments (including social and political developments) have accentuated the insecurities experienced by people across the world, and particularly in developing countries. It is observed that the neoliberal policy regime is actually dependent on insecurity, as there is no state-based social and economic security, portrayed as the welfare state and a complex way of protective regulations and institutions in the new policy regime. The present society is "a risk society" (ILO, 2004), as most groups, and particularly the groups at the bottom, are exposed to the uncertainty and risks, which have emanated from the new policy regime. Work related insecurity is an important component of economic insecurity. It comprises employment insecurity, income insecurity, work insecurity, job insecurity, and skill related insecurity. How to provide protection and support, particularly to the poor at the bottom, in this uncertain environment, is the third major challenge for policymakers.

Lastly, the new developments in the economies have not treated women well, in the sense that women have lost in several ways as compared to men. As it is, women suffer from segregation as well as discrimination in most labour markets due to their low human capital, labour market segmentation, socio-cultural biases on the part of employers and domestic responsibilities, which restrict their supply in multiple ways, with the result that women workers lag behind men in most labour market outcomes. Liberalisation seems to have accentuated these gender inequalities in the labour market. How to reduce gender inequalities in the labour market in the face of liberalisation is one more challenge to policymakers.

Alternative Approaches

One finds several alternative approaches presented in the literature to address the slow growth of employment, the deteriorating quality of employment, and the increased economic insecurity of people—particularly at the bottom.

For raising the rate of growth of employment, one approach could be to mainstream employment in developing strategy and policies by treating it as the primary objective of development and making other dimensions, *viz.*, growth rate, technology, balance of payments etc. dependent upon it. For this approach to be applied, the amount of employment required to be generated has to be assessed as also the employment likely to be generated by any given rate and structure of growth. Such an approach has not been found feasible and has, therefore, never been attempted (Papola, 2008). This is because: (1) the economic growth required to generate the needed employment during a given period of time, may be much higher than the available resources, (2) the structure of output resulting from purely employment oriented growth may not correspond to the pattern of demand, and (3) such an approach in an economy with low level of income and high incidence of poverty may prove self-defeating, as it may not ensure a reasonable level of income from work.

Promotion of labour-intensive sectors is, yet another approach recommended by many experts. This approach ensures that economic growth tends to be labour-intensive, along with rising labour productivity. This in turn ensures that the levels of incomes of the workforce improves, raising the aggregate demand in the economy. In other words, this approach generates productive employment for the unemployed on the one hand, and raises the aggregate demand to push the economy upwards on the other. The Government of India has adopted this strategy and it is to be implemented with fresh efforts in the Eleventh Five Year Plan (Planning Commission, 2008). According to the Plan, this has to be achieved: (1) by encouraging the corporate sector to move into more labour-intensive sectors and (2) by facilitating expansion of employment and output of the unorganised enterprises that operate in the labour-intensive sectors.

Two important questions need to be asked in this context: (1) what will happen to the people at the bottom till the labour-intensive sectors are developed enough to generate adequate employment opportunities in the economy? Do we leave them to their fate? And (2) is it feasible to use the labour of the un/underemployed to promote the labour-intensive sectors in the economy? Can we use an EGP to move towards labour intensive economic growth? We believe that a well designed EGP, preferably with the legal component of guarantee to work, can reply both these questions positively.

Right-to-Income Approach *versus* Right-to-Work Approach

It is frequently argued, however, that the right to income approach (i.e. the cash transfer approach), under which the needy are given a right to a minimum income for maintaining a living standard, is better than the right to employment approach or EGP approach[2] under which a legal right to employment is given by the state, to all those who are willing and ready to work at a certain (minimum) level of wages.[3] It is argued by the proponents of the cash transfer approach that this is the best tool to address shocks, hazards and insecurities faced by people under globalisation, because: (1) it has low administrative costs, (2) it can reach directly to the least secure and most vulnerable, (3) it gives the poor freedom to use the cash as per their own priorities and emergencies, (4) it does not force the poor to do the hard work which is usually the case under an EGP, and (5) it respects human dignity and human freedom.

Cash transfer schemes have been used in Latin American countries like Brazil, Mexico, Chile, Bolivia, Peru etc. and several African countries like Zimbabwe, Zambia, Ghana, South Africa, Uganda, Burkina Faso, Botswana, Ethiopia, Malawi etc. as well as in Asian countries like India, Bangladesh, Sri Lanka and few East Asian countries (during the last financial crisis).[4] Several evaluation studies of these programmes have shown that these programmes have been largely successful in poverty reduction, particularly of the destitute, critically poor and incapacitated. In other words, cash transfers appear to be the most appropriate and cost-effective tool to reduce hunger and the suffering of households that are at the bottom of the rung (Standing, 2007; ILO, 2004; Farrington and Slater, 2006; Mitchel, 2007; Tcherneva and Wray, 2006; Kakwani and

---

2. or the Employer of the Last Resort (ELR) approach.
3. There is a third approach, the communitarian model, where the workers are entitled to their minimum needs by belonging to a communal society. The Chinese model in the past was close to this model. This model, however is not relevant here, as it requires specific political conditions not prevailing in most developing countries. However, a few lessons which can be learnt from the Chinese experience is that: (1) surplus manpower, if utilised systematically for land and water resource management, can lead to agricultural growth and promotion to growth of allied activities and (2) collective self-interest can play an important role in the success of public works programmes (Hirway and Terhal, 1994).
4. Important cash transfer programmes are: Cash for Relief Programme, Ethiopia (2003); Emergency Cash Relief Programme, Somalia (2003); Social Cash Transfer, Zambia (2003); Cash for Herds Scheme, Mongolia; Bosla Familia, Brazil; Cash for Education, Bangladesh; Cash for School Attendance, South Africa; Schooling Subsidy, Mexico; Social Pensions, Latin America etc.

Soares, 2005). Some of the problems faced under cash transfer are in terms of targeting (there are leakages), pilferage (corruption) of funds and delays. However, geographical or universal targeting, use of bank accounts etc. help considerably (Kakwani and Soares, 2005; Farrington and Slater, 2006).

There are basically three types of cash transfers, namely, social assistance, i.e. cash transfer to households without bread winners, (i.e. destitute and incapacitated households); cash transfer for specific objectives, such as for promoting children's education, malnutrition etc. and cash transfer to households, who have workers but are not able to get work or earn enough to live on. Out of these, the first and second type of cash transfers are desirable, but need to be managed efficiently. The third type of cash transfers have been a point of controversy. These transfers have been observed to encourage complacency among beneficiaries, promote corruption and kill incentive to work. Again, there is a question of affordability of these transfers. Since cash transfers through deficit financing can prove to be highly inflationary, these have to be financed by government budgets. However, government budgets in developing countries cannot usually afford large scale cash transfers. It is necessary therefore, to limit cash transfers to the needy groups, i.e. destitute, incapacitated and those unable to work.

What is more important however is that the poor need work to lead a life of dignity and not just for cash (even if as a right). As seen earlier, employment has many advantages, which cash in hand does not have. Also, the poor in developing countries do not have many employment opportunities to choose productive work with cash in hand, as the economies are not developed enough to provide such opportunities or choices on a scale. These countries need infrastructure development and natural resources management that contribute towards expansion of employment opportunities in these economies. And this can happen only if the labour of the poor is used in a planned manner, through an EGP, to create such opportunities.

An EGP has clearly an edge over cash transfers, particularly in the case of the unemployed, for achieving poverty reduction and for promoting employment-intensive growth in developing countries.

EGP as Tool to Move towards Full Employment

Under an EGP, the national government provides/guarantee work to all those who are willing and ready to work at a fixed minimum level of wages. Such programmes have been used by developed and developing countries for different reasons: to ameliorate the after-effects of financial crisis (for example, Jefes programme in Argentina, Padat Karya in Indonesia, Master Plan for Tackling Unemployment in South Korea), to ensure food security (Rural Maintenance Programme and Food for Work Programme in Bangladesh, Ethiopia and in many other countries); to stabilise economy during the downward trend of business cycles in developed countries (the Netherlands, Sweden and USA) and to address structural poverty (labour based infrastructural programmes in Ghana, Zimbabwe and many other African countries, including Expanded Public Works Programme in South Africa). India also has used this programme for ameliorating effects of droughts, to ensure food security during the lean season, and to address structural poverty (NREGA). Guaranteeing employment, by national governments, to ensure full employment has emerged as an important strategy at the global level.

In the case of developing countries, these programmes are designed to meet the immediate needs like ensuring a minimum income to the households affected by economic crisis, eliminating starvation in the face of structural poverty, and providing supplementary employment to the under-employed or seasonally unemployed. After meeting this objective, however, these programmes are also used for achieving different objectives in different countries:

- South Africa, Malawi, Ghana, Zimbabwe, Uganda and several other African countries have designed public works programmes for constructing socioeconomic infrastructure facilities, following the ILO strategy of constructing labour based infrastructure. Expanded Public Works Programme (EPWP) of South Africa is worth noting here. The EPWP includes social services and natural resource management also under its purview.
- Argentina, Brazil and some other Latin American countries have used wage employment programmes for providing support to the families affected by financial crisis. They provide employment in

social services related to child care, health and nutrition for the poor, education and skill training etc. These temporary programmes are expected: (1) to protect the crisis affected families and (2) to improve employability of the participants so that they can get a job outside as the situation improves. Jefes of Argentina is one of the most famous programmes here.

- Indonesia and South Korea designed a wage employment programme (Padat Karya of Indonesia and Master Plan for Tackling Unemployment in South Korea) following the financial crisis in the late 1990s. This programme included construction of socioeconomic infrastructure as well as social services in the areas of education & skill training, health & nutrition etc. to help the crisis affected households in their respective countries.
- Countries like Bangladesh have used public employment programmes for maintenance of public roads on a massive scale. These programmes provide regular employment along with ensuring good maintenance of public roads.
- India has designed an EGP to guarantee employment at a minimum wages for manual work. The programme neither includes skill training nor social services.

A common feature of all the programmes is ensuring employment to all in crisis (immediate objective) and expansion of employment opportunities in the medium/long term, by constructing productive assets which promote growth of labour-intensive sectors, such as agriculture; allied activities like animal husbandry and dairying, forestry, fishery etc. and promote small enterprises in food processing, textile and garments, leather and leather goods, basic social services etc.

Size of EGP/Employment Programmes and their Impact

The impact of an EGP or a wage employment programme (or public works programme) on an economy in the second and third rounds in terms of generation of mainstream employment depends on the size of the EGP. In fact, an EGP can play an important role in promoting full employment only if it is implemented on a scale so that it can generate a significant number of assets that can expand the labour absorbing capacity of the mainstream economy. In order to ensure a large impact of an EGP therefore, there is a need to expand the programme to its full potential. Incorporation of a guarantee component can help here, as the programme becomes demand driven and flexible, allowing it to expand to meet the total demand for wage employment in the economy.

However, even a small EGP can have a positive impact on the level of employment if it is planned well. What needs to be underlined is that an EGP or a wage employment programme needs to be planned well, keeping in mind its long-term goals.

Looking into the conditions of most developing countries at present, one can suggest that an EGP should have the following activities included in its purview: (1) strong natural resource management on a massive scale, for promoting agriculture and allied activities as well as for producing raw materials for several labour-intensive industries like textiles and garments, dairying and animal husbandry, leather and leather products, food processing etc. (2) basic infrastructural facilities like rural and urban roads, feeder roads etc. to promote tiny, small and medium enterprises, and (3) drinking water, sanitation and other infrastructure for health and education to improve labour productivity. A well-designed employment guarantee programme can incorporate these features along with guaranteeing productive employment to all at minimum wages with good working conditions. Since, these are the sectors in which majority of the poor in developing countries are located are covered here. There is, therefore, considerable overlapping between promotion of labour-intensive sectors and increase in the productivity, and incomes of the poor.

It needs to be underlined therefore that the role of an EGP is much more than guaranteeing work to the poor, because guarantee alone will have limited impact on employment generation in the economy. The guarantee can be treated as an end itself only under the assumption that the development process of the developing economies under the neoliberal policy regime will generate adequate employment opportunities in the medium term to absorb the surplus manpower, including additions to the labour force. However, looking into the experiences in recent past, this assumption does not seem to be realistic. If, however, developing economies focus on an EGP without worrying about strengthening its links with the macroeconomic development process, the EGP can end up as a permanent burden on the national exchequer, as it will always be needed for the growing size of the bypassed and marginalised labour force.

STRENGTHENING LINKS BETWEEN EGP AND FULL EMPLOYMENT PATH

There are several possible links between an EGP and a full employment growth path in developing countries. That is, in addition to the immediate impact in terms of poverty reduction, a well-designed employment guarantee programme can lead the economy towards labour intensive growth path that is also a pro-poor growth path.

Strengthening the Sectors in which the Poor are Predominant

One common feature of most developing countries, at present, is that the majority of the poor and the marginalised are located in agriculture and allied activities, which suffer from low productivity as well as uncertainty arising from fluctuating production and incomes. Population depending on these sectors, therefore, experiences a high incidence of poverty and vulnerability. For example, agricultural sector in India suffers from low productivity in most parts of the country; it is highly unstable as it is subjected to fluctuations in rainfall (majority of cropped area in India is rainfed, without surety of water supply); and majority of the poor (working poor and un/under-employed) are located in this sector (Bhalla, 2007).

An employment guarantee programme can be planned in a way that it stabilises these sectors by reducing fluctuations and promotes their growth by raising labour productivity.

This can be done by undertaking the following works under an EGP:

- Irrigation schemes, including minor irrigation schemes to ensure water availability,
- Construction of water harvesting structures including farm ponds as well as revival of traditional structures like ponds and tanks,

- Watershed development for improving land and water management to enhance productivity of land,
- Regeneration of common lands for achieving higher productivity in forestry, fishery, animal husbandry, dairy etc.—by digging fishponds, undertaking plantations, promoting fodder farms,
- Undertaking forestation on wastelands etc. and
- Improving connectivity through construction of feeder roads, milk roads etc. infrastructure facilities.

The long experience of natural resource management (NRM) in developing countries however shows that ad hoc selection of NRM works at a local level can distort and harm natural systems, some times irreparably; can create conflicts between villages or between regions; and can become non-sustainable. It is necessary, therefore, to see that natural resources are planned systematically. To start with, NRM needs to be viewed in the context of a larger scene. For example, water conservation and water harvesting structures at the village level need to be planned with reference to macro watershed and the relevant river basin. Water harvesting structures like check dams planned at the village level in isolation may corner water at the cost of neighbouring villages. Also, an isolated structure here and another there is not likely to lead to systematic water harvesting or systematic watershed development. Similarly, drought-proofing has to be promoted under a sound regional strategy. Isolated forestation or water structures will not lead to drought proofing.

In short, ad hoc works without any context of the macro watershed and river basin, will not be of much use. The lessons learnt from the long experience of NRM present some "non-negotiable principles of development and management of natural resources in sustainable manner" (Development Support Centre, 2000).[5] These principles

5. These 8 principles include: (1) community based organisations of primary stakeholders at the centre of planning, budgeting, implementation and management of natural resources, (2) management of natural resources for achieving social, economic equity, (3) decentralisation in the planning and management of natural resources, (4) appointing a facilitating agency (NGO) with professional and multiple skills for motivating and organising people, (5) participatory evaluation and monitoring—concurrent, midcourse and outcome based, through independent expert agency, (6) allocation of resources for training and software inputs, (7) ensuring use of the works completed and (8) organisational restructuring for implementing these principles.

underscore the importance of systematic planning on the one hand and emphasise the role of community participation on the other.

Systematic regeneration of natural resources will have multiple impact on the sectors in which the majority of the poor are located: (1) it will stabilise agriculture, encourage multiple cropping and enhance its productivity, (2) increase employment opportunities in agriculture in general and particularly in the lean season, and (3) promote diversification within the primary sector. The surplus generated in the process will also enable diversification of economic activities into non-farm sectors. The EGP will, thus, create an enabling environment for the growth of the sectors which are predominated by the poor including working poor, unemployed and under-employed.

In addition, as Figure 1.1 shows, these assets generated under an EGP can improve the asset base of poor farmers and the poor engaged in animal husbandry, fishery etc. thereby, reduce their vulnerability, improve their access to credit, technology etc.

Figure 1.1

Impact of EGP on Agriculture and Allied Sectors

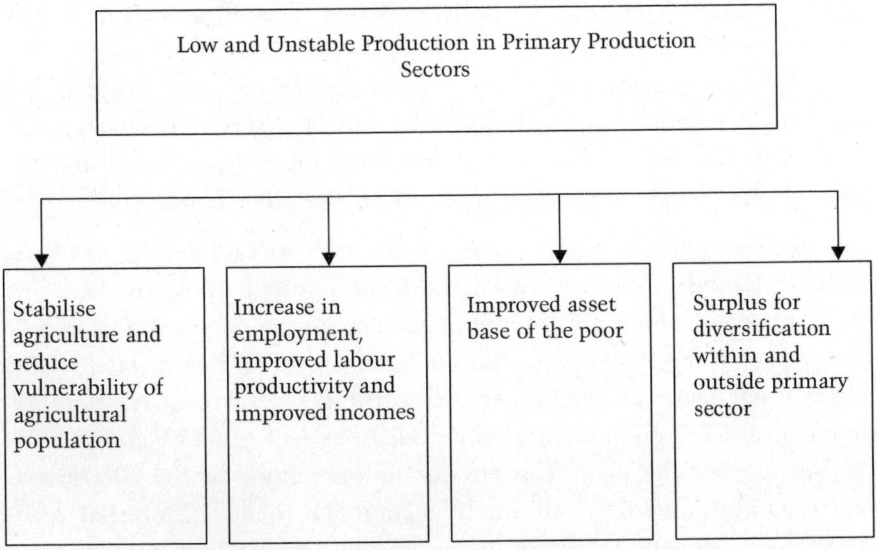

Construction of Socioeconomic Infrastructure for Promoting Employment-Intensive Development

Absence of adequate socioeconomic infrastructure is one of the major causes of low level of development, of developing economies. Construction of these basic infrastructure facilities under an EGP can be a good link between labour-intensive construction of infrastructure and employment-intensive economic development.

Socioeconomic infrastructure will include: (1) approach road and other roads, i.e. feeder roads, milk roads that improve connectivity, (2) water harvesting for ensuring water supply and construction of pipelines for ensuring water supply at the doorstep, (3) drainage, sanitation and arrangements for disposal of solid and liquid waste, (4) internal roads including paving of internal roads, (5) housing for the poor, (6) construction of buildings for basic educational and health services, and (7) economic infrastructure like marketing yards, godowns, community centres etc.

Once again, there is a need to plan these systematically. Construction of infrastructure at different levels requires a systematic and a multilevel approach. Ad hoc selection of works, based on the 'needs' of local people can be both inefficient as well as expensive. All infrastructure facilities cannot be located anywhere and everywhere. For example, each village cannot have a secondary school, or a hospital or a godown or a marketing yard. The location of a service/infrastructure, thus, depends on the threshold population on the one hand and the distance that people are willing to travel on the other hand.

According to the service centre approach, primary service centre or each settlement should have all the basic physical infrastructure and social services, which are important for ensuring a minimum quality of life to people, particularly to the poor (for example, health facility and educational facility) and for ensuring their access to developmental opportunities. Construction of these facilities will generate considerable employment for the poor. The physical infrastructure at the village level will broadly include: (1) all weather approach road, (2) internal roads connecting different localities in the village, (3) drinking water facility, preferably from local sources, from rainwater harvesting structures and distribution of drinking water within the village, (4) village drainage system for disposal of used water and its reuse, (5) sanitation and public hygiene including arrangement for waste disposal etc. The basic social infrastructure in the village will include pre-school, primary school, midday meal arrangements, drinking water and toilet in schools, as well as drinking water, sanitation and public hygiene. Similarly, the secondary and tertiary services at the block level will have to be planned in an optimum manner. These services will include educational services like a secondary school or a higher secondary school, hostel, health services will include a public health centre with beds, a maternity ward etc. and the physical infrastructure like inter-connecting roads for villages, godown and market, a (cooperative) bank, a post office etc. The territory service centres will provide much higher level of services.

Figure 1.2

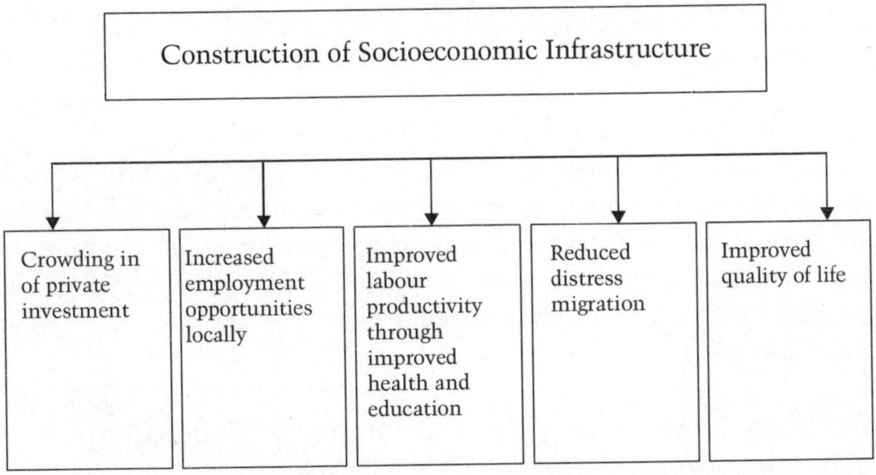

The first major impact of construction of basic socioeconomic infrastructure facilities will be crowding in of private investments, as better opportunities will be available for starting new enterprises. This will increase employment opportunities locally. And since the new employment will increase purchasing power of the masses, it will increase production of wage goods that will be labour-intensive in character.

Improved health and educational facilities will enhance labour productivity, which will, in turn, give a push to economic growth. It will also improve access of the poor to skilled employment with higher productivity.

Another impact will be in terms of reduced distress migration of the poor. It has been observed that the neoliberal policies have increased seasonal or short-term national and international migration of people in search of work. This distress migration has been frequently at low wages, at poor terms of employment, trapping the poor in low income equilibrium. A well-designed EGP, with a guarantee of local employment, can reduce distress migration considerably. Alternatively, it can raise the wages in their jobs in the destinations. Reduction in distress migration will improve access of the poor to local health and educational opportunities (particularly children) and to developmental opportunities.

Improved local infrastructure will improve quality of life of people in multiple ways. It is usually the poor, and the areas in which the poor live, that suffer from inadequate basic socioeconomic infrastructure facilities, like drinking water, sanitation, roads etc. This is because local bodies do not have funds or willingness to spend on infrastructure for the poor. A well-designed EGP can change this situation radically. An EGP can thus, bring about radical changes in the quality of life of the poor, which in turn can bring about considerable increase in their productivity.

Addressing Unpaid Work of Women for Promoting Women's Work in the Labour Market

The third major link between an EGP and the development process is through reduction in the unpaid work. Unpaid work essentially means the work that does not receive any direct remuneration. It includes unpaid SNA (Systems of National Accounts) work, covered under the production boundary of the UNSNA as well as unpaid non-SNA work. Unpaid SNA work includes non-marketed production of goods (which has been included under the UNSNA after the expansion of the production boundary), such as collection of free consumption goods like water, fuel wood etc. raw materials for income generating activities like fodder for animal husbandry, leaves, bamboo or wood for crafts and other manufacturing, and other subsistence work on farms, in forestry, fishery etc. Unpaid SNA work usually has low productivity—is time consuming and involves drudgery. Unpaid non-SNA work includes domestic work consisting of household upkeep (washing, cleaning, cooking and shopping for household etc.) and care of children, the sick, old, disabled in the household, and community services.

Women in general and women in developing countries in particular spend considerable time on unpaid SNA activities and unpaid non-SNA activities. Time use studies in Latin America (Brazil, Mexico, Chile, Nicaragua, Argentina), Africa (Benin, Malawi, Guinea, Morocco, Tanzania, Nigeria, Madagascar, Mauritius) and Asia (Mongolia, Nepal, Thailand, India, Philippines) have shown that unpaid work, both SNA and non-SNA, is highly unequally distributed between men and women with women carrying the major burden of this work (Hirway, 2007). It has been observed that women spend up to 20-25 per cent of their productive time in the labour market on collection of basic goods like fuel wood, water, fruits, vegetables, leaves etc. as well as on collection of raw materials like fodder, wood etc. for family enterprise. Also, women spend up to 30-40 per cent of their time on non-SNA activities (men spend much less time on these activities). These activities are usually time consuming drudgery that restrict women's access to high productivity work in the labour market and consume their energy resulting in their time stress. Consequently, women's workforce participation as well as intensity of their participation in the mainstream labour market declines considerably.

Since this work of women is invisible in statistics and is unpaid (as it does not receive any remuneration) in nature, women's work is not recognised and they are assigned inferior status (subordinate) at home, leading to patriarchal values in the household.

This inferior status at home is reflected in their inferior status in the labour market, because: (1) women enter the labour market with the burden of domestic responsibilities that deprives them of level playing field in the labour market, (2) women experience less opportunities for human capital formation due to the patriarchal values at home, as well as limited time and energy to access opportunities for skills in the labour market, (3) women are less mobile in their job due to domestic responsibilities, and (4) women tend to be subordinate to men and tend to become meek and docile as workers. As a consequence of all this, women enjoy lower status in the labour market in terms of their participation, employment status, the incidence of unemployment, wage rates, diversification and opportunities for upward mobility. Though women's lower status in the labour market has been attributed by scholars to their lower human capital, discrimination against women, segmentation of labour market for women and low access to information for women, at the root of these explanations is the higher burden of unpaid work on women and the consequences thereof.

An EGP can reduce women's unpaid work in multiple ways, as shown in Appendix A-1.1 at the end of this chapter. It indicates that the time spent by poor/women on non-market unpaid economic activities such as: (1) acquiring basic needs like fuel wood, water etc. and (2) on collecting raw material for income generating activities, can be reduced by suitable public assets like regeneration of common lands, construction of water harvesting structures etc. Similarly, the time spent on unpaid domestic services like care of children, care of the old, the sick and the disabled, maintenance of non-durable houses etc. can be reduced by constructing suitable infrastructural facilities. A well-designed EGP can relieve unpaid workers from their drudgery and provide them a better access to the labour market, and a better status in the labour market. That is, an EGP can reduce gender inequalities in the labour market by empowering women.

A paradox observed in developing countries is the simultaneous existence of sizeable un/under-employment on the one hand and sizeable unpaid work, on the other. If a part of unpaid work is brought into public domain through constructing suitable infrastructure, unpaid workers can be released for productive work in the labour market.

Figure 1.3 presents how this can happen. When an EGP reduces women's work, the first major impact will be that women will have more time available to take up more productive work in the market.

Secondly, reduction in time stress of women will enable them to access leisure and educational/skill related opportunities. This will improve women's labour productivity in the labour market. Thirdly, reduction in the unpaid work of women and their participation in the market activities will help women to improve their status at home, with their higher incomes. Fourthly, all this will promote gender equality in the labour market, women will be in a better position to access opportunities coming their way.

Figure 1.3

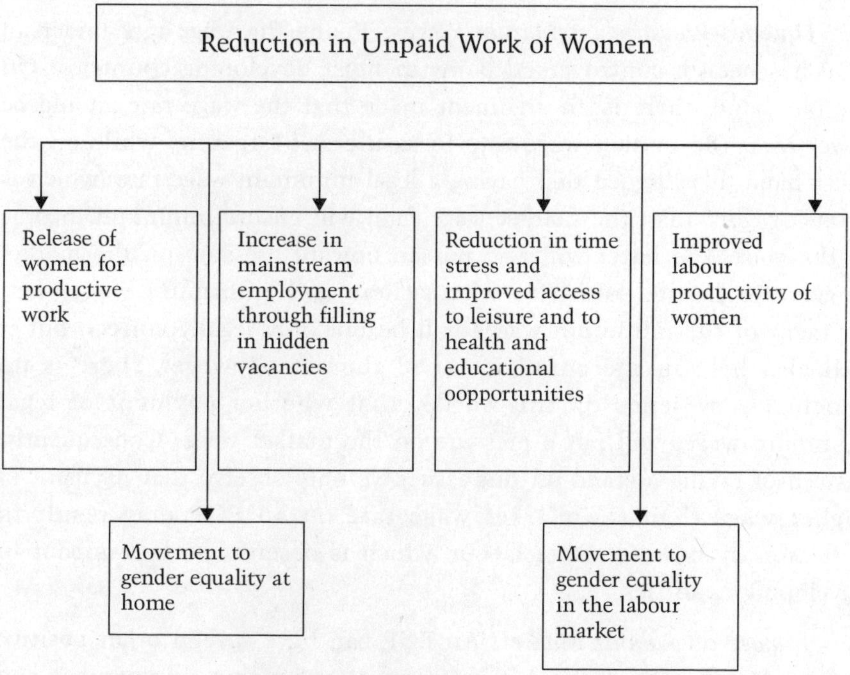

And lastly, these developments will increase mainstream employment opportunities in the labour market, as the "hidden vacancies" of unpaid work, so far filled in by women, will appear openly in the labour market. That is, larger employment opportunities will be created in the labour market in the basic services like child care services, managing local water supply, organising sanitation services etc. (Antonopoulous and Fontana, 2006).

In short, an employment guarantee programme will contribute significantly towards engendering the growth process in developing countries, along with enhancing employment opportunities in the labour market.

Other Links between EGP and Labour-Intensive Development Process

There are several other possible links between an EGP and labour intensive development process in developing countries.

Upward Pressure on Market Wages: Fixing the wage rate under an EGP has been a controversial point in most developing countries. On the one hand, there is an argument made that the wage rate should be lower than the market wage rate to assure self-targeting, while on the other hand, it is argued that paying a legal minimum wage rate (which is usually higher than the market wage rate) will ensure minimum income to the poor. The latter will also put an upward pressure on the market wage rate. In the countries where there is a minimum wages act, payment of the minimum wages will be not only legally correct, but it will also help in the enforcement of the act. However, there is no conclusive evidence on this so far, that whether payment of legal minimum wages will put a pressure on the market wage. Consequently, instead of taking a stand on this issue, we only observe that payment of higher wage than the market wage rate on an EGP may result in reduction in exploitation of labour, which is observed to be rampant in developing countries.

Impact on Labour Market: An EGP can have several other positive impacts on the labour market in terms of enhancing employment and quality of employment.

- By paying legal minimum wages, an EGP can help in the effective enforcement of the minimum wages act.
- Since the wage rates on an EGP are equal for all, throughout the year, the programme will reduce/remove wage rate inequalities across seasons as well as across different socioeconomic groups including gender.

- An EGP can improve the quality of employment, as the government programme can ensure a minimum package of entitlements of workers, namely, social security, working conditions and facilities, and amenities at work sites.
- Large number of workers working together for a long time are likely to form labour unions. That is, an EGP/EGS can encourage workers to develop their collective strength and bargaining power in the labour market. This can also improve the bargaining strength of workers outside the EGP.

Women's Empowerment and Gender Equality: There will be another link will be between EGP and women's empowerment and reduced inequalities. This link will be in addition to the impact on unpaid work. Women will be empowered under an EGP in multiple ways:

- In almost all countries, the participation of women has been very high in EGP works, and in most cases, women's participation has been higher than that of men. This participation is likely to improve women's status at home.
- Working outside home is likely to improve women's exposure to the outside world. This exposure, along with cash in hand, is likely to improve their clothing, as well as their confidence and self esteem (Dandekar, 1983).
- The overall employability of women is likely to improve after they get work experience in EGP.
- Large scale participation of women on EGP can encourage them to form unions. This collective strength, in the long run, can improve women's bargaining power in the labour market.
- As seen earlier, reduction in unpaid work is likely to improve their employment and labour market status, along with enhancement in the employment opportunities in the economy.

In short, an EGP can promote integration of women in the labour market.

Directing Economic Growth towards Domestic Markets

The linkages between an EGP and the macro development path as seen above, are likely to expand domestic employment and domestic market, strengthening the domestic economy in the process: expansion of agriculture and allied activities will generate large scale demand for wage goods, and this will give a push to labour-intensive agriculture as well as labour-intensive industries. Secondly, infrastructure development, including basic services, will once again expand local markets by attracting private investment. An EGP can, thus, trigger a process that will enrich the domestic economy and domestic market.

The Guarantee Component

The guarantee component underlying the programme has several advantages in this context. A legal guarantee can give a legal right to the poor to demand work, rather than wait for the officials to provide work. That is, the demand for work (by workers) and not the supply of work (by officials) will determine the size of the programme. Starvation deaths and related sufferings can, therefore, be avoided only through the guarantee. Secondly, the element of guarantee will provide the required flexibility to the programme, as the size of the programme will expand when the demand for work increases and vice versa. Thirdly, the guarantee also will reduce delays in starting works and in wage payment; as such delays can be challenged in the court of law. Fourthly, the guarantee element can also reduce distress migration, as workers are ensured of the availability of work during the lean season. This, in turn, can improve the access of the workers' households to education, health and other welfare facilities. And lastly, the guarantee of work can ensure massive asset generation, particularly for ecological regeneration and infrastructure development in backward regions, both of which can promote economic growth of the regions. The element of guarantee can thus, ensure that the programme reaches the poor at the bottom on the one hand, and promotes development of backward/poor regions on the other. It also ensures that the programme does not end up in creating a permanent army of unskilled labour.

IMPLICATIONS FOR DESIGNING EMPLOYMENT GUARANTEE PROGRAMMES

The above discussion has important implications for the designing of employment guarantee programmes in developing countries:

Long Term Perspective: An EGP will have to be viewed in terms of its medium and long-term impact on the economy, and its design will have to facilitate this long-term role. Consequently, the EGP will have to be planned keeping in mind its role in the development process. Such a plan can be indicative at the macro level and concrete at the lower levels.

Strong Planning Component: Designing long-term perspective plan, organising horizontal coordination and ensuring convergence of EGP with ongoing programmes and processes, will have to be an essential element of the programme. Also, it will be necessary to use multi-level planning when necessary, for example, in infrastructure planning and in natural resources management.

Decentralised Planning and Implementation: Decentralisation will help in: (1) ensuring local participation, (2) incorporating local needs for assets, (3) bringing transparency and accountability, and (3) in systematic monitoring.

Guarantee of Work: Looking to the multiple advantages of the element of guarantee in the programme, one can strongly recommend the inclusion of guarantee in these programmes.

In addition, an EGP should have the following features so as to enable it to play the desired role.

Skill Training: It is an important component of most employment programmes (EGPs) in developing countries. (For example, EPWP in South Africa, *Jefes* in Argentina, labour-based infrastructure programmes in many African countries). Inclusion of skill training will improve productivity as well as employability of workers, and this will ensure that the programme does not end up in creating a large army of unskilled workers. Again, it is only the skilled workers, who will be able to create durable quality infrastructure, and systematic and scientific natural resources management. A small component of skill training of workers will have to be an essential part of an EGP.

Inclusion of Maintenance of Public Assets: Several countries have designed EGP or wage employment programmes for maintenance of public assets like roads (for example, rural maintenance programme in Bangladesh, Padata Karya in Indonesia and infrastructure based programmes in Africa). Considering the fact that lack of proper maintenance of roads and other infrastructure is a common problem in many developing countries, this results in serious losses in the economy, and (2) regular maintenance can generate regular wage employment, it is very desirable that maintenance of roads and other infrastructure is incorporated in the design of EGP.

Labour-based Infrastructural Development: ILO has initiated a very useful programme on labour-based infrastructural development in many African countries (Miller, 2006; Islam, 2006). The EPWP of South Africa is a good success story in this context. The rationale of this programme is to maximise employment in the construction of infrastructure like roads, buildings, airport etc. The programme uses light equipments in the place of heavy machines, but ensures that the quality of infrastructure like roads, buildings, airport etc. is up to the mark, i.e. the quality of infrastructure is not compromised to generate employment. The issue of the ratio of labour cost and material cost is important here. Though the programmes like EPWP are not very clear on this, one can fix a ratio (say at 60:40) and stick to it for several infrastructure facilities. Some of the advantages of this approach are: (1) relatively large employment is created[6], (2) skill training is given to workers, raising their employability, and (3) higher multiplier impact can be achieved through such an approach.

Inclusion of Services in Employment Guarantee Programme: Several countries have included services, such as child care, care of the old and the sick (particularly HIV-AIDS patients), cooking for community, and other social services as a part of employment guarantee. Argentina (Jefes), Indonesia (Padat Karya), South Africa (EPWP) are some of the examples of this. This employment is created for a short period, 3-4 months or so. The rationale behind the inclusion of services is that:

---

6. The labour cost rises to 60 per cent of total costs in many infrastructure construction, which usually has 30-40 per cent labour cost (Miller, 2006).

(1) the persons performing these services are trained on the job so that their employability improves, (2) with the persons providing these services after every few months, these services are provided to the community continuously, and (3) in the long run these services can be converted into permanent services available to communities.

EGP is only a Component of Full Employment Strategy

In the end, it needs to be underlined that though a well-designed EGP can contribute significantly towards pro-poor growth in developing economies, it can only be a component, though a critical component, of a pro-poor growth strategy. In order that an EGP is able to establish meaningful linkages with the growth process, it is necessary that the EGP is integrated with the development process and productive use of the assets generated is ensured. This can be organised mainly through supplementary policies and programmes. One famous example here is the development of horticulture that happened in Maharashtra when the land and water development works under the Maharashtra Employment Guarantee Scheme, were supplemented by the supply of the required inputs and technology along with loans for horticulture.

Summing Up

The discussion above has shown that a well-designed EGP can take on, to a considerable extent, the challenges posed by the changing employment scene in developing countries under the neoliberal policies. An EGP, can not only address the immediate problem of ensuring employment and wages to the poor at the bottom, but it can also contribute towards labour intensive and pro-poor economic growth. The planning under an EGP, therefore, requires a long-term perspective and systematic approach to create and strengthen meaningful linkages between the EGP and the macroeconomic growth process.

It is important to note that the guarantee component can add significantly to the achievements. It can accelerate the linkages and ensure the goals.

Present Study

The present study has been taken up to show, how an EGP can help in taking an economy towards labour-intensive growth path. This has been done by studying the impact of National Rural Employment Guarantee Act (NREGA) in India. A social accounting matrix (SAM) model has been constructed for a selected village, to study the multiplier impact of the assets created under the NREGA on the employment, output and incomes in the village.

Appendix A-1.1

Unpaid Work and Its Implications for Public EGPs

Type of Activity	*Description of Activities*	*Implications for EGPs: Works/Assets*	*Impact*
1. Non-market economic activities: Acquiring/collecting basic necessities	1. Fetching water	1. Construction of water harvesting structures	Public provisioning of necessities
		2. Deepening tank/improving traditional structures	
		3. Organising distribution of water supply and laying pipelines	
	2. Fetching fuel wood from common lands	1. Regeneration of common lands & plantation: social forestry	1. Access to low cost healthy energy
		2. Regeneration of forest lands	2. Promotion to income generating activities
		3. Constructing smokeless stoves/improved stoves	3. Improved environmental resources
		4. Constructing biogas plants running on cowdung, biomass	
		5. Plantation of biofuel trees	
	3. Walking long distance for relieving activities	1. Construction of latrines	1. Improved health facilities
		2. Construction of drainages	
2. Non-market economic activities: Collection of raw material for income generating activities	1. Collection of fodder from common lands	1. Regeneration of common lands for fodder crops or fodder farms	1. Improved income/ productive employment
	2. Collection of wood/bamboo etc. for crafts/manufacturing	1. Regeneration of common lands: social forestry goods	1. Improved income/ productive employment

Contd...

...contd...

Type of Activity	*Description of Activities*	*Implications for EGPs: Works/Assets*	*Impact*
		2. Regeneration of forest lands	2. Improved environmental resources
		3. Waste land (public) development	
3. Unpaid domestic work: Care related activities	1. Child care	1. Constructing child care centres	1. Improved child health
		2. Constructing child development centres for children below 5	2. More time for women to rest or to work in productive employment
		3. Constructing school rooms & school facilities	3. Improved education: More enrolment & less dropout
		4. Construction of midday meal kitchens	
	2. Care of the sick, old and disabled in the household	1. Constructing health centres/ dispensaries	1. Improved health facilities
		2. Improving/repairing expanding existing health facilities	
		3. Constructing facilities for public sanitation and hygiene	
5. Unpaid domestic work: Household repair in non-durable shelter	1. Repair and maintenance of house: Floor, walls & ceiling	1. Construction of durable housing for the poor	1. Improved homes of people
			2. More time available for rest/work
6. Unpaid work: Travelling	1. Travelling for different reasons on foot	1. Construction of roads: Approach roads, feeder roads, paving of internal roads	1. Less drudgery of walking
			2. More time for rest/ work

2 The Employment Challenge and NREGA in India

The Employment Challenge in India

India has achieved a high rate of economic growth in the recent decade. The economy came out of the "Hindu rate of growth" syndrome of 3.5 per cent rate growth in the 1980s, and registered an average annual growth rate of 5.8 per cent during 1981-2005. In the recent years, the growth rate has shown continuous acceleration, from an annual average of 5.5 per cent during the Ninth Plan (1997/98-2001/02) to 7.7 per cent during the Tenth Plan (2002/03-2006/07), with 8.7 per cent growth rate in the last four years of the plan. Though the rate of growth declined temporarily during the global financial crisis in 2008 and 2009, it has rose again and is soon likely to reach the previous rate of growth.

With this kind of growth, India is one of the fastest growing countries in the world, and with per capita GDP of US $1033, it is now regarded as a middle income developing country (Planning Commission, 2008).

One of the major characteristics of the rapid economic growth experienced by the Indian economy during the recent decades is the highly unbalanced structural transformation of the economy. Though the overall average annual growth rate has been higher than 8.00 per cent (reaching 9.00 per cent in the last years of the Eleventh Plan), the rate of growth of agriculture has been 2.00 per cent per year in the Ninth Plan, and 1.7 per cent in the Tenth Plan. Also, agriculture, which contributes less than 20 per cent to the national GDP, houses about 57 per cent of the workforce implying very low average labour productivity in this sector, as compared to the other sectors. Since the majority of the cultivated area is rainfed, depending on the erratic behaviour of the Indian monsoon (thanks to the low level of assured water supply through irrigation), agriculture is also unstable and uncertain. Consequently, the highest incidence of poverty as well as vulnerability in India is observed to be among agricultural population, mainly marginal and small farmers, and agricultural labourers. The incidence of rural poverty in India, therefore, is much higher than that of urban poverty.

Apart from the predominance of lagging agriculture, the rural economy also suffers from poor diversification within agriculture as well as outside, limiting the opportunities of productive employment for the rural labour force. There are several reasons for this state of affairs. Firstly, the natural resources, such as land, water and vegetation on which the livelihoods of majority of people depend, are depleted and degraded in many parts of the country. Consequently, there is low and uncertain productivity in crop cultivation in many regions on the one hand, and there is low productivity and limited diversification in the primary sector activities like animal husbandry, dairying, horticulture, fishery, forestry etc. on the other. Secondly, there is limited development of socioeconomic infrastructure in rural areas that can support and promote productive economic activities. Some of the major gaps in infrastructure are in connectivity through roads and transportation; marketing facilities like cold storage, ware housing, marketing yards etc. water supply and irrigation; energy; and in health and educational services. In short, many rural areas lack in parts of the kind of support that is required for promoting agricultural growth and diversification of the rural economy into non-agricultural areas. The Lewisian transformation of labour from primary to non-primary activities is therefore, stagnated.

The long-term annual rate of growth of employment has declined from 2.1 per cent during 1983-1993/94 to 1.84 per cent during 1993/94-2004/05. Though one observes a marked improvement in the recent years, i.e. during 1999/2000-2004/05, during which period the employment increased by an annual rate of 2.46 per cent, this increase cannot be considered as a positive development, firstly, because a large part of this new employment is in self-employment, which is emerging as a residual sector for all those who cannot get any work in the labour market; secondly, a significant part of this increase is of subsidiary employment, i.e. part time, marginal employment, and thirdly, because almost the entire increase (60 million) is of informal employment—either in the informal sector or in informal jobs in the formal sector. The official data indicate that there has been a decline in the employment in the organised sector by 0.31 per cent per year during 1993/94–2004/05 (Planning Commission, 2008). As G.S. Bhalla observes, the increase in the rate of growth of employment in the recent years cannot be interpreted as India's faster move towards industrial revolution, and diversification of its employment to higher productivity non-agricultural sectors (Bhalla, 2007).

Table 2.1

Sector-wise Share of Employment by Current Daily Status

	CDS Basis (%)		
Industry	*1983*	*1993-94*	*2004-05*
Agriculture	65.42	61.03	56.06
Mining and quarrying	0.66	0.78	0.63
Manufacturing	11.27	11.10	12.90
Electricity, water etc.	0.34	0.41	0.35
Construction	2.56	3.63	5.57
Trade, hotel and restaurant	6.98	8.26	12.62
Transport, storage and comm.	2.88	3.22	4.61
Financial, insurance, real estate and business services	0.78	1.08	2.00
Community, social and personal services	9.10	10.50	9.24
Total	100	100	100

The changes in the structure of employment in the Indian economy have not been very positive. For example, the share of agriculture in the national GDP has declined to less than one-fifth of the GDP, while its share in the total employment still remains high, at 56.67 per cent, and it declined at a very low rate, from 65.42 per cent in 1993 to 61.03 per cent in 1993/94 and to 56.67 per cent in 2004/05. Conversely, the share of industry in total GDP increased by 10 percentage points, while its share in employment increased by only 1.00 per cent (from 11.24 per cent in 1983 to 12.20 per cent in 2004/05). This indicates the wide as well as widening gap between the labour productivities in agriculture and manufacturing sectors. As the official data show, the rate of increase in the per worker productivity in agriculture during 1993/94–2004/05 has been 1.80 per cent, as against 3.48 per cent in manufacturing and 4.51 per cent in the territory sector. It is not surprising, therefore, that the poverty in India is concentrated in rural areas, and particularly among agricultural/rural labour and small/marginal farmers (Bhalla, 2007). The agricultural sector, which houses more than 55 per cent of the workforce has experienced low rate of growth of labour productivity and a high level of un/under employment.

Table 2.2

Per Worker Productivity (Rs.) (At 2000 Prices)

Sector	*1983*	*1993/94*	*2004/05*	*% Increase (1993/94–2004/05)*
Agriculture and allied	12907	15343	18668	1.80
Mining and quarrying	91348	11178	204902	5.71
Manufacturing	32383	44345	64612	3.48
Secondary	42191	54930	72776	2.59
Territory	53004	69569	113002	4.51
All sectors	47723	63479	95726	3.80
Non–agriculture	22961	31309	50451	4.43

A related problem is the low and fast declining employment elasticity of economic growth in all the major sectors in the economy. The overall employment elasticity in the Indian economy was 0.40 during the period 1983-1993/94. It declined to 0.32 during 1993/94–2004/05. The sectoral elasticities also show a decline during this period.

Table 2.3

Employment Elasticity with Respect to GDP

	1983-1993/94	*1993/94 to 2004/05*
Primary sector	0.50	0.33
Secondary sector	0.53	0.51
Tertiary sector	0.58	0.44
Total	0.40	0.32

The low and rapidly declining employment elasticity implies that the Indian economy will have to grow at a very fast rate if it has to achieve satisfactory employment levels within 5-7 years.

Another worrisome feature of the employment scene in India is the rising incidence of unemployment. The overall rate of unemployment has increased from 6.1 per cent in 1993/94 to 8.3 per cent in 2004/05. The unemployment rate of agricultural labour households has risen to 9.5 per cent in 2004/05 while the rate of unemployment of women in rural and urban areas has increased to 8.7 per cent and 11.6 per cent respectively in 2004/05.

Table 2.4

Unemployment Rates by Usual Status (US), Current Weekly Status (CWS) and Current Daily Status (CDS)

	Rural Male			*Rural Female*		
	US	*CWS*	*CDS*	*US*	*CWS*	*CDS*
1983	2.1	3.7	7.5	1.4	4.3	9
1993-94	2	3.1	5.6	1.3	2.9	5.6
1999-2000	2.1	3.9	7.2	1.5	3.7	7.0
2004-05	2.1	3.8	8.0	3.1	4.2	8.7
	Urban Male			*Urban Female*		
	US	*CWS*	*CDS*	*US*	*CWS*	*CDS*
1983	5.9	6.7	9.2	6.9	7.5	11
1993-94	5.4	5.2	6.7	8.3	7.9	10.4
1999-2000	4.8	5.6	7.3	7.1	7.3	9.4
2004-05	4.4	5.2	7.5	9.1	9.0	11.6

Source: Mitra (2008).

The impact of the overall high growth has not been very positive on poverty reduction either. One does not observe any acceleration in poverty reduction, along with the acceleration of the GDP. The incidence of poverty declined from 30.00 per cent in 1993/94 to 27.8 per cent in 2004/05, implying a very small rate of decline of 0.74 per cent per year during the period. The elasticity of poverty reduction with respect to per capita GDP growth has also declined from 1.13 per cent during 1993/94–1999/2000 to 0.69 per cent during 1999/2000-2004/05. In the case of some marginalised groups like the scheduled tribes, the reduction in poverty has been almost zero. The absolute number of the poor declined from 320 million in 1993/94 to 302 million in 2004/05. In short, the glorious performance of economic growth is not really reflected in poverty reduction.

To sum up, the major areas of concern in the field of employment in India are: (1) the low and declining rate of growth of employment, (2) the rising incidence of unemployment, (3) the rapid deterioration in the quality of employment, and (4) the negligible increase in the real wages of workers. The major employment challenges, therefore, are (Planning Commission, 2008) how to ensure faster growth of (productive) employment than the rate of growth of labour force so as to reduce unemployment; and how to ensure faster growth of employment with "decent work"?

Quantifying the Employment Challenge

T.S. Papola has estimated the size of the employment that needs to be generated in the economy on the basis of the: (1) unemployment rates and (2) under-employment rates of the workforce. This is estimated at 76.8 million in 2007 (Papola, 2008). Adding the working poor, who are too vulnerable in their present jobs and who need new employment, the total employment required to be generated during the plan has been estimated at 92.3 million (Papola, 2008).[1]

As against this demand, the supply of employment that will be generated in the economy will depend on the economic growth and the labour coefficients (employment elasticities) of this growth. Given the pattern of growth and the low and declining elasticity, it is clear that the present growth will not be able to generate adequate employment in the economy. It has been estimated, that with the employment elasticity of 0.25 (which seems to be realistic), the Indian economy will have to grow

1. Employment required to be generated in Eleventh Plan

a Unemployment 2007	21.6 million
b Addition to labour force (2007-2012)	44.7 million
c Working poor that need employment	26.0 million
Total	92.3 million

at 11.00 per cent just to absorb the new labour force, and the openly unemployed (at 2.7 per cent growth of employment). This growth will not offer employment to the vulnerable working poor. Considering the fact, that this growth is neither feasible nor adequate for the required employment generation, one has to look for alternatives.

A useful strategy in this context, as seen in the earlier chapter, would be of promoting labour intensive sectors in the economy, so that the overall employment elasticity of growth improves. This is the approach adopted by the Government of India, and it is going to be intensified in the Eleventh Five Year Plan (2007–2012). It has been estimated by T.S. Papola, that 9.3 per cent growth at the 0.44 overall employment elasticity during the Eleventh Plan will enable the employment to grow at 4.09 per cent and it will be able to generate adequate employment in the economy during the Eleventh Plan. The primary, secondary and tertiary sectors will have to grow at 4.00, 11.00 and 10.00 annual rates respectively with 0.45, 0.68 and 0.58 employment elasticities respectively.

The required overall growth rate of the economy (9.3 per cent) seems to be realistic, looking at the recent trends. Shifting the employment elasticities in the different sectors to the required levels however, appears to be a tall order! How can we reach this rate and pattern of economic growth? In other words, promotion of labour intensive sectors is a sound strategy, but achieving this is a big challenge. According to the Eleventh Plan, this has to be achieved by encouraging the corporate sector to move into more labour-intensive sector, and by facilitating expansion of employment and output of the unorganised enterprises that operate in the labour-intensive sectors[2] (Planning Commission, 2008). The National Commission for Enterprises in the Unorganised Sector (NCEUS) has recommended a 13-point

---

2. The NCEUS has also recommended a Thirteen Point Action Plan for Employment in the unorganised sector. This plan consists of: (1) protective measures for workers (conditions of work and social security), (2) measures for small and marginal farmers (targeted programmes for SF/MF, land and water management, credit to farmers and debt relief), (3) measures to improve growth of non-agricultural sector (improve credit flows, encourage self-help groups (SHGs) and micro-finance institutions (MFIs), and cluster development), and (4) expand employment and improve employability (strengthen self-employment, NREGA, skill development) (Planning Commission, 2008).
Give details p.80.

strategy, which also supports this approach, along with suggesting other supportive measures (NCEUS, 2009).

Two Critical Questions

There are two critical questions that need to be answered in this context: Firstly, what will happen to the poor till this massive employment is generated? How will they survive till then? And secondly, what kind of interventions/inputs is needed to promote labour-intensive sectors? Is it possible to use the present surplus labour to create an enabling environment for the purpose of promoting the labour-intensive sectors?

As seen in the first chapter, large scale wage employment programmes can contribute significantly towards creating an enabling environment for the growth of labour-intensive sectors. The effective promotion of labour-intensive sectors, i.e. agriculture and allied activities like animal husbandry and dairying, forestry, fishery; food processing; textile and garments, leather and leather goods and other similar industries; basic social services etc. requires three major inputs: (1) strong natural resource management on a massive scale, for raising productivity and acquiring stability in agriculture and allied activities; producing raw materials for several labour-intensive industries like textiles and garments, (2) basic infrastructural facilities to promote tiny, small and medium enterprises, and (3) drinking water, sanitation and infrastructure for health and education to improve labour productivity. Though there are several flagship programmes of the Government of India in these three areas, (such as SSA, NHM, Bharat Nirman etc.), there are several critical gaps in these programmes. A well-designed employment guarantee programme can fill in these gaps effectively, along with guaranteeing productive employment at the minimum wages and with good working conditions. Also, by providing work at the minimum wages, with decent working conditions as well as social protection, such a programme can provide a bottom line of decent work for workers.

In addition massive employment generated under such a programme can raise demand for wage goods in the economy, which in turn, will need labour-intensive industrialisation.

From Public Works Programmes to NREGA

India has a long history of public works programme. These programmes started as "relief works" during the pre-British and British period when disasters like drought, floods etc. threatened the survival of people. These relief works provided employment at minimum wages to enable affected people to survive. Since the need to provide relief was always urgent and since the works were organised at a short notice focusing on reaching the most vulnerable groups of people, considerations such as appropriateness of assets was secondary. Assets were selected in an ad hoc manner keeping in mind largely the convenience of affected people.

After Independence, however, public employment programmes were viewed as a means of generating employment, to address the structural un/under-employment as well as means of creating productive assets for expanding the labour absorbing capacity, of the mainstream economy. The first public works programme, Rural Works Programme (RWP) was introduced in the 1960s with a view to generating employment for the unemployed. A series of wage employment programmes followed in the 1960s and 1970s, each trying to improve upon the earlier ones. The important of these were Crash Scheme for Rural Employment (CSRE) and the Pilot Rural Employment Project (PIREP). Based on these experiences, two national employment programmes were introduced in the 1980s, namely the National Rural Employment Programme (NREP) from 1980-81 to 1989 and the Rural Landless Employment Guarantee Programme (RLEGP) during 1982-83–1989. In order to involve local elected bodies like Panchayati Raj Institutions (PRIs), in this programme, a new programme, Jawahar Rozgar (employment) Yojana (programme) was introduced in the mid-nineties. A modified version of this programme, Sampoorna Grameen Rozgar Yojana (SGRY) was introduced in the late 1990s to provide massive wage employment to rural population in public works (Hirway and Terhal, 1994).

All the above programmes basically aimed at reducing poverty at the bottom, by providing employment at reasonable wages to the poor on the one hand and at generating productive assets of different kinds on the other. In a way, these programmes aimed at using surplus manpower in generating productive assets to expand the labour absorbing capacity of the mainstream economy, though not very systematically, in line with the approach recommended by R. Nurkse or Hirschman in the 1950s and 1960s (Nurkse, 1957; Hirschman, 1958).

The working of these programmes has been evaluated by a large number of official and non-official agencies. An important observation coming out of these studies is that these programmes have definitely helped the poor, at least in selected pockets, by raising their employment and wage incomes. However, they have not made much significant impact at the macro level. These programmes, therefore, cannot be rated as highly successful programmes. Some of the weaknesses of the programmes are as follows (Hirway, 2003):

- The programmes have recorded a limited impact at the macro level in terms of generation of employment per worker.
- They also have made a limited impact in terms of production of durable, good quality assets.
- The planning component of the programmes has been weak in terms of selection and sequencing of assets, with the result that the selected assets have not been the best assets to expand the labour absorbing capacity of the mainstream economy.

These studies have observed that if wage employment in public works has to result in poverty reduction, it is necessary that the employment made available is on a scale that meets the demand for work; work is provided at a minimum wage rate and for adequate number of days to ensure minimum incomes; the employment is made available locally so as to reduce distress out-migration; the employment is accompanied by a minimum package social security (i.e. security against injury, sickness and death, old age, maternity); there is a good Public Distribution System (PDS) to ensure access of workers to food grains etc. the assets created are owned and maintained well by workers community; and the distribution of the benefits/incomes from the assets generated is equitable (Hirway, 2003).

Studies have also shown that if the use of surplus labour under wage employment programmes has to result in capital formation, i.e. in generation of productive assets that generate employment in the medium and long run (by expanding the labour absorbing capacity of the mainstream economy), it is necessary that the selection and sequencing of assets/works is done systematically. That is, the assets selected are labour-intensive during the construction phase, they have short gestation periods, and they generate sustainable employment in the mainstream subsequently. Since the productive assets are not likely to generate mainstream employment automatically, there is a need to ensure their productive use systematically by providing appropriate support measures in terms of finance/credit, institutions and infrastructure, and skill training and capacity building of workforce to improve labour productivity and wage incomes of workers. It is important to see, that the programmes do not end up in generating a large army of unskilled workers on a permanent basis. In other words, a wage employment programme is successful, if it is needed less and less over time. In short, if planned and implemented well, these programmes can promote strategic use of surplus labour to promote labour-intensive, sustainable development in the economy.

Maharashtra Employment Guarantee Scheme (MEGS)

Maharashtra's Employment Guarantee Scheme, (MEGS) is important in this context, as it has several useful features not found in early employment programmes. Maharashtra, a major state in India, introduced MEGS with multiple objectives of guaranteeing work to all those who are willing to work at the fixed wage rate in rural areas, producing water and land based assets to fight droughts and promote agricultural growth, and generating productive assets in general for promoting economic growth that would generate significant mainstream employment. It was felt that a wage employment programme, with a legal guarantee of work can remove many of the weaknesses discussed above. As seen in the first chapter, the element of guarantee can ensure that the programme reaches the poor at the bottom on the one hand and can promote development of backward/poor regions on the other. The other objectives of MEGS aimed to see that the programme does not end up in creating a permanent army of unskilled labour, and it promotes gradual absorption of surplus labour in the mainstream economy.

MEGS was introduced in the early 1970s as a scheme, and a legal support was provided to it in 1974. The MEGS is perhaps the biggest employment guarantee programme in the world that has been implemented for the longest period, more than 30 years. So far, more than Rs. 10,0000 million have been spent on the scheme and about 3700 million person days of employment has been generated. The amount spent on the scheme in the year 2001-02 was Rs. 9417 m., which was 107 per cent of the total rural development budget and 4.57 per cent of the total development budget of the state (Krishnaraj *et al.*, 2006).

The MEGS has shown some important achievements in terms of: its long life that reflects the long term commitment of its leaders; financial sustainability arising from the separate funds: organisation of EGS workers and their impressive collective strength in some pockets; generation of supplementary income and employment for many workers by way of relief, and some pockets of successes in terms of agricultural growth, development of dairy industry, horticulture etc. emanating from the assets generated under the scheme (Datar, 2007; Krishnaraj *et al.*, 2006; Dev, 1995; Acharya, 1990; Hirway and Terhal, 1994; Sathe, 2001 etc). Some of the sub-schemes of the EGS, like Jawahar Well Scheme, Horticulture Scheme, Watershed Development Programmes etc. have done well in some pockets in the state.

In spite of these achievements, however, there have been several failures of the scheme particularly after the introduction of the economic reforms: (1) the scheme has continued for more than 30 years, without any decline in the demand for unskilled wage work under the scheme. In 1975, it generated 110 m. person days, in 2000-01, it generated 111 m. person days and in 2001-02, it generated 162 m. person days, (2) no dramatic achievements have been made in poverty reduction or in unemployment reduction in the state. In fact, the state has done poorly as compared to other states in these areas. The incidence of rural poverty in Maharashtra was 29.6 per cent in 2004-05, which put the state at 13th position among the major 20 states in India. The state was 7th in this rank in 1973-74. The rate of decline in poverty was much less in Maharashtra than in many other states, (3) distress seasonal migration of workers from backward regions continues, as the guarantee is not really implemented in many areas, (4) social security measures, maternity benefits, facilities at work sites, etc. are implemented poorly, (5) skill training is given, if at all, on a negligible scale, (6) unemployment allowance has not been paid to anybody so far, as continuous work of 75 days (which is a pre-condition for unemployment allowance) is not provided to most persons, and even when provided, adequate records from one site to another are not maintained, and finally, (7) quality of the assets created and their maintenance/use are frequently not satisfactory.

Pre-conditions for Success of Employment Guarantee Programmes

The Maharashtra experience as well as the long experience of wage employment programmes in India has indicated that there are several pre-conditions that need to be fulfilled, to achieve short-term and long-term goals of these programmes.

Ensuring Guarantee of Work: The first important pre-condition is that suitable systems should be established for ensuring the guarantee of work under the programme. That is, if demanded, work should be provided throughout the year; continuous work should be ensured by systematic planning of series of work and by minimising delays in taking up such works; and the stipulated wages should be paid regularly without undue delays.

Planning for Assets: It is important to plan works under these programmes, in a way that the programmes generate employment during the construction phase, and the completed works also generate employment in the mainstream economy in the post-construction phase. It is important, therefore, to select assets with a short gestation period so that the expansion of the mainstream employment starts early.

Promoting Productive Use of Assets: Another important pre-condition is to see that the assets generated, are used productively to create the expected employment in the mainstream economy. An asset generated under the programme will not be used productively, unless efforts are made to organise its productive use. For example, a minor irrigation tank/pond constructed under an employment programme will expand the mainstream employment, only when the farmers in the command area are helped in accessing the water through the supply of credit and other required inputs. In other words, it will be necessary to create enabling conditions for the use of the assets generated.

Skill Training and Capacity Building: It is frequently argued that a large scale wage employment programme is likely to end up as a programme that generates a large army of unskilled workers in the economy. This can happen, when the workers on the programme are deprived of skill training and capacity building. The logic of the programme requires that the workers are trained in different skills, like masonry, carpentry etc. so that they are able to construct the assets (almost all assets will need some skilled labour) and are equipped to use these assets productively. The required training for skills and capacity can be organised in the job as well as outside the job.

Support for Infrastructure, Finance and Institutions: Productive use of the assets generated under an employment programme can be ensured, if there is adequate support in the areas of infrastructure, finance and institutions. This support needs to be planned systematically, preferably in a project mode.

Involving Women: The general experience is that women are attracted to these programmes largely because, in the absence of ownership of assets and poor access to credit, women frequently prefer wage employment to self-employment. Women also prefer to work when it is available locally, is manual and does not need any specialised skills. However, women need support in the form of shade, crèche etc. all of which need to be ensured under these programmes. There is also a need to undertake works, which reduce women's drudgery. In short, there is a need to strengthen the gender sensitivity in planning and implementing such programmes.

Asset Ownership and Construction of Private Assets under the Programme

Ownership and use of assets created under an employment guarantee programme is important from equity considerations. It frequently happens, that the benefits of the assets occur only to those with assets (for example, farmers will benefit from water harvesting structures) and the assetless do not gain anything but the wages. This tends to increase asset inequalities in the region. In order to avoid widening asset inequalities under the programme, it is necessary that: (1) as far as possible, the assets generated under the programme are owned by all the workers including the assetless and (2) the distribution of benefits is done equitably between the households with and without assets. This calls for setting up of suitable institutions for the management of the assets.

It is not always possible to create only public assets under the programme, firstly because it is not always feasible under some NRM programmes (i.e. a watershed development project will have to cover lands of private farmers also) and secondly, because there is a need to develop private assets, particularly of the poor to promote economic growth. For example, Jawaharlal Well Scheme, under the EGS of Maharashtra, has benefited small and marginal farmers. Also, development of horticulture in Maharashtra has been possible largely due to the use of EGS on private lands. What one can do, however, is to see that: (1) private works are taken up only after public works are exhausted, (2) private works focus on the works that strengthen the asset base of the poor, (3) proper institutions are set up to assure that benefits of public works are equally distributed to all, (4) asset uses are charged for the use of the assets and/or (5) part of the cost of construction is recovered from private asset owners, whose assets are built under the programme.

Unpaid Work and Wage Employment Programmes

The above discussion has suggested, that an employment guarantee programme is expected to create short term and long term employment for those who are under-employed (i.e. seasonally unemployed or do not get employment for adequate number of days) or unemployed in the labour market. That is, it is expected to generate employment for those who are looking for work (or additional work), or are available for work (or additional work). This approach, however, does not address unpaid drudgery of the poor, and particularly, poor women. As seen in the earlier chapter, there is simultaneous existence of un/under-employment and unpaid work in developing countries. If this unpaid work is converted into paid market work, it will raise the level of employment in the mainstream on the one hand, and relieve unpaid workers (mainly poor women) from the drudgery of unpaid work and enable them to participate in the mainstream productive work on the other.

In other words, there is a need to expand the purview of employment guarantee programmes to include unpaid workers engaged in unpaid SNA and non-SNA work to release them for accessing better opportunities in the labour market.

National Rural Employment Guarantee Act, 2005 and NREGS

Learning from the past experiences of wage employment programmes in the country on the one hand, and the experiences of implementing an employment guarantee programme, i.e. MEGS, on the other, the Central government in India decided to introduce an employment guarantee scheme in 2006 under the National Rural Employment Guarantee Act, 2005. Under the act every rural household living in the most backward 200 districts of the country was guaranteed at least 100 days of wage employment at the minimum wage rate of the concerned state. This Act was extended to 100 more districts in the second year, and to the entire country (rural areas) from April 2008. The Act was followed by formulation of national guidelines, on the basis of which each state government was asked to design an employment guarantee scheme. All the state governments subsequently designed the schemes, which are now being implemented in the respective states.

This legal commitment is a landmark event in the history of poverty reduction strategies in India. It is also a unique event in the pro-poor strategies in the world, as no country in the world has ever given a right of this kind to such a large section of the population so far. The major features of the act and the schemes are as follows:

Guarantee of Work: Under the Act: (1) the guarantee is given for casual and manual work of 100 days at the legal minimum wage on public works (and on private works under specified situations) to all households (all members above 18 years) living in rural India, (2) the work should be provided within 15 days of demanding it, and (3) it should be located within 5 kilometre of distance. If work is not provided to anybody within the given time, he/she will be paid a daily unemployment allowance, which will be at least one-third of the minimum wages. Also, if work is provided outside the limit of 5 kilometre, the worker will get an allowance for travelling and living there.

Other Entitlements: Workers on public works under the Employment Guarantee Act, are entitled to several amenities, facilities and allowances: (1) Medical treatment and hospitalisation costs in case of injury on work, along with a daily allowance of not less than half of the statutory minimum wages, and (2) work site facilities like safe drinking water, shade for small children and workers for rest period, a first aid box with adequate material for emergency treatment of minor injuries, strokes, body ache and other health hazards and crèche for babies. The other entitlements include payment of compensation in case there is a delay in the payment of wages; deduction of five per cent of wages as contribution to welfare schemes like health insurance, accident insurance, survivor benefits, maternity benefits and social security schemes, and unemployment allowance if work is not provided within 15 days of demand at the rate of one-third of the statutory minimum wages. Strict penalties have been laid down in the Act for non-compliance of the rules relating to employment guarantee, terms of employment, and entitlement of workers.

Planning for Works and Funding: A Central Employment Guarantee Council (CEGC) has been constituted at the national level to implement the Act. The council, which has adequate representation from women and Dalits: (1) advises Central government on all matters concerning implementation of the Act, (2) establishes central evaluation and monitoring systems, and (3) organises regular monitoring. At the state level, there is a state council which advises the state government on all matters concerning the Employment Guarantee Programme and its implementation. At the district level, the collector or the chief executive officer (CEO) is responsible for the implementations of the programme. All other officers of the state government and local authorities within the district are ultimately responsible to the collector. At the block level, there is a programme officer and *panchayat samiti* in charge of the implementation of the Act.

Village *panchayat* (the local elected body) at the village level, is supposed to be the most important institution in the planning and implementation of the programme. The village *panchayat* is expected to prepare a perspective plan (for five years), an annual plan and a shelf of projects/works in a participatory manner in consultation with the *gram sabha* (consisting of all adults in the village) and technical experts. It has been laid down that 50 per cent of the works will be planned at the village level, while 25 per cent each will be planned at the block and the district levels, in consultation with people and experts. Each person wanting employment gets registered with the village *panchayat* and gets a job card along with his/her photograph. Work is to be provided to all registered persons, as per the rules laid down in the state.

As regards finances, a separate National Employment Guarantee Fund has been set up at the Centre. Also, state level funds at the state level will be created to ensure the availability of funds for the programme. The wage component will be paid by the Central fund while the material component will be shared by the Centre and state government.

Transparency and Accountability: The Act lays down detailed clauses for ensuing transparency of implementation and accountability of implementers: (1) The district collector/CEO in the district will be responsible for the programme at the district level, (2) each village *panchayat* will prepare an annual report on the implementation of the programme, which will be made available for public scrutiny, (3) all accounts and records relating to the programme will be available in convenient form for public scrutiny, (4) the details of each project, including accounts, will be displayed prominently on a board close to the site and at the office of the village *panchayat*, (5) the *gram sabha* (village assembly) will monitor the work by way of social audit, and the productive assets created under the programme will be evaluated by technically qualified personnel to ensure that they meet the required technical standards and measurements. Heavy penalties have been laid down for non-compliance of any rules under the Act (a fine not less than Rs. 1000 or imprisonment up to six months or both).

In short, the NREGA is seen as an effective instrument for eradicating poverty of the poor at the bottom, and a tool of empowering them as well as a programme that generates assets for enhancing livelihood for people. The long term objectives of the programme, however, are not very explicit. That the programme can promote labour-intensive growth in the economy in the medium and long term; can address unpaid drudgery of women to relieve them to enjoy better access to productive work; or can enhance health and education status of the poor by filling in the critical gaps in the required infrastructure projects etc. is not recognised well by policymakers. However, we believe that, it is important to recognise this programme as a transitional programme that "contributes towards transformation of our labour surplus economy in to a full employment economy through 'strategic use of surplus labour' that generates productive assets and expand employment avenues in the mainstream economy" (Tinbergen, 1994).

NREGS: Overview of First Four Years

Table 2.5 presents the data on the overall performance of NREGA during the past four years, i.e. from 2006-07 to 2009-10.

Table 2.5

Performance of NREGA during 2006-07 to 2009-10

Item	*2006-07*	*2007-08*	*2008-09*	*2009-10*
No. of districts	200	331	615	615
HH provided work (in million)	21.02	33.91	45.11	52.57
NREGA income per HH	1920.0	2972.4	3899.0	4400.7
Person days (in million)	905.06	1436.8	2163.35	2830.35
Person days per HH	43.05	42.37	47.96	53.54
Women days (in million)	367.90	610.91	1035.72	1377.84
% women days	40.65	42.52	47.88	48.68
SC days (in million)	229.50	394.23	633.59	863.85
% SC days	25.36	27.44	29.29	30.52
ST days (in million)	329.88	420.56	550.16	586.97
% ST days	36.45	29.27	25.43	20.74
Funds allotted (in million)	120736	192788	363005	496437
Funds used (in million)	88233.6	159998	272501	379483
% of funds used	73.08	81.98	75.07	76.44
Works: total (in lakh)	8.42	17.92	39.89	46.03
Ongoing	4.49	9.69	27.75	23.70
Completed	3.97	8.24	12.14	20.95

Note: The statistics for 2009-10 are up to February 2010.

Source: Based on official website data on NREGA.

Table 2.5 shows that the overall performance of NREGS has been significant in quantitative terms. The number of households participating in the programme has increased continuously from 21.02 million in 2006-07 to 45.11 million in 2008-09 to 52.57 million in 2009-2010. The last figure comes to more than 70 per cent of BPL households in the country. The expenditure on NREGA reached Rs. 379483 crore in 2009-10 and it generated 2830 million person days of work. In all, about Rs. 90,000 crore has been spent on NREGS in the country so far, and about 45 million works (assets) have been completed and more than 60 million works are under construction.

The table also shows that there has been continuous improvement in the working of NREGA at the aggregate level: the person days of employment per households has increased from 43.05 in 2006-07 to 47.96 in 2008-09 to 53.54 in 2009-10; the percentage share of women in total person days has increased from 40.65 in 2006-07 to 48.68 in 2009-2010; the share of SC and ST days has remained significant at around 50-55 per cent; and NREGS income per household has increased from Rs. 3899 in 2008-09 to Rs. 4400 in 2009-10.

Most of the assets generated under NREGA are related to natural resource management. In Figure 2.1, 54 per cent assets are related to water supply, 6 per cent are for drought proofing and 7 per cent are for construction of irrigation facilities on the lands of SC/ST/BPL households. In other words, 67 per cent of the total 80 million assets constructed or under construction in NREGA are for improving and using natural resources in the country. Of the rest, 21 per cent assets have been for construction of rural roads to improve connectivity in rural areas and 8 per cent assets have been constructed for flood control. The overall selection of assets under NREGA appears to match with its objective of promoting better management of natural resources and improving rural connectivity.[3] Though there are several problems about the implementation of NREGS in many states, there are some pockets of successes, showing several positive impacts, such as reduction in distress migration, increase in the local wage rate, improvement in local

3. 27 per cent assets are for water conservation and water harvesting; 12 per cent assets are for land development; 10 per cent are for renovating traditional water bodies; 5 per cent are for desilting—maintaining—repairing irrigation canals.

agriculture and allied activities, women's empowerment and empowerment of the poor etc. In short, NREGS has emerged as a major scheme in the economy. With the expanded coverage to 615 districts and the expected rise in demand for work, the size of the scheme is likely to increase considerably in the near future.

Figure 2.1

Assets constructed under NREGS during 2006-07 to 2009-10 (February 2010)

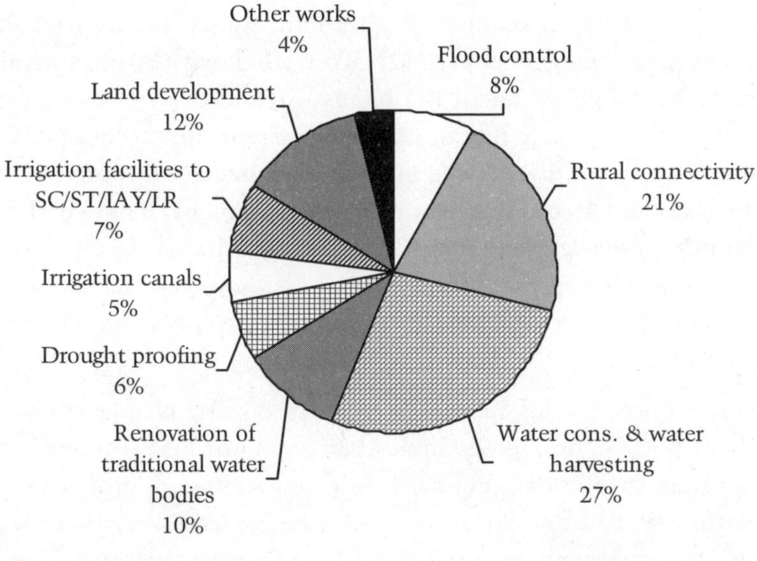

Note: IAY= Indira Awaas Yojana.
Source: Employment Challenge and NREGA in India.

This is not to say that the scheme does not have any problems. The report of Comptroller and Auditor General (CAG) as well as large number of studies have brought out many weaknesses of the scheme ranging from non-delivery of the basic entitlements to people (work on demand, payment of minimum wages, timely payment of wages, payment of unemployment allowances and worksite facilities), to poor performance in self-targeting, weak planning and ad hoc selection of works, top-down implementation rather than participatory, low transparency, poor accountability, corruption etc. The scheme is likely to improve its performance when these problems are addressed even in parts.

A serious problem with NREGS, however, is that its role of generating productive assets in the economy and in promoting labour-intensive and pro-poor growth is not yet taken seriously enough. There is a need to appreciate this role and use NREGS to achieve the long-term goals of the Indian economy.

The Empirical Study

The three critical features of NREGS, according to us are: (1) empowerment of the workers by guaranteeing them basic entitlements like work on demand, payment of minimum wages, timely payment of wages, worksite facilities etc. (2) strengthening the decentralised democracy by giving power in the hands of Panchayati Raj Institutions (PRIs) and making their functioning transparent and accountable, and (3) strengthening the livelihoods of people, ultimately leading to labour-intensive, broad-based and sustainable development. Though the first two features are recognised officially, the last feature has not yet received adequate importance. Our discussion so far, however, has shown that NREGS can play a critical role in promoting pro-poor development in the economy.

The empirical study presented in the following chapters highlights the role of NREGS as a programme that promotes labour-intensive pro-poor growth in a local economy. The concepts of multiplier and accelerator effects from macroeconomic theory have been borrowed to illustrate the enormous potential of NREGS in the economy. It has been argued that the performance of NREGS needs to be judged by its multiplier impacts in terms of growth of income, output and employment. The study illustrates that by putting cash in the hands of people, NREGS triggers a process of growth in the economy by increasing the effective demand that pushes production of the wage goods in the economy. The increase in the effective demand accelerates investment creating a virtual cycle of multiplier-accelerator of NREGS investments.

The study involves construction of a village social accounting matrix (SAM) to understand the village economy and to assess the impact of NREGP works on the household production, income and employment as well as on the village economy through multiplier analysis. The NREGP works are treated as external shocks in the analysis. The study also examines how portions of unpaid SNA and non-SNA work, can be substituted by NREGA works and what impact it can make on the incomes and employment of households, and on the economy. This has been done by estimating the multiplier impact of the substitution of unpaid work by NREGP assets/infrastructure, on the village economy.

Nana Kotda village, a medium size village located in north Gujarat, has been selected for the in-depth study. There are several reasons for selecting this village: Firstly, this village (and the district) is covered under the NREGA right from the first year, as it is a backward tribal village (located in a backward tribal district) that has a high incidence of poverty, and needs the employment guarantee programme urgently. This village is also selected as a case study under the concurrent monitoring of NREGS by CFDA.[4] In addition, the district of Sabarkantha is also covered under the time use survey that was conducted in India in 1998-99 on a pilot basis. We, therefore, have detailed data on the time use pattern of the population of the district. In short, we have good database of the village economy and the village society. This has helped in the data analysis and its interpretation.

Chapters 3 and 4 describe the economy of Nana Kotda based on the secondary data as well as the social accounting matrix (SAM), which has been constructed based on a complete census of the village. The SAM provides a comprehensive picture of the village economy as well as helps in identifying the gaps or the need for NREGA kind of works in the village on the one hand and the nature and characteristics of surplus labour and the potential demand for NREGA works on the other.

Chapters 5 and 6 discuss the time use of the villagers, based on the survey done earlier as well as the recent data collection, and identify the extent of unpaid work of men and particularly women that can be reduced through NREGS works. Both these chapters are based on primary data collection from the village.

---

4. While conducting the concurrent monitoring of the NREGA, a few village-level studies were conducted. Nana Kotda was one such village.

Chapter 7 presents the multiplier impacts of the NREGA interventions on the village economy in terms of output, income and employment. The chapter also discusses analysis that goes beyond the multiplier impact, to show how the value of such multipliers can be maximised, the increase in subsequent years, and presents the impacts that go beyond to present the multiple impacts that cannot be captured through multiplier analysis alone.

Finally, in the last chapter, apart from presenting major conclusions, efforts are made to indicate the changes which are needed to make NREGA more effective for achieving its long-term goals.

3 Employment, Poverty and Human Development in Nana Kotda

Nana Kotda Village

Nana Kotda is a mid size village, with 1870 population, located in Idar block (*taluka*) in Sabarkantha district of Gujarat state. Sabarkantha district is located in north Gujarat and is one of the 200 most backward districts of India, selected for implementing the NREGA in its first year, from February 2006.

Of the total population, 946 are men (51.07 per cent), while 906 are women. About 27.75 per cent population is below 14 years while 66.5 per cent population is between 15-60 years and only 5.83 per cent population is above 60 years. The majority of the population belongs to low social groups, i.e. low castes and tribes. Of the total 404 households in the village, 283 belong to other backward castes (OBC), 94 belong to scheduled castes (SC) and 4 households belong to scheduled tribes (ST).

Table 3.1

Population by Age and Sex in Nana Kotda

Age Group	*Male*	*% to Total*	*Female*	*% to Total*	*Total*	*%*
0–6	110	10.47	119	13.13	229	100
7–14	165	17.44	131	14.46	296	100
15–30	314	33.19	307	33.89	621	100
30–45	191	19.77	174	18.87	365	100
46–60	126	13.32	125	13.80	251	100
En–	55	5.81	53	5.85	108	100
Total	961	100.00	909	100.00	1870	100

The rest of the households, i.e. 23 households belong to middle and high castes. The village has 9 wards (*falias*), which are inhabited by different castes.[1]

Village Level Amenities and Facilities in Nana Kotda

With respect to basic services, the village has an all weather *pucca* road connecting the village to the highway going to Idar, the block headquarter 9 km away. There is a regular bus service from the state transport department that comes to the village three times a day. However, there is a "dip", a low bridge on the small nearby river, 2 km away from the village. In the monsoon season, when water flows over the dip, the village gets cut off from the rest of the world. Though a proposal has been made to raise the level of the bridge to improve connectivity to the village, no decision has been taken so far.

The internal roads in the village are paved only in half the wards, and drainage facility is not available to any ward at all. There is no public system for disposing off solid and liquid waste, though some households manage it for themselves. The result is that the village is vulnerable to water-borne and air-borne diseases.

The village does not have any local health facility. It neither has a PHC (primary health centre) nor a sub-PHC nor a family welfare centre. There is no qualified private doctor or a private dispensary in the village. The only professional health facility available to the village is a nurse, from the health department, who is expected to visit the village once in a week. The nurse usually visits the Anganvadi (the pre-school) when she visits the village. People are expected to contact her there, if they need her help. It was reported by villagers that she was not regular and not everybody was aware when she visited the village.

Since the nurse is available only once in a week and is not dependable, villagers go to Idar town to one of the private clinics. They prefer to go to a private doctor and not to the government hospital because the timings of the public hospital are inconvenient (9.00 to

1. The settlement pattern in the village is caste based. Each settlement or a *falia* is inhabited by one catse. A few settlements are mixed.

12.00 noon), and the doctors are not always available even during the fixed timings.

There are however four "medical practioners", unqualified medical persons (quacks), who give some medicines for common diseases in the village. As was pointed out by the *sarpanch* (village head), people go to them 'at their own risk'.

The educational facilities in the village are better than the health facilities. The village has two pre-schools (for children between 3-6), one elementary school (1st to 7th standard) and one residential school (1st to 7th standard), which is known as Ashramshala. The Ashramshala, which is located in the outskirts of the village, serves only outside students from neighbouring villages. Except for a peon, no staff in the Ashramshala is from the village. Children have to go to Idar town, for secondary and other higher education.

The two pre-schools do not have a proper building. One pre-school is running in a private house, and the other in a rented room. Both the facilities are small and inadequate. The elementary school in the village also needs a few extra rooms.

The village has electricity for agriculture as well as for domestic use. 351 households (about 86 per cent) have electric connection to their homes. There are streetlights on all major internal roads. Recently, the village has introduced the low voltage CFL lights, which give more light but consume less electricity.

There is only one source of drinking water in the village, the group scheme that covers a group of 15 villages and brings water to the village from the Dharoi Dam on Sabarmati river located 50 km from the village. There is only one outlet, a stand post, for water supply in the village that is constructed by the GWSSB (Gujarat Water Supply and Sewerage Board) of the Government of Gujarat. All women of the village come to this stand post for fetching water and stand in long queues. Some of them walk up to 1 km distance to the stand post. Most households use this water for drinking and cooking, and use the other local sources for washing and cleaning. This is because, the water coming from Dharoi Dam is treated by GWSSB, while there is no provision of treating the local water supply.

Since the pipelines under the group scheme are not maintained well, there are frequent breakages and leakages, resulting in irregular and non-dependable water supply. As was pointed out by the *sarpanch*, there are one or two breakages every month, resulting in the lack of water supply for 4–6 days every month. The breakages increase in the summer, when there is general scarcity of water supply.

The other local sources are also not adequate for all the wards in the village. Out of the total nine wards, only two wards reported daily and satisfactory water supply. The wards belonging to low castes, like Vaghari, Raval, Thakarada and Vankar reported general shortage of water supply throughout the year.

Most villagers believe that the local sources are adequate (with about 800 mm annual average rainfall and a rivulet passing by the village) and if harnessed well, the village can augment its own water supply. Deepening of the two tanks, and construction of wells may solve their problem for ever.

Household Level Facilities: As far as individual/household level amenities and facilities are concerned, 240 households (about 60 per cent) have individual water connection, 351 households (85 per cent) have electricity connection, 156 households (34 per cent) have individual bathrooms. Not a single household has a drainage connection.

The major gaps in the basic amenities and facilities can be listed as follows:

- The village does not have dependable, reliable and sustainable supply of water supply in all the wards, and in all the seasons.
- The village lacks in drainage facility and in clean arrangement for disposal of solid and liquid waste.
- The village does not have internal paved roads in all the wards.
- Most households lack in toilets and bathrooms.
- The two pre-schools do not have room as well as related facilities like toilets and drinking water.
- The village elementary school does not have adequate number of rooms.

- There is no health facility in the village.
- The village has a small *panchayat* office, but there is no community hall with a library for people's use.

Poverty and Human Development in Nana Kotda

Income Poverty: According to the official data, 67 households have been declared as below poverty line or BPL households.[2] This comes to 16.58 per cent of the total households. This figure however is misleading, as the concept of poverty line is extremely narrow here. It is primarily based on the norms of calorie consumption, 2100 calories per capita per day. The poverty line neither includes adequate nutrition nor other basic needs like clothing, housing etc. nor basic literacy & education, health and basic well-being.

Table 3.2

Incidence of Poverty (Official) in Nana Kotda

Occupation	*% of BPL HH*
Agriculture	11.76
Marginal	14.76
Small	4.05
Other	0.00
Self-employed in non-professional non-agriculture	17.14
Agricultural labour	21.23
Other labour	33.33
Service (govt.)	0.00
Service (private)	3.4
Animal husbandry	12.50
Interest/royalties income	15.00
Pension income	50.00
Beggar	100.00
Destitute	82.50
Total	16.58

2. Poverty line is basically determined primarily on the basis of the calorie norms.

As expected, the incidence of poverty is the highest on agricultural labour households and other labour households, the incidence being 21.23 and 33.33 per cent respectively. This is followed by self-employed in non-agriculture and marginal farmers, and then by households employed in animal husbandry. The beggar households and the destitute are clearly below the poverty line. The pensioner households also are poor, as the old age pension given to the old belonging to BPL households is not enough to remain above the poverty line.

As regards the social groups of the poor, the data show that 5 out of the total 67 BPL households (7 per cent) belong to middle and high castes. In other words, 93 per cent of the poor belong to the low castes such as the SCs, the STs and the OBCs. It is also worth noting that out of the total 67 BPL households, 12 are female headed households (15 per cent). This indicates vulnerability of female headed households. In all, there are 35 female headed households in the village (about 9 per cent), of which 10 are BPL households. Of these, 2 are single person destitute households. Three households depend on government pension, 4 households own a small piece of land (less than 1 ha), and 3 households depend on manual labour for living.

Educational Achievements: Educational achievement reflects the quality of life enjoyed by people on the one hand and the level of their skills and productivity of workers on the other. Nana Kotda is very poor in terms of educational achievements. About half of the adult women in the village are illiterate, 17.76 per cent women have studied up to 5th standard and only 8 per cent women have studied above tenth standard. The condition of men is slightly better, with 22.35 per cent adult being illiterate and more than 14 per cent of adult men having education above tenth standard (Table 3.3). The table also indicates that not all boys and girls in the age group 6-14 go to school. About 9.65 boys and 24.78 per cent girls (almost one-fourth girls) in this age group do not go to school. That is, 17.62 per cent children of school-going age do not attend the school.

Table 3.3

Distribution of Population by Education Levels

Education Code	*Male*	*Female*	*Total % (M+F)*	*Children (6-14)* *Boys*	*Girls*	*Total % (B+G)*
Illiterates	22.37	49.92	35.83	9.65	24.78	17.62
Up to primary (Std. 5)	19.15	17.76	18.47	56.22	51.78	54.52
Up to secondary (Std. 10)	35.82	24.35	30.22	32.43	22.22	27.40
Up to higher secondary	11.70	4.59	8.23	1.70	1.22	1.47
University degree holder (graduate)	6.73	1.84	4.34	0.00	0.00	0.00
Technical diploma/certificate	0.58	0.46	0.52	0.00	0.00	0.00
Professional education	0.58	0.15	0.37	0.00	0.00	0.00
Other higher education	3.07	0.92	2.02	0.00	0.00	0.00
Total	100.00	100.00	100.00	100.00	100.00	100.00
Total	684	653	1337	185	180	365

Note: Children below 6 years are excluded.

When one looks at educational achievements of the different social groups, one observes that the ST population is the least educated social group with 33 per cent of them being illiterate. They are followed by the OBC and the SC population. The rest of the population (i.e. higher castes) is relatively more educated in terms of literacy as well as years of schooling/education. The achievements of higher castes, however, are also far from impressive, as only 2.9 per cent of them have higher education. Again, the poorer occupational groups like the self-employed in non-agriculture (non-professional), and rural and agricultural labour households have the highest incidence of illiteracy. Households engaged in government service (no government jobs are available without a minimum level of education) and agriculture (larger farmers) have higher educational achievements.

Health Status in Nana Kotda: We do not have data on health outcomes such as life expectancy at birth (LIB), infant mortality rate (IMR) etc. in Nana Kotda. However, our investigation reveals that the major health problems in the village are water-borne diseases (diarrhoea, typhoid, gastroenteritis etc.), malaria and the diseases related to unclean environment. As we have discussed, the village does not have any reliable health facility in the village. One of the major causes of indebtedness in the village is sickness, and this has been a major source of vulnerability and poverty in the village.

LABOUR AND EMPLOYMENT IN NANA KOTDA

Major Occupations in Nana Kotda

The village economy of Nana Kotda is predominantly agricultural in nature, with most households engaged in crop cultivation and animal husbandry (Table 3.4). There are 102 households whose main occupation is crop cultivation and 45 others whose secondary occupation is crop cultivation, bringing the total to 147 farming households. Animal husbandry is another important activity, which is taken up by villagers mainly as a secondary occupation. About 16 households have animal husbandry as their main occupation and 107 households have it as secondary occupation, implying a total of 123 households engaged in animal husbandry. The households engaged in animal husbandry earn a living from selling milk (cow, buffalo, goat etc.), selling meat and wool, and from using animals for transportation. In all, 270 households (about two-third of the households) depend on these two activities, as a main source or as a secondary source of income.

The most important occupation in the village, however, is labour: agricultural labour and other manual labour. In all, 203 households (51 per cent) use labour as their main source of income, mainly in agriculture. In addition, 68 households (16.83), usually with small land holding or small income sources, depend on labour for supplementing their income. This labour includes agricultural work on farms, in construction, in animal husbandry etc.

In short, 325 households out of the total 404 households (80 per cent) have a primary sector activity as their main source of income either as owners/employers or as labourers. There are about 43 households whose main occupation is in the non-primary sector but also have a primary sector activity (farming, animal husbandry, agricultural labour) as their secondary activities. That is, about 91 per cent of the households, to a small or large extent, depend on primary sector activities for their living.

Table 3.4

Household Occupations in Nana Kotda

Main Occupation	*Details of Secondary Occupations*										
	Agri.	*Agri. Lab.*	*Other Lab.*	*Animal Husb.*	*Self-empl. Non-agri.*	*Govt. Serv.*	*Pvt. Serv.*	*Insurance*	*Rent etc.*	*Others*	*Total*
Agriculture	102	12	0	4	25	1	49	3	7	1	204
Agricultural labour	203	83	30	4	0	33	49	2	2	0	406
Other labour	4	2	0	0	2	0	0	0	0	0	8
Animal husbandry	16	3	5	2	5	0	0	0	1	0	32
Sub-total primary (a)	325	100	35	10	32	34	98	5	10	1	650
Self employed non-professional in non-agriculture	28	18	5	0	2	0	3	0	0	0	56
Service (govt.)	8	2	3	0	0	0	2	0	1	0	16
Service (private)	23	9	10	0	0	0	4	0	0	0	46
Insurance	0	0	0	0	0	0	0	0	0	0	0
Rent Income	0	0	0	0	0	0	0	0	0	0	0
Sub-total non-primary (b)	59	29	18	0	2	0	9	0	1	0	118
Pension income	3	0	0	2	0	0	0	1	0	0	6
Interest/royalties income	2	0	0	1	0	0	0	0	1	0	4
Beggar	3	0	0	0	0	0	0	0	0	0	3
Servant	1	0	0	0	0	0	0	0	0	0	1
Destitute	8	0	0	0	0	0	0	0	0	0	8
Sub-total dependent (c)	17	0	0	3	0	0	0	1	1	0	22
Closed house (d)	3	0	0	0	0	0	0	0	0	0	3
Total (a+b+c+d)	404	129	53	13	34	34	107	6	12	1	793

About 28 households have self-employment in non-agriculture, i.e. in the manufacturing sector as well as in trade and services as their main source of income. Many of them go to Idar, the block headquarter, for service and business. There are only a few shops in the village that include a bangle vendor, a fruits and vegetable vendor, carpenter, a cloth shop, a *paan* shop and a PDS shop. The trades include transportation of passengers and goods by *auto-rickshaws*, donkeys and by tractors. Services include government services in and outside the village, and private services like hiring of tractors and threshers, domestic service, helpers in tailoring shops and in the flour mill, catering, astrologer, priest and other services. About 19 households depend on pension, interest/rent income, or on help from relatives or on begging.

It is interesting to note that 275 households (69 per cent) have more than one source of income. Many of them have two, three or even more than three subsidiary occupations. Household members get employed in multiple jobs, mainly because one job does not provide them full time employment or, income from one job is not adequate to meet their needs or, because there are multiple earners in the household.

In short, the economy of Nana Kotda is predominantly agricultural in character, with a very small non-agricultural sector. In the absence of assured water supply, the agriculture depends mainly on rainfall, which is low and erratic. The economy suffers from low and fluctuating incomes in agriculture and in animal husbandry, resulting in high vulnerability of majority of the agricultural population. The average annual income in the village is Rs. 45296 (US $1160) per household, which is not very high by any standards. The highest average income, earned by large farmers is Rs. 108264 (US $2776) which is also not very high.

The NREGS can promote growth of agriculture and animal husbandry through watershed development, and regeneration of common lands and wastelands.

Under-employment of Workers

Table 3.5 presents the overall employment scene in Nana Kotda. Calculation of workforce participation rates are 78.38 and 64.52 per cent for men and women respectively. Though these rates are high, most of them get employment only for a limited number of days. On an average, a worker gets employment of 132 days in a year. There is not much difference in the days of work for men and women.

Except for those employed in government services, no occupation provides full employment (except for begging). The highest man-days are provided by government services (365 days), followed by private services (225 days) and self-employed in non-agriculture (207 days).

The low employment of large farmers (141 days) is perhaps voluntary as their annual income is quite large, more than Rs.1.0 lakh per year. The low employment of agricultural labour households (128 days), marginal farmer households (121 days) and small farmers (160 days) does indicate a significant level of under-employment and seasonal unemployment, arising from the predominance of single cropped farming in the village. In the absence of assured water supply, most farmers in the village grow only *kharif* crop. Landless agricultural labourers, however, are observed to be migrating or commuting to distant villages to work. Similarly, households with animal husbandry (as their main occupation) also are highly under-employed with 121 days of employment in the year. If 270 days of employment is considered as full employment, almost all occupations in the village (except government service) fail to provide full employment. Even though men and women work for more or less equal number of days in a year, women in farm households seem to work for higher number of days, 129 days as against 113 days of men. This is true for all categories of farm households—marginal, small and large farmers.

It is clear, that there is a need to at least double the level of employment in the village. Also, the data indicate that the total number of workers wanting additional wage work would easily exceed 700.

Diversification of Work

Even within the poor diversification of work in the village, men's work is relatively more diversified than that of women. Men spend 42 per cent days on agriculture (crop farming) compared to 70 per cent of women. Again, men spend 2 per cent of their days on animal husbandry,

Table 3.5

Employment of Workforce in Nana Kotda by HH Occupation

Main Occupation of HHs	*No. of HHS*	*No. of HH Members*			*No. of Workers*			*No. of Work Days*			*Average No. of Work Days*		
		M	*F*	*T*	*M*	*F*	*T*	*M*	*F*	*T*	*M*	*F*	*T*
Agriculture (i+ii+iii)	102	347	308	655	343	287	630	38747	36914	75661	113.0	128.6	120.10
(i) Marginal farmer	63	220	201	210	144	119	263	15572	16342	31914	108.14	137.33	121.35
(ii) Small farmer	30	77	59	105	53	41	94	7711	7360	15071	145.49	179.51	160.33
(iii) Large farmer	9	50	48	39	17	15	32	1915	2604	4519	112.65	173.60	141.22
Self-employed in non-agriculture	27	64	54	118	44	10	54	9625	1585	11210	218.8	158.5	207.59″
Agricultural labour	192	460	451	911	308	263	571	37586	35083	72669	122.0	133.4	127.27
Other labour	1	3	2	5	7	7	14	981	726	1707	140.1	103.7	121.93
Service (govt.)	6	18	11	29	13	3	16	4745	1095	5840	365.0	365.0	365.00
Service (pvt.)	18	48	37	85	30	8	38	6627	1907	8534	220.9	238.4	224.58
Animal husbandry	5	13	15	28	4	0	4	485	0	485	121.3	0.0	121.25
Interest	2	0	2	2	0	2	2	0	365	365	0.0	182.5	182.50
Pension	3	0	3	3	4	0	4	1095	0	1095	273.8	0.0	273.75
Beggar	1	0	1	1	2	0	2	730	0	730	365.0	0.0	365.00
Destitute	8	2	7	9	0	0	0	0	0	0	0.0	0.0	0.00
Closed house	0	0	0	0	0	0	0	0	0	0	0.0	0.0	0.00
Total	404	968	902	1870	758	582	1340	99560	77174	176734	132.3	132.6	132.4

against 8 per cent of women. On the other hand, men spend almost half of their days (of work) on non-agricultural activities (including services) as against, a mere 11 per cent by women. In short, women workers are crowded in agriculture and animal husbandry, with 78 per cent of their person days of employment spent on these activities. For men and women together, 51 per cent of their person days are spent on agriculture, 4 per cent on animal husbandry and 37 per cent on non-agricultural activities in Nana Kotda (Figure 3.1).

Education Level of the Workforce

Of the total workforce in the village, 34 per cent (one-third) is illiterate, 20 per cent has studied up to the primary level, and 30 per cent has studied up to secondary level. The rest 16 per cent of workforce has higher qualification. As regards technical education, the situation is much worse. The traditional activities like farming, animal husbandry, rural artisan work etc. do require skills, but these are acquired by workers while working on the job. They do not possess any formal technical qualifications. In fact, there is not a single worker in the village with formal technical qualifications.

Except for government service, no other occupation seems to need high and formal educational qualifications. All persons employed in government service are, therefore, educated: 20 per cent are university graduates, 20 per cent have other higher qualifications while 60 per cent have studied up to the secondary level (i.e. up to 10th standard). Labour households (agricultural labour and other labour) are the least educated: 35 per cent are illiterate, 25 per cent have studied up to 4th standard and another 25 per cent have studied up to 7th standard. The rest are educated up to higher secondary level (i.e. 12th standard). Similarly, self-employed in non-agriculture (i.e. in shops, vending, petty-trade etc.) are also less educated: 40 per cent are illiterate, 40 per cent have studied up to secondary level, and the rest have studied up to higher secondary level. The educational status of large farmers is slightly better: 25 per cent of all farmers are illiterate and another 25 per cent have studied to the primary level. Of the rest, 30 per cent have studied up to secondary level and the rest have studied beyond that level.

Figure 3.1

Sectoral Distribution of Employment by Gender

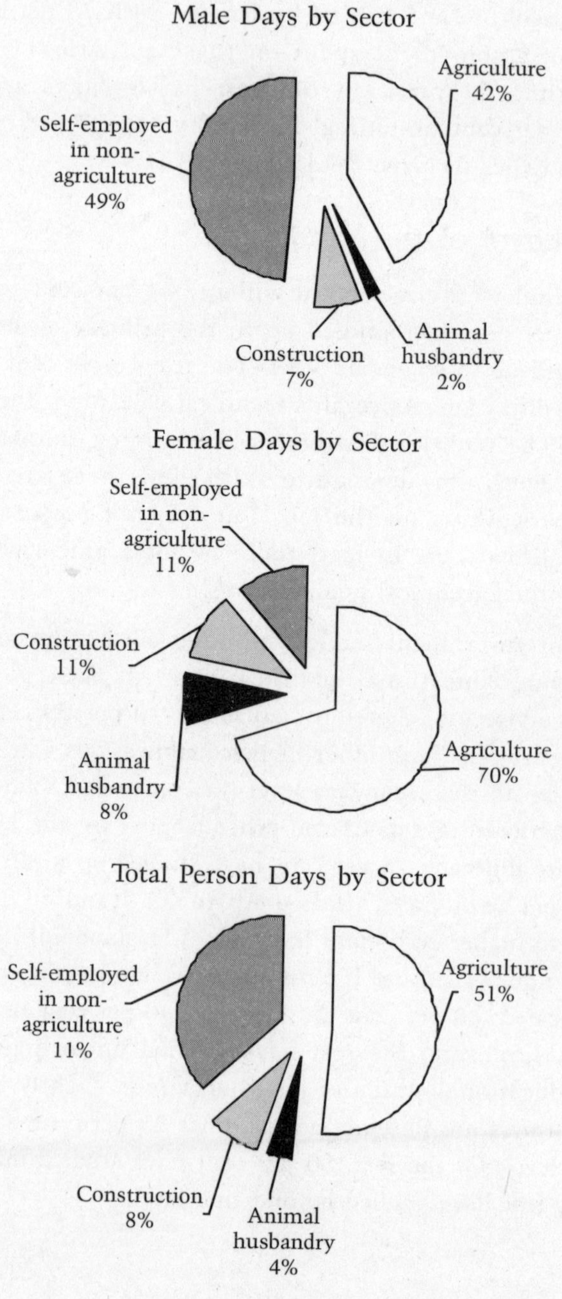

Absence of technical education, even among youth is a matter of concern, as it indicates limited employability of the labour force in the modern sectors of the economy.

Hired and Family Labour

Family labour constitutes an important part of the total workforce in Nana Kotda, as it is a common practice to work on family farms/ enterprises. Table 3.6 presents the distribution of total labour income of hired and family labour by sex, in Nana Kotda. The labour income for family labour has been imputed using the prevalent market wage rate (daily) of Rs. 50.00.

Table 3.6

Sector-wise and Sex-wise Distribution of Labour Income

	Labour M Family	*Labour F Family*	*Labour M Hired*	*Labour F Hired*	*Total M*	*Total F*
Wheat	911	817	6033.02	4480.96	6944.02	5297.96
Jowar	517	447	858.16	618.72	1375.16	1065.72
Bajra	10	10	75.24	75.24	85.24	85.24
Maize	1887	1429	4609.08	3915.92	6496.08	5344.92
Tur	61	61	796.74	796.74	857.74	857.74
Pulses	35	35	168.08	137.52	203.08	172.52
Castor	49	33	346.14	346.14	395.14	379.14
Groundnut	59	59	264	264	323	323
Cotton	3612	2654	10627.54	10145.58	14239.54	12799.58
Fruits & vegetables	101	101	161.54	161.54	262.54	262.54
Animal husbandry	14388.4	5467.6	5979.62	0	20368.02	5467.6
Other crop	0	0	1426.26	1426.26	1426.26	1426.26
Cotton ginning	0	0	8301.98	2197.26	8301.98	2197.26
Construction	0	0	9240	0	9240	0
Education	0	0	1102.44	0	1102.44	0
Bangle vendor	480	0	0	0	480	0
Fruit & vegetable vendor	816	1016	0	0	816	1016
Barber	1435	0	0	0	1435	0
Carpenter	5584	0	1.6	0	5585.6	0
Cloth shop	320	0	320	0	640	0
Paan shop	876	0	0	0	876	0
PDS shop	288	0	120	0	408	0
Transport	1210	165	0	0	1210	165
Other service	2545	0	60	0	2605	0
Total	35184.4	12294.6	50491.42	24565.86	85675.82	36860.46

As the table as well as Figure 3.2 shows, hired labour income and family labour income constitute 61.36 per cent and 38.74 per cent shares respectively of the total labour incomes in the village. Of these, women's shares are 20.05 and 10.03 respectively. In other words, women contribute 34.94 per cent in the total family labour income and 25.89 per cent of the total hired labour income. To put it differently, women contribute 30.08 per cent of the total labour income in the village. Of this, one-third is family labour and two-third is hired labour. In the case of men, they contribute about 70 per cent of total labour income in the village, and of this 60 per cent is hired labour income.

Figure 3.2

Distribution of Labour Income by Hired/Family Labour Status and Sex

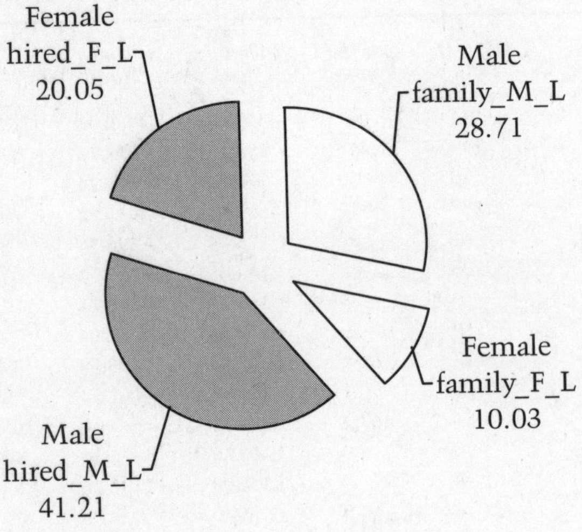

The table also presents sector-wise share of hired and family labour by sex. It shows that women's share in the total labour is zero in the sectors like shops and vendors, government services (including education), either as hired labour or as family labour. Women's participation is zero also as hired labour in animal husbandry (women provide family labour in this sector), as helpers in shops and in small trade and transportation, as they provide unpaid family labour in these sectors.

As regards crop cultivation, women work as hired labour as well as family labour. In fact, women's participation is much more as hired labour than as family labour in the production of crops like cotton (cotton picking), groundnut, castor, fruits and vegetables etc.

In- and Out-Migration of Workers

All workers including labourers in the village are local—except for a few school teachers and majority of workers in the ginning factory who come from outside. The ginning factory gets workers from outside mainly because, as reported by the owner, migrant workers come at a lower wage rate.

There is not much out-migration from the village for work. However, there is a lot of commuting for work. All the government servants who work in Idar, commute from the village. Those engaged in small business or in private services also commute mainly to Idar. In addition, about 200 workers commute to nearby villages for agricultural and non-agricultural unskilled work. Our discussion with the commuting unskilled workers indicated that they would prefer to work in their own village, if work is available. The percentage of women migrating out of the village is very small, as they prefer to work in the village so as to take care of domestic responsibilities along with working in the labour market.

Wages and Wage Structure

The average wage rate in agriculture and other unskilled work in the village is Rs. 50.00 per day (2006-07). However, the working hours are usually much longer than eight hours. There are no seasonal differences in the wage rate, but farmers usually employ workers for half a day during the lean season and make them work for more than four hours. This comes to lower wage rates in the lean season.

Workers migrating to nearby villages for agricultural work earn up to Rs. 55.00 per day. However, they prefer work in the village because: (1) it saves time and money in travelling, and (2) the wage difference is not big enough. They commute, as no work is available at home.

Women in the Labour Market

Women's participation in the labour market, though lower than that of men, is significant (their WPR is 64.52). Their share is about one-third of the total hired work and one-fourth in the total family labour in family enterprises. Women also commute much less than men largely because of their domestic responsibilities. They are less skilled and less educated compared to men, and as seen above, their work is less diversified. Women are, therefore, better candidates for NREGS works.

Quality of Employment

All employment except for employment of some government servants (60 per cent of them are permanent) in the village is temporary, contractual or casual employment. Some operations in crop cultivation are paid on the basis of the work performed, i.e. by work rates. There is no social protection or social security provided to workers, and there is no legal regulation of work conditions implemented effectively in the village except in government services, where there are rules regarding working hours, leave and sometimes social protection.

CONSUMPTION AND SAVINGS AND INDEBTEDNESS

Household Consumption Expenditure

The average household consumption expenditure in the village is Rs. 34035 (at 2006-07 prices). This comes to Rs. 7608 per capita per year, which is indeed very low. As expected, the large farmers enjoy the highest average consumption expenditure per household, Rs. 71389 (2006-07). They are followed by the service households (Rs. 62953) and small farmers (Rs. 51367). The labour households have the lowest average annual consumption expenditure, Rs. 34176, along with the "the other households" (which include pensioners, destitute etc.), whose expenditure is Rs. 20061.

At the village level, almost half of the total expenditure is incurred on food items. This is followed by consumer durables (like beds, utensils, cupboards, fan etc.), and then by health & education. As one would expect, the proportion of expenditure on food is the minimum for large farmers (35.37 per cent) and maximum for the self-employed in non-agriculture (SENA) households (57.81 per cent). The proportions are almost the same for SENA and labour households. However, labour households spend relatively higher proportion on food grains and less on milk and milk products when compared with SENA households. Service households spend relatively much less on food grains.

Households belonging to lowest income groups, i.e. labour households, marginal farmers and self-employed in non-agriculture, spend a very high percentage on health and medical services. Marginal farmers spend 10.05 per cent (Rs. 3575), small farmers spend 8.63 per cent (Rs. 4433) and labour households spend 8.17 per cent of their expenditure (Rs. 1758) on health. These amounts are larger than the corresponding amounts spent by large farmers and those employed in government services. In fact, Table 3.7 shows that the percentage of expenditure on health is the lowest for the richest groups, namely large farmers and government service households. This indicates the poor health conditions and a high incidence of morbidity of the poorer groups on the one hand and their very low access to government health services (where they get medical services almost free) on the other. It appears that the better off groups, have a better access to free/subsidised government health facilities. As we shall soon see, the high proportion of health expenditure is an important cause of the indebtedness, vulnerability and poverty of the poorer groups.

The fact that almost 8 per cent of the total expenditure of village households is on health and medical services clearly indicates that free health services of the government are not really reaching the village.

The high percentage of expenditure incurred on health and medical services also indicate that there is a good scope for strengthening health related infrastructure in the village. Provision of potable drinking water to all, drainage facilities, toilets and paving of internal roads can contribute towards improving the overall health status of people. The NREGS can help here.

As regards expenditure on education, the percentage of average household expenditure spent on education is 5.09. For the poorer groups it varies between 2 to 5 per cent. This implies that even free education is not free, as households have to spend on books and stationery. Households employed in government services spend a high portion (12.38 per cent) of their total expenditure on education, as they send their children out for higher education.

Table 3.7

Consumption Expenditure of Households by Occupation (%)

	Marginal Farmer	*Small Farmer*	*Large Farmer*	*Self-employed in Non-agriculture*	*Labour*	*Services*	*All Other HHs*	*Total*
Food crops	11.22	12.67	10.89	10.77	23.35	7.13	10.71	14.90
Fruits & veg., milk etc./animal product	12.98	17.35	12.97	20.95	9.12	15.86	17.74	13.13
Other food items	3.75	3.03	2.20	4.54	5.52	3.11	4.73	4.12
Total fuel	15.91	14.43	9.10	21.54	18.54	10.52	18.31	15.77
Sub-total	43.86	47.49	35.37	57.81	56.54	36.63	51.49	47.92
Clothing & cosmetics	4.34	3.61	2.35	5.89	7.87	3.58	4.60	5.26
Consumer durables	26.61	27.68	51.67	17.42	10.03	31.87	23.54	23.67
Health & medical services	10.05	8.63	2.02	4.89	8.17	5.21	5.87	7.88
Education	5.28	2.76	3.37	4.35	4.30	12.38	2.33	5.09
Rent & Elec.	6.64	6.89	4.44	6.58	10.97	6.30	9.00	7.93
Grand total	100.00	100.00	100.00	100.00	100.00	100.00	100.00	100.00
Cons. expenditure (per household) Rs.	39506	51367	71389	34176	24514	62953	20061	34035

The other important features of the consumption pattern of different economic groups are: (1) the poorer groups incur low expenditure on consumer durables, (2) they spend considerable percentages on tobacco and *paan*, and (3) they incur very low expenditure on fuel, as they get free firewood from common lands.

Household Savings

The total savings of all the households in the village is Rs. 25.9 lakh. It is the large farmers who save the most, followed by services households. The labour households are mostly hand to mouth, and have almost negligible savings. All other households have negative savings. It needs to be noted, that the savings refer to the average of the two normal years in agriculture.

Table 3.8

Summary Statistics for SAM Household Groups (Rs.)

Household Group	*Total Income (Rs.)*	*Total Expenditure (Rs.)*	*Savings (Rs.)*	*% of Expenditure*	*% of Savings*
Marginal farmer	3879411	3515993	293055	90.63	7.55
Small farmer	2043283	1438279	581882	70.39	28.48
Large farmer	2057010	1356384	684992	65.94	33.30
Self-employed in non-agriculture	1423202	922763	489909	64.84	34.42
Labour	4744524	4706603	37920	99.20	0.80
Services	2176760	1510861	650618	69.41	29.89
All others	472098	541652	-123622	114.73	-26.19

Indebtedness of Households

The low income and consumption levels, unstable and less developed agriculture, which is the main occupation in the village, and lack of adequate employment avenues for the people have pushed many households in to incurring debts. Households seem to incur debts for two reasons: first for consumption, i.e. for consumption of food—for survival; for social functions like death, marriage etc; for emergencies like ill health; and for other reasons like education. The second reason for incurring debt is for production, i.e. for buying capital or inputs etc. for production. Since financial institutions do not give loans for consumption purposes, the household have incurred consumption debts from private sources like the local money lenders, employers, large farmers, relatives etc. The term of such loans are usually unfavourable, in term of rate of interest and other conditions, as a result of which these households frequently find it difficult to get out of the debt trap. They become vulnerable and poor.

Debts for Consumption: Table 3.9 indicates that 193 households out of the total 404 (about 48 per cent) have incurred debts for consumption (the average amount of the debt being Rs. 33667) and only

37 households (9.01 per cent) have incurred debt for production purposes. That is, the number of households incurring debt for consumption is more than five times the number incurring debt for production. This reveals the vulnerability and poverty of the village on the one hand and the poor access of households to developmental opportunities on the other.

Table 3.9

Indebtedness in Nana Kotda

Main Occupation of HH	*Total HH*	*No of HH Debt for Consumption*	*Total Amount for Cons.*	*No. of HH Debt for Production*	*Total Amount for Prod.*	*Average of Consumption Amount*	*Average of Product Amount*
Agriculture	102	35	2446304	26	1087000	69894.4	41807.7
SENA	28	7	66500	2	50000	9500	25000
Agricultural labour	203	125	2703600	6	96200	21628.8	16033.3
Other labour	4	4	65000		0	16250	0
Service (govt.)	8	5	385000		0	77000	0
Service (pvt.)	24	9	433300	2	12000	48144.4444	6000
Animal husbandry	16	4	345000	1	30000	86250	30000
Interest/royalties income	2	0	0	0	0	0	0
Pension income	3	1	2000	0	0	2000	0
Beggar	3	2	31000	0	0	15500	0
Destitute	8	1	20000	0	0	20000	0
Total	401	193	6497704	37	1275200	33666,65	34464

The total amount of the debt incurred for consumption in the village is Rs. 64.97 lakh, which comes to about 84 per cent of the total debt in the village. That is, the debt/loans for production constitute only 16 per cent of the total debt and only 9 per cent of the households could access it.

About 65 per cent of the indebted households (for consumption loan) are labour households and 19 per cent are farmers (all marginal farmers). The rest of the households are service (private) households, households employed in animal husbandry, and in self-employment in non-agriculture. The highest incidence of indebtedness is in agricultural labour households and on small farmers.

Table 3.10

Occupation-wise HH Debt for Consumption

Main	Count of HH No.	Debt for		Debt for		Debt of		Debt for		Other Debt		Mortgage of		Sale of Assets		Loan	
		No. of HH	Total Amount (Rs.)	No. of HH	Total Amount (Rs.)	No. of HH	Total Amount (Rs.)	No. of HH	Total Amount (Rs.)	No. of HH	Total Amount (Rs.)	No. of HH	Total Amount (Rs.)	No. of HH	Total Amount (Rs.)	No. of HH	Total Amount (Rs.)
Agriculture	102	9	102800	1	80000	19	1078000	11	758504	1	50000	1	20000			1	200000
SENA	28					3	19000	1	5000	3	42500						
Agricultural labour	203	31	288900	5	72000	66	1515600	42	848100	2	25000	3	46000				
Other labour	4	2	30000			1	30000	1	5000								
Service (govt.)	8			1	80000			4	305000							2	400000
Service (pvt.)	24	3	158300			5	213300	2	80000								
Animal husbandry	16					5	149000	2	250000								
Interest/ royalties income	2													1	54000		
Pension income	3	1	2000														
Beggar	3	1	1000			1	30000										
Destitute	8	1	20000														
Total	401	48	603000	7	232000	100	3034900	63	2251604	6	117500	4	66000	1	54000	3	600000

Figure 3.3

Purpose of Incurring Debts (% of the Total Amount of Debt)

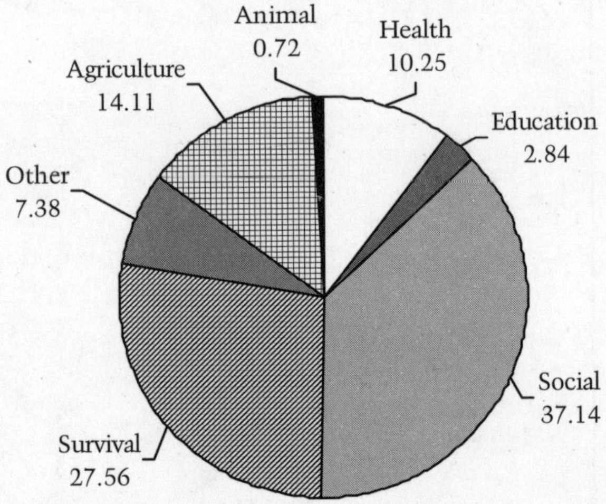

The most important reason for incurring debt is social functions, such as marriage, death and other social celebrations. 37.14 per cent of the debt is incurred for this reason. This is followed by survival, i.e. for buying food and other basic necessities (27.56 per cent), and ill health (10.25 per cent). That is, about one-third households have borrowed money to survive, for food and basic necessities in life and about one-fourth of the indebted households have incurred debt for health reasons and the amount of this debt is 10 per cent of the total debt. Agricultural labour households and farmer households are predominant in these households. Social functions reflect the seriousness of this social problem in the village society.

Debts for Production: Less than 10 per cent households have incurred debt for production. This debt is incurred mainly by farmers (mostly large farmers and a few small farmers) in the form of bank loans. In fact, 70 per cent of borrowing households are farmer households. Since banks are not willing to give loans to small and marginal farmers and to poor households, their share is very low. The other borrowers are agricultural labour households (6 households) and (private) service households. About 80 per cent households have incurred debt for agriculture, i.e. for buying equipment and machinery, inputs and irrigation facility. The rest have incurred debt for buying animals.

Table 3.11

Occupation-wise HH Debt for Production

Sr. No.	Main Occupation of HH	Count of HH No.	Debt for Agriculture		Debt for Animal		Other Debt	
			No. of HH	Total Amount (Rs.)	No. of HH	Total Amount (Rs.)	No. of HH	Total Amount (Rs.)
1	Agriculture	102	24	997000	3	55000	1	15000
3	Self employed non-professional in non-agriculture	28	2	50000				
4	Agricultural labour	203	5	66200			1	30000
5	Other labour	4						
7	Service (Govt.)	8						
8	Service (pvt.)	24	1	10000	1	2000		
9	Animal husbandry	16	1	30000	1	2000		
11	Interest/ royalties income	2						
13	Pension income	3						
17	Beggar	3						
19	Destitute	8						
	Total	401	33	1153200	5	59000	2	45000

In short, the poverty and vulnerability on the one hand and the lack of health facilities on the other, are primarily responsible for the high incidence of indebtedness in the village. The average amount of debt incurred for consumption is Rs. 33666 per indebted household. The average debt for production is almost the same, Rs. 34464 per household, but it is available to about 9 per cent of the total households.

Conclusion

Nana Kotda is a typical mid size village in Gujarat. It lacks in basic facilities like health and education, drinking water, sanitation, public hygiene, connectivity etc. It, therefore lags in human development achievements. Also, though the village economy is agricultural and majority of the workforce is engaged in agriculture, the agriculture in the village is rainfed, more than 70 per cent cultivated land depending on erratic rainfall. Well-selected NREGS works can help in human development as well as in agriculture by ensuring water to agriculture.

There is significant under-employment in the village as most farmers grow only one crop, the *kharif* crop, and there are not many employment avenues in the non-agricultural sectors. Consequently, there is a huge potential demand for NREGA kind of work in the village.

The insecurity and vulnerability of the village is reflected in the high incidence of indebtedness (for consumption) and the highly unfavourable terms of this debt incurred by about half of the households. The access of households to bank loans, which are usually for production purposes, is limited with the result that there is a limited investment made in agriculture in the village.

4 Village Economy: Nana Kotda

As seen in the earlier chapter, the village economy of Nana Kotda is predominantly agricultural in nature, with most households engaged in crop cultivation and animal husbandry. The most important occupation in the village, however, is labour: agricultural labour and other manual labour. About 51 per cent of the village households use labour as their main source of income and about 16 per cent households, mostly small and marginal farmers, depend on labour for supplementing their income. This labour includes agricultural work on farms, in construction, in animal husbandry etc.

The village economy is poorly diversified with about 80 per cent households having a primary sector activity as their main source of income either as owners/employers or as labourers. Only 28 households have self-employment in non-agriculture sector, i.e. in the manufacturing sector as well as in trade and services as their main source of income, and 31 households depend on government and private services for living. The rest of the households depend on income from pension, interest/ rent income, or on help from relatives or on begging. More than 69 per cent households have more than one source of income, many of them having two, three or even more than three subsidiary occupations. This is because one job does not provide them full time employment or income from one job is not adequate to meet their needs or because there are multiple earners in the household.

The village has about 1392 acres land of which 1188 acres (85.40 per cent) is under cultivation; 42.12 acres (3.02 per cent) is village common land/grazing land, and 3.66 acres (0.26 per cent) is government wasteland. The rest of the land is under non-agricultural use, largely under human settlement.

Social Accounting Matrix (SAM) for the Village[1]

We constructed a social accounting matrix (SAM) for Nana Kotda to understand the dynamics of the village economy through analysing its different sectors.

A SAM can be defined as an organised matrix representation of all transactions and transfers between different production activities, factors of production and institutions (like households, corporate sector and government) within the economy and with respect to the rest of the world. A SAM is thus a comprehensive accounting framework within which the full circular flow of income from production to factor incomes, household income to household consumption and back to production is captured. All the transactions in the economy are presented in the form of a matrix. Each row of the SAM gives receipts of an account while the column gives the expenditure. The total of each row is supposed to be equal to the total of each corresponding column. An entry in row i and column j represents the receipts of account i from account j.

A SAM can be regarded as an extension of input-output (I-O) tables. I-O tables are a widely used framework to provide detailed information on the flow of goods and services as well as on the structure of production costs. In this matrix, final consumption expenditure, capital formation and trade are shown by product or industry of origin and intermediate consumption both by product or industry of origin and destination. Income generation is shown by value added. However, it is worth noting that the symmetric I-O table is based on the absorption (use) matrix and make (supply) matrix. Absorption matrix gives the inputs of the commodities into industries (activities) while each row of the make matrix gives the distribution of the output of different commodities produced by the industry of that row. Each column of this matrix gives the values of output of that commodity produced by different industries. Symmetric I-O table is obtained from these two matrices by making certain mathematical assumptions regarding technologies (CSO, 2008). The I-O matrix does not show the

1. The full technical details are presented in Appendix A-4.1 at the end of this chapter.

interrelationship between value added and final expenditures. By extending an I-O table, showing an entire circular flow of income at macro level, one captures the essential features of a SAM.

Previous attempts to build a SAM for India have been made by Sarkar and Subbarao (1981), and Sarkar and Panda (1986), where the private income of the economy is divided into three parts, namely: (i) agricultural wage income, (ii) non-agricultural wage income, and (iii) non-agricultural non-wage income. Given the nature of their income classification, this does not help in the analysis of the size distribution of income. However, the SAM for 1977-78 by De Janvy and Subbarao (1986) had grouped households into seven social classes characterised by sources of income, *viz.:* (1) rural landless agricultural workers, (2) rural small farmers, (3) rural medium size farmers, (4) rural large farmers, (5) urban workers, (6) urban marginal workers, and (7) urban capitalists. This SAM was later updated to 1981 and expanded by Subramanian (1993). Another recent SAM by Pradhan and Sahoo (1996) do consider the income distribution of households according to their occupational classification. But they have only one urban category. Further, all of them do not have very detailed production sectors (for references of all these works, see Pradhan *et al.*, 2006).

A detailed SAM was constructed for the Indian economy for 1994-1995 for 60 sectors of the economy with two factors of production and six categories of occupational households, separately, for rural and urban areas. This SAM was updated to 1997-98 and to 2002-03 (Pradhan *et al.*, 2006). A SAM has been also constructed recently by Saluja and Yadav (2003-04).

At the village level, however, there is only one SAM in India, according to our knowledge. This is constructed by Subramanian and Sadoulet (1990) for Kanzara village of Maharashtra state to examine effects of investments on the village economy. This SAM covered 40 households and in that sense it did not cover the entire village.

Village Level SAM

The village SAM has the following account structure: (1) commodity accounts, (2) factor accounts, (3) institutional accounts, (4) capital accounts, and (5) rest of the world accounts. The SAM constructed for this study covers the entire village. The basic structure of this SAM is based on the following transactions and transfers in the economy given in Table 4.1.

Production requires intermediate goods and the primary factors of production, i.e. labour and capital. These factor endowments are contributed by the institutions (*viz.*, households, firms and government), which in turn, receive factor payment as value added. Apart from the value added, village institutions get income from other sources such as transfers from the government and from rest of the world. The income is spent as the consumption expenditure on goods and services and for payment of taxes and the rest is saved for the future. The total supply in the economy has to be matched by the demand made by the institutions and capital formation, i.e. purchase of investment goods. In the SAM, extra breakdown of the household sector is done to reflect the role of people in the economy

Table 4.1

The Structure of the SAM

	Expenditures						
	Endogenous			*Exogenous*			*Totals*
Receipts or Incomes	*Factors*	*Households*	*Productive Activities*	*Government*	*Rest of the World*	*Capital Account*	
Endogenous							
Factors	0	0	T_{13}	X_{14}	X_{15}	X_{16}	Y_1
Households	T_{21}	T_{22}	0	X_{24}	X_{25}	X_{26}	Y_2
Product. activities	0	T_{32}	T_{33}	X_{34}	X_{35}	X_{36}	Y_3
Exogenous							
Government	L_{41}	L_{42}	L_{43}	t_{44}	t_{45}	t_{46}	Y_4
Rest of world	L_{51}	L_{52}	L_{53}	t_{54}	t_{55}	t_{56}	Y_5
Capital acts.	L_{61}	L_{62}	L_{63}	t_{44}	t_{45}	t_{46}	Y_6
Totals	Y_1	Y_2	Y_3	Y_4	Y_5	Y_6	

Designing a SAM for Nana Kotda Village

The village SAM for Nana Kotda consists of the following components.

1. *Production activities:* The following production sectors are included in the SAM.
   - *Crop husbandry:* Wheat, *jowar*, *bajra*, maize, *tur*, other pulses, oilseeds, cotton, fruits & vegetables and other crops. Cultivation of these crops is divided for irrigated and rainfed areas, but in SAM we have only one column for each crop.
   - *Animal husbandry:* Milk and milk products, wool and meat, cow dung manure and bullocks.
   - *Construction*
   - *Service providers and self-employed:* Fruit & vegetable vendor, bangle vendor, cloth shop, *paan* shop, PDS shop, transport, carpenter and other services.
   - *Manufacturing:* Cotton ginning factory.
   - *Services:* Government services (education, welfare), private services (petty services).
2. *Factors of Production:* The following factors of production have been included.
   - *Labour:* By sex: Males and females.
   - *Capital:* Capital includes mixed income of self-employed.
3. *Institutions:* The following institutions have been covered in the SAM.
   - *Households:* By occupation: Small farmers, medium farmers, large farmers.
   - Labour
   - Self employed in non-agriculture
   - Service
   - Other households

(Note: The farmers are divided into three categories based on the cultivatable land owned by them. These categories are: marginal farmers up to 2.5 acres, small farmer with land from 2.5 to 5.0 acres, and large farmers with land above 5.0 acres).

- *Government:* Only village *panchayat* (local body) is taken as the government.

The village *panchayat* receives land tax and house tax from households as income and government grants from other sources outside the village. It gives grants for the development activities like that for house construction, which are treated as expenditure for the *panchayat* along with its other expenditures.

Savings in the economy including depreciation on capital consist mainly of household savings.

4. *Outside the village:* Consists of values of sectors and labour going out of the village and coming into the village.

Construction of SAM for the village Nana Kotda, required data on the output in different sectors, the value added by these sectors and sector-wise consumption of different components of final demand. The value added for each sector is divided into labour income (hired) by gender and capital income (including mixed income). Although sex-wise value of labour is separately available, for inverting SAM we have made it a single row for the entire hired labour.

In all there are 55 producing sectors. First 13 sectors from rice to animal husbandry correspond to agriculture where many of the items are produced in the village. For the construction of SAM, the normal yield for the crops has been taken for last two years, because 2006-07 happened to be a drought year. Sectors 14 to 38 are manufacturing sectors where all the items are brought from outside the village except for cotton ginning (for which there is only one factory), which produces cotton inside the village and sends the entire production, including that of cotton seed outside the village. The other remaining sectors are the service providing sectors in the village. The activities could not be separated from commodities because the data available was directly on commodity basis both for inputs as well as outputs. Hence, the SAM is directly in the commodity X commodity form, which is derived from the use and supply matrices.

A complete census of all households in the village was carried out to collect data on all entities and sector-wise expenditure of different types of households and data about occupation and education level of all household members. Except for salaried and wage labour households, the details of costs and revenue earned were collected for all households.

For example, data collected from wheat producers included data on the value of the output of wheat produced in the fields (area X yield X price), value of the byproducts, and consumption of different inputs like seed, fertilisers, pesticides, etc. For salaried and wage labour households, the details of their income were collected.

In addition, detailed information was collected from all institutions /organisations like schools, cooperative societies and *panchayats* about their activities, costs and revenues. Details were also collected about the working of NREGA in the village.

In the SAM for cultivators there is one row under capital for each crop. This is the total for different categories of cultivators. In the column under capital, these values have been given separately for different types of cultivators. The entry in the cell of capital and self-employed row is equal to the total of capital column for all self-employed non-agricultural categories. For all other households, the entire earnings are put under capital. The earning under labour, consists of the labour as well as some helpers getting salaries. There are some labourers who go to nearby villages/Idar town to earn money. The major income from outside the village, however, is from services. The total of their income is put under service households.

For trading activities like fruit, vegetable and bangle vendor, income is calculated as net profits earned by deducting the value of inputs from the gross receipts. In the case of fruits and vegetables, the expenditure obtained from the census of household is adjusted for the expenditure by the fruits and vegetables vendors. Similar adjustments have been done in the cases of the cloth shop, the *paan* shop and PDS shops.

There are two cooperatives in the village, namely, the milk cooperative and the farmers' service society. The income shown in the column is their profit. This profit is divided into its members who are agriculturists. There is a separate column for this in the SAM, in order to show the importance of cooperatives in the village. For the construction of the SAM as well as for using it for multiplier analysis, we have merged the column with the different columns under crop production (Refer to Appendix A-4.1).

Table 4.2

Aggregated SAM 2006-07 (Rs.)

	Expenditures						
	Endogenous			*Exogenous*			*Totals*
Receipts or Incomes	*Factors*	*Households*	*Productive Activities*	*Government*	*Rest of the World*	*Capital Account*	
Endogenous							
Factors	0	0	29515186	80146	-14317045	0	15278287
Households	15278287	0	0	1512000	0	0	16790287
Product. activity	0	13992534	158621685	128600	172692294	1440525	346875638
Exogenous							
Government	0	183000	0	0	0	0	183000
Rest of world	0	0	158738767	0	0	0	158738767
Capital acts.	0	2614753	0	-1537746	363518	0	1440525
Totals	15278287	16790287	346875638	183000	158738767	1440525	

SAM is a double entry table, where each row of the table details the receipts of an account while the columns details the corresponding expenditure. A SAM is always a square matrix. SAM provides information on interactions between production activities (by sectors), factors of production (capital and labour), institutions (households by occupations, local government) capital account, and rest of the world (imports, exports). These accounts are symmetrically arranged (in rows and columns) forming a square matrix that traces the origin and destinations of expenditure and receipts. A simplified aggregate SAM for the economy of Nana Kotda, is given in Table 4.2.

The first row, gives the income of factors of production. This income consists of the income of male labour, female labour working in the village, the income of labour working outside the village, and capital income including the mixed income of the self-employed (e.g. income of family labour of cultivators). The second row, shows the income of the households, which is mainly in the form of the income of the factors of production. It also includes the grants from the government. The corresponding column gives the expenditure of households, taxes paid, and the saving of the household.

The third row gives the income of the productive activities. This income is in the form of the consumption by households, consumption by the production activities in the form of intermediate consumption and exports. The corresponding column gives the expenditure in the form of payments to factors of production, expenditure on inputs on item produced in the village and payments to outside world in the form of imports of inputs of materials and labour. The fourth row gives the income of the local government from taxes and the fourth column gives the expenditure of the government. The fifth row as well as the fifth column tells about the exports from the village and imports to the village. The last row as well as the last column deals with the capital account which is in the form of saving of the households, local government and from outside.

From the perspective of this study, a SAM is a powerful tool in that it can include sufficient details to point out gender differences—and biases—in the division of labour, patterns of income received and expenditures incurred, etc. In addition to the transparency of income distribution and the labour composition of production (as it emerges from the description of the productive structure of the economy), it allows one via simulations of hypothetical policy intervention scenarios to examine the impact of different NREGA works.

Contribution of Different Sectors to Village Economy

The SAM for the village consists of 55 producing sectors. The total production of all the sectors produced inside the village is Rs. 186.00 m (million) and items worth Rs. 158.9 m comes from outside the village. The high value of the internal production of the village economy is mainly because of the cotton ginning factory whose output is Rs. 167.0 m and which forms 90 per cent of the output produced in the village. Similarly, the huge import figure is because the cotton ginning factory imports raw cotton of worth Rs. 145.0 m which forms 91.2 per cent of the imported items. Contribution of agriculture sector in the economy is 5.3 per cent and the rest is contributed by animal husbandry, construction, and other self-employed sectors. However, if we exclude the cotton ginning factory, the total output in the village is Rs. 18.62 m. The contribution of agriculture and other sectors has been presented in Table 4.3 and in Figure 4.1.

Table 4.3

Contribution of Major Sectors in the Total Production

Sector	*Output (Rs.)*	*% Contribution in Total*
Agriculture	10019976	54
Animal husbandry	2989812	16
Construction	1927027	10
Non-agriculture	3687510	20
Total	18624325	100

Figure 4.1

Sectoral Distribution of Output

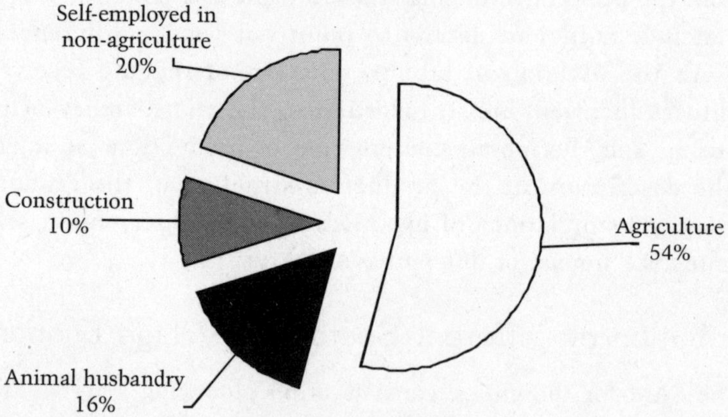

Agriculture forms 54 per cent of the total value of output of all sectors followed by 20 per cent in self-employed in non-agriculture, 16 per cent in animal husbandry and 10 per cent in construction. It needs to be noted that though more than 72 per cent of the households in the village depend on agriculture (crop cultivation), the contribution of agriculture to the village output is 54 per cent only.

The average annual income per household in the village is Rs. 41355, which comes to Rs. 8989 per capita (Table 4.4). The highest income per household is earned by large farmers, followed by that of service households, small farmers, self-employed in non-agriculture households, and marginal farmer households in that order. Per household income, is the lowest in the case of "other" households, followed by that of labour households.

The table also shows that the labour households, which constitute 47.3 per cent of the total households, earn only about one-fourth of the total village income. On the other end, large farmers who constitute 4.7 per cent of the total households, earn more than 11 per cent of the total village income. The households engaged in services and small farmer households also earn disproportionately higher income. Figures 4.2 and 4.3 depict this clearly.

Table 4.4

Income Distribution among Households by Occupation

	Total Income (Rs.)	% to Total Income	No. of households (Nos.)	Percentage of Households	Income per HH (Rs.)
Marginal farmers	3879411	23	89	22	43589
Small farmers	2043283	12	28	7	72974
Large farmers	2057010	12	19	5	108264
Self-employed in non-agriculture	1423202	9	27	7	52711
Labour	4744524	28	192	47	24711
Services	2170760	13	24	6	90448
All Other HH	472098	3	27	7	17485
	16790288	100	406	100	41355

Figure 4.2

% Share of Different Occupations in Total Income

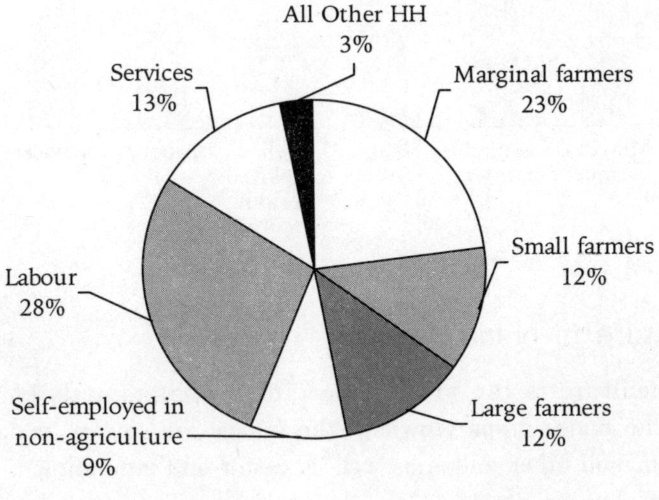

Figure 4.3

% Share of Different Occupations in Total Households

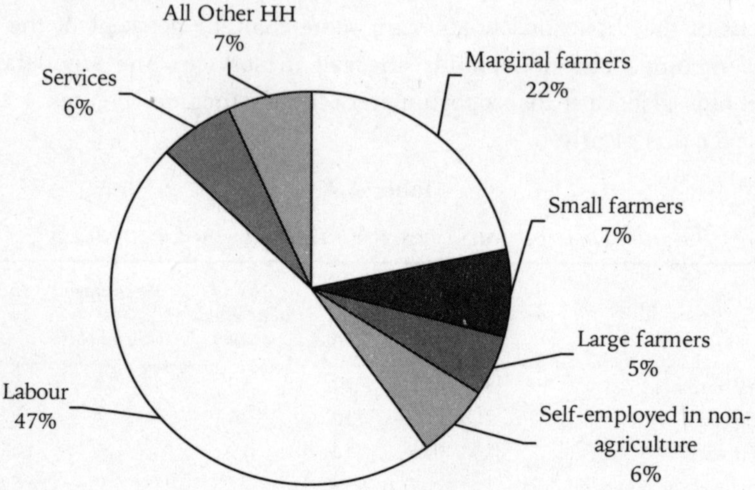

Figure 4.4

Average Household Income by Occupation

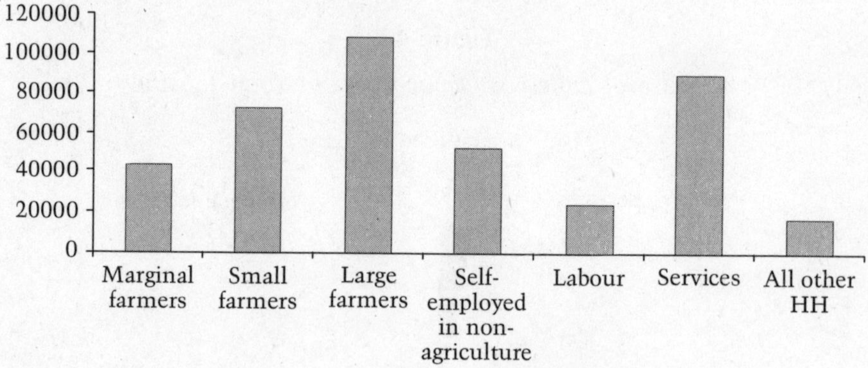

Agriculture in Nana Kotda

Agriculture is the most important economic activity, in Nana Kotda. The major crops grown in the village are cotton, maize, *jowar*, wheat, *tur*, and other pulses as well as castor and groundnut.

Table 4.5

Crops Grown in Nana Kotda

Name of Crop	*Irrigated Area (in acres)*	*Non-Irrigated Area (in acres)*	*Total Area (in acres)*
Maize	24.7	81.51	106.21
Cotton	24.7	49.4	74.1
Jowar	12.35	34.58	46.93
Tur	19.76	37.05	56.81
Urad /Moong	7.41	14.82	22.23
Wheat	19.76	61.75	81.51
Tomato	9.88	19.76	29.64
Castor	44.46	93.86	138.32
Groundnut	9.88	24.7	34.58
Bajra	0	2.47	2.47
Total	172.9	419.9	592.8

About 30 per cent of the cultivated area is irrigated and 70 per cent area is rainfed. Agricultural production in the village, therefore shows wide annual fluctuations due to the variations in the rainfall. In every five years there are 2-3 years of droughts or floods that result in agricultural losses. For example, in the year 2006-07, the year of investigation, the farmers in the village had experienced huge losses due to floods and diseases. The total agricultural production was Rs.40 lakh, as against the total costs of Rs. 49.88 lakh. The net loss was of Rs. 9.88 lakh. As Table 4.6 presents data on the losses made by small farmers and large farmers. The rate of returns were -29.00 per cent for marginal farmers, -36.00 per cent for small farmers and -11.00 per cent for large farmers. The marginal farmer household, on an average made a loss of Rs. 3814, while the small farmer household made a loss of Rs. 10941 and the large farmer made a loss of Rs. 6470.

Such losses, result in farmers mortgaging or selling their land and, as we will shortly see, in incurring debts. In short, fluctuating crop production makes cultivation non-viable for farmers, which makes small and marginal farmers highly vulnerable.

Table 4.6

Returns on Agriculture by Marginal, Small and Large Farmers in 2006-07 (Bad year) (Rs.)

	Marginal Farmers	*Small Farmers*	*Large Farmers*
Production	1517140	1097350	1385510
Inputs	903686	555692	579513
Female hired labour	309234	344996	423672
Male hired labour	342171	441796	441796
Female family labour	184150	60250	37900
Male family labour	216500	88500	57900
Profits	-438602	-393884	-155271
Profit per household (Annual)	-3814	-10941	-6470
No. of households	115	36	24
Returns (profit/output) %	-29	-36	-11

In a normal year, however, crop cultivation is viable with positive returns. The average production of two normal years (2003-04 and 2004-2005) has been used as normal production in our analysis. As Table 4.7 indicates, the total output in the normal years is Rs. 100.20 lakh and the net profit is of Rs. 50.32 lakh. The rate of returns (profits) is 49.00 per cent, 46.00 per cent and 56.00 per cent for marginal, small and large farmers respectively. The average annual income earned by a marginal farmer (Rs. 16041) is almost one-fifth of the income earned by a large farmer (Rs. 80413), from crop cultivation.

In short, agriculture in Nana Kotda has low productivity, earns low income and is highly unstable. Controlling fluctuations and ensuring stable supply of water is a major need in the village. Ensured and increased water supply will also improve cropping intensity (by promoting multiple cropping) as well as crop yields in the village.

Value-added by Different Crops: The details of the output and value added (labour + capital) by different crops and the inputs consumed by the crops are presented in Table 4.8. The maximum production in the village, is of cotton (Rs. 50 lakh), followed by wheat (Rs. 21.04 lakh) and maize (Rs. 14.6 lakh). The other crops like *jowar*, *bajra*, *tur* etc. have much less production.

Table 4.7

Returns on Agriculture by Marginal, Small and Large Farmers in Normal Year (Rs.)

	Marginal Farmers	*Small Farmers*	*Large Farmers*
Production	3800427	2748855	3470694
Inputs	903686	555692	579513
Female hired labour	309234	344996	423672
Male hired labour	342171	441796	441796
Female family labour	184150	60250	37900
Male family labour	216500	88500	57900
Profits	1844685	1257622	1929913
Profit per household (Annual)	16041	34934	80413
No. of households	115	36	24
Returns (profit/output) %	49	46	56

Farmers Service Society: There is a farmers service society (FSS) or the Nana Kotda Service Cooperative Society, which provides inputs as well as marketing services to farmers. It has 410 members, and a small executive committee of 9 to manage the society. The FSS buys fertiliser [urea, DAP (diammoniun phosphate), Narmada force, biogold, superforse etc.], seeds and pesticides in bulk from outside, and sells these to farmers with a small profit. The FSS also borrows money from outside, and lends it to local farmers at a slightly higher interest rate. In the year 2006-07, the FSS sold fertilisers worth Rs. 2.25 lakh and seeds (maize, cotton, *jowar*) worth Rs. 1.25 lakh to farmers. It also lent Rs. 45.00 lakh to local farmers by borrowing it from outside and made a small profit of Rs. 52068.

The FSS also supports the Department of Agriculture in organising meetings, demonstrations, training programmes etc. and thereby helps farmers in adopting new technologies.

Animal Husbandry and Milk Cooperative Society

Animal husbandry is an important occupation in the village that provides main or secondary incomes to a large number of households. Since milk is a major output, there is a full fledged milk cooperative society in the village with more than 410 members (sometimes there are

Table 4.8

Crop-wise Value of Output, Value Added and Inputs Consumed (Rs.)

	Wheat	*Jowar*	*Bajra*	*Maize*	*Tur*	*Pulses*	*Castor*	*Groundnut*	*Cotton*	*Fruits & Vegetables*	*Other Crops*
Seed	198450	7580	350	33510	4932	350	4900	800	233490	5720	17828
Animal husbandry	91200	21872	4100	145200	36785	3450	5000	3200	260180	6250	17828
Fertiliser	67900	19600	1500	84175	24115	1275	5500	1500	174840	4425	
Pesticide	15600	2400	0	7250	0	0	1100	500	104250	2150	
Electricity	5179	0	0	5179	0	0	0	0	0		
Other exp.	5612	0	0	5612	0	0	0	0	0		
Equipment S. repair	1897	0	0	1897	0	0	0	0	0		
Transport	48675	10450	1200	61975	30518	0	4600	1600	126800	1500	
Other ser.	48971	600	500	49381	1900	0	50050	500	500	1900	
Labour M	301651	42908	3762	230454	39837	8404	17307	13200	531377	8077	71313
Labour F	224048	30936	3762	195796	39837	6876	17307	13200	507279	8077	71313
Capital	1095425	98249	19476	642538	68360	51910	123982	97500	3055835	42673	534848
Total	2104608	234595	34650	1462967	246284	72265	229746	132000	4994551	80772	713130

more than one member from a household). It collects all surplus milk from the village to send it to the district diary, Sabar Dairy. The Sabar Dairy processes it, and sells milk and milk products to outside markets. In 2006-07, about 4.15 lakh litre milk was collected by the cooperative society. Of this, 36.4 per cent was cow milk and the rest was buffalo milk. The milk society provides veterinary services, cattle feed and medicines etc. for milch animals. The cooperative society earned a profit of Rs. 1.14 lakh in 2006-07. This came to an average of Rs. 285 per member (in addition to milk price), which is a pittance.

It is clear that like agriculture, this sector also suffers from low productivity and low incomes. There is a need to raise the productivity in this sector by improving the breed, ensuring water supply and quality fodder, and by increasing the number of milch animals. NREGS can play a role here.

Animals are also used for carrying loads and transporting people/ luggage, as well as for wool. The total returns from animal husbandry are presented in Table 4.9. In all, 170 households are engaged in it and the total returns (profits) are Rs. 3.48 lakh, which gives, on an average, an annual income of Rs. 2049. It is clear, that the activity yields low income, and there is a need to increase it by increasing the number of animals as well as their productivity.

Table 4.9

Animal Husbandry in Nana Kotda

	(Rs.)
Output	2989812
Inputs	1349730
Hired labour M	298981
Hired labour F	0
Family labour M	273380
Family labour F	719420
Profits	348301
No. of households having animal	170
Profits per household (annual)	2049
Returns (profits/output)	0.116

Note: It is assumed that a person spends on an average 4 hrs a day on animal husbandry activities and gets Rs. 4 for an hour.

It is important to note that family labour is predominant in animal husbandry. Of the total person days of employment in this sector, 76.9 per cent are of family labour. Of these, 73 per cent is women's labour. Hired labour is of men only. This is largely in animal grazing and related activities. Women's share in the total labour is 56 per cent.

Non-Agricultural Sectors

Non-agricultural sectors include non-agricultural enterprises, located in the village, and non-agricultural employment, which is located inside and outside the village. The value of the total output produced in non-agricultural sectors is Rs. 3687510 and the value of the total inputs is Rs. 2079695. This sector contributes 37 per cent of the total output in the village. The different occupations under this group are vendors (bangle vendors, fruits and vegetable vendors, barbers), rural artisans/manufacturing (carpenter), shops (a cloth shop, *paan* shops, a PDS shop) and services. Their total revenue and income are given in Table 4.10.

Table 4.10

Self-employed in Non-agriculture: Annual Revenue and Income (Rs.)

	No. of HH with Main Occupation as	*Revenue*	*Income*	*Income per Household*
Bangle vendor	2	112000	32000	16000
Fruits and veg. vendor	6	278000	146600	24433
Barber	3	90000	74875	24958
Carpenter	8	721200	276000	34500
Cloth shop	1	560000	137700	137700
Paan shop	2	588000	84000	42000
PDS shop	1	408000	20480	20480
Transport	5	619000	485640	97128
Govt. services	16		674140	42134
Pvt. service	35		956980	27342

Note: Revenue-Expenditure = Income.

The value of output in the reference year is the maximum for the carpenter (Rs. 721200 followed by that for transport, *paan* shop, cloth shop, other services and the PDS shop. The income is the highest for the transport owner (Rs. 485640), followed by that of 'other services'. As regards income earned per household, the highest annual income is earned by the cloth shop owner (Rs. 137700), followed by transporters. Households of government servants also earn relatively good money (Rs. 42134). The others, engaged in petty trade and petty services earn less than Rs. 25000 a year. This barely meets their basic needs.

The PDS Shop: There is a fair price shop, or a shop set up by the Government under the public distribution system (PDS). It acquires supplies of essential commodities from the government and sells these to the villagers. There are two sets of buyers, namely, the below poverty line households (BPL) and the above poverty line households (APL). The commodities are sold at fixed (fair) prices and in limited quotas. These commodities include wheat, rice, sugar and kerosene. All the supplies come from outside the village and are sold within the village.

In the year 2006-07, the PDS shop sold commodities worth Rs. 3.40 lakh and made a small profit of Rs. 20480 for itself. The shop is fully managed by the shopkeeper, who is supported by a servant who works for 10 days a month. The low earnings of the PDS shop is because of its limited business. However, managing the shop is a part time business, as the shop opens for a few hours in the morning.

Figure 4.5 presents the income per household by non-agricultural occupations.

Figure 4.5

Income per Household by Occupation

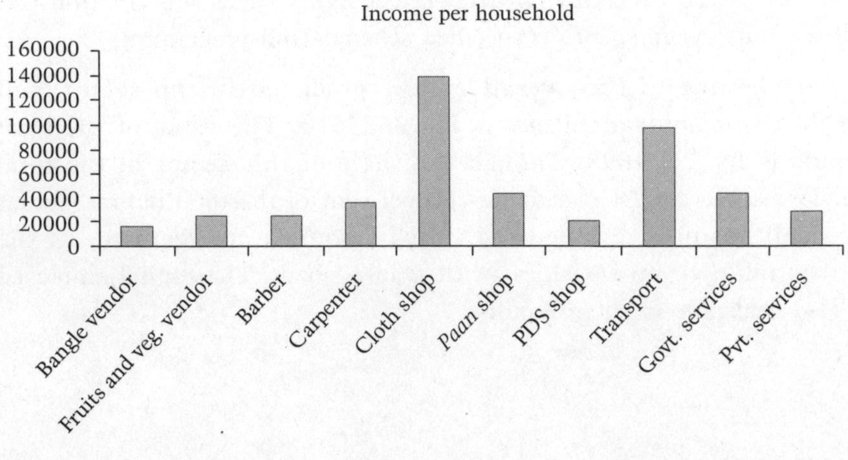

The Ginning Factory: Since this district/block produces cotton in bulk, there are quite a few ginning factories in the region. The Surod Ginning and Pressing Factory in Nana Kotda, works seasonally (8 months a year). It buys cotton from all the surrounding villages, produces cotton bales which are then sold to spinning mills in the state. Since there is a huge demand for the bales, purchasers come to Nana Kotda to buy these.

The factory was set up in 1968. It employs 64 workers on contract basis and has a manager, supported by a small permanent staff of 4 persons (an accountant, an office boy and two watchmen). Of the contract workers, 44 are men and 20 are women. In the year 2006-07, the factory purchased 750,000 kg cotton and sold 15000 cotton bales (each with 165 kg) and 4.8 million kg cotton seeds. The factory made a profit worth Rs. 15.0 million for the year.

Village Panchayat (Local Body): The local elected government, the village *panchayat*, is a local body that is responsible for the affairs of the village. It is headed by *sarpanch*, the elected head of the village and has eight other elected members to support him. The *panchayat* is supported by a *talati*, who acts as secretary of the *panchayat*. The *talati* (the revenue man) is the secretary to four other village *panchayats*.

The income of the *panchayat* comes from government grants for different schemes and programmes, local taxes and donations made by local people or, the MLA/MP. In the year 2006-07, the village *panchayat* received a grant of Rs. 19.4 lakh for different programmes like housing schemes (Rs.15.12 lakh), NREGS, street lights, road construction etc. All the funds were spent on specified schemes and programmes.

The value of the overall output produced in the sector 'self employed in non-agriculture' is Rs. 3687510. The value of the total inputs is Rs. 2079695. Though the share of this sector in the total employment is low, it contributes 56 per cent of the total output. As far as small business is concerned, hired labour is not required, as the owners run their own business with family labour. The capital employed is also negligible in these sectors.

Consumption Expenditure of Different Categories of Households

Table 4.11 presents the patterns of consumption expenditure of village households by categories of households. The table is revealing in many ways. To start with, labour households spend the highest percentage of their consumption expenditure on total food (52.94), followed by self employed in non agriculture and all other households (50.09 and 43.52 respectively). The households with services as their main occupation and large farmers spend the lowest percentage on food items, 31.52 and 32.19 percentages respectively. The composition of the food items, however, reveals that self employed in non agriculture, medium farmers and all other households spend larger percentage on fruits, milk and vegetables, while the labour households spend the highest percentage on food grains.

Another interesting point, emerging from the table is that, on an average, households spend more than one-fifth of their expenditure (21.46 per cent) on consumer durables. The highest percentage is spent by large farmers (43.67 per cent), followed by households in services. Labour households spent the lowest percentage (7.88 per cent) on these items. The high percentage of expenditure on health and education is by service households (17.88 per cent) followed by small farmers (14.33) indicates the non-availability of free health and educational services in the village. As we have already seen, people in the village have a poor access to public health services, as a result they have to spend huge amounts on health. The same is the case with educational services, with the difference that people cannot avoid spending on medicines if there is illness in the family, while they can avoid paying for education if they do not want to spend on school fees, or books. Finally, at the village level, food items have the maximum share in the total consumption expenditure (about half the expenditure is on food items), followed by consumer durables (21.46 per cent), such as beds, tables, chairs and other furniture as well as radio/TV/mobiles etc. Around 11.10 per cent is spent on health and education, and 3.35 per cent on housing and mainly electricity.

It is clear, that except for some food items and housing, most of the consumption goods and services come from outside the village, this tends to restrict the impact of NREGS works on the village economy.

Table 4.11

Percentage Distribution of Consumption of Commodities and *Services by Different Categories of Households, 2006-07*

	Marginal Farmers	*Small Farmers*	*Large Farmers*	*Self-Employed in Non-Agriculture*	*Labour*	*Services*	*All Other HH*
Food grains	11.02	12.32	11.29	10.34	22.77	7.37	10.06
Fruits & veg. milk/ animal product	11.61	15.76	12.06	17.61	9.86	14.48	15.12
Other food Items	16.92	14.26	8.84	22.13	20.32	9.67	18.33
Sub total	39.54	42.34	32.19	50.09	52.94	31.52	43.52
Total fuel	2.90	2.41	1.86	3.40	4.34	2.54	3.41
Clothing & cosmetics	6.84	5.87	4.09	9.08	11.70	6.02	6.26
Consumer durables	20.56	22.00	43.67	13.08	7.88	26.06	16.96
Health & education	14.33	11.39	5.39	9.24	11.47	17.68	8.19
Rent & elec.	3.11	3.16	2.23	2.80	4.98	2.68	4.50
Grand total	87.28	87.17	89.44	87.68	93.31	86.50	82.84
Others	12.72	12.83	10.56	12.32	6.69	13.50	17.16
Total (Rs.)	3516011	1438279	1356384	922761	4706605	1510862	541651

Exports from and Imports to Nana Kotda

The total exports from the village are worth Rs. 1726.92 lakh, of which cotton along with cotton seeds form the major part (the ginning factory). If we exclude the ginning factory, the highest exports are of agricultural crops like maize, wheat, castor, *jowar* etc. The next sector is animal husbandry, the exports from which are of Rs. 1238029. The other sectors are carpentry, and education (Table 4.12).

The total imports to the village are worth Rs. 1609.21 lakh, of which cotton is most important with the value of Rs. 1453.20 lakh. The imports include food grains (including rice and wheat not grown in the village); fruits and vegetables; other food items like tea, coffee, spices, sugar etc; textiles; consumer durables like furniture, bicycles and two/

four wheelers; and construction material. The village also depends on outside for health and medical services, for agricultural inputs like fertilisers, pesticides, equipments etc. and for other miscellaneous items.

Table 4.12

Exports and Imports from the Village

Sector	*Value (Rs.)*	*Percentage*
A. Exports		
Wheat	885285	0.51
Jowar	106475	0.06
Maize	1105109	0.64
Tur	54773	0.03
Castor	175995	0.10
Groundnut	131200	0.08
Total crops	2458837	1.42
Animal husbandry	1238029	0.72
Cotton ginning	167948438	97.25
Education	614330	0.36
Carpenter	432660	0.25
Total	172692294	100
B. Imports		
Food grains and other food items	3235902	2.01
Fuel wood, LPG, kerosene, electricity	3186380	1.98
Consumer durables	2732771	1.70
Construction material: bricks, sand, cement, metal sheets etc.	1176000	0.73
Medical and health services	970204	0.60
Others	4229549	2.63
House rent	69200	0.04
Cotton	145321035	90.31
Total	160921041	100

Total gross value added (GVA) of the village economy is Rs. 152.00 lakh. Income from labour contributes 39.3 per cent of this and the rest is capital amounting to Rs. 92.63 lakh. About 36.2 per cent of labour income comes from outside the village and the rest, Rs. 3.83 m is earned inside the village, the major part is earned by the labour households. 91.7 per cent of the income earned outside the village comes from the income earned by the service households. The rest of the GVA which is formed by way of capital amounting to Rs. 92.63 lakh is distributed among different categories of cultivator households, self-employed and other households.

Land and house tax paid by the village households comes to Rs. 183000 except for the labour households who do not pay the tax since they do not have land. This is taken as the total income of the *panchayat*. In addition, *panchayat* gets grants from outside sources and distributes these to various sections of people as help for construction.

Summing Up

Nana Kotda is a typical village, the economy of which is predominantly agricultural, with agriculture suffering from low and fluctuating yields. Animal husbandry, the second most important activity in the village also earns low income. The village economy is poorly diversified, thanks to its low and unstable income, and poor infrastructure. The village economy is far from a closed economy. The village exports its surplus agricultural products outside and a significant number of village households depend on government and private services in Idar town or commute as unskilled workers in nearby villages to earn. About half of the products consumed in the village come from outside, as the village has a poor production base.

The urgent needs of the village can be identified as stabilisation and enhancement in agricultural production, strengthening natural resource base to promote as well as diversify the primary sector, and improving socioeconomic infrastructure to provide enabling conditions to promote diversification of the village economy into non-primary sectors. Any programme for promoting enterprises, or any small and big project for diversifying the village economy requires these inputs. Improvement in the quality of life of people, is critical for the village to ensure good life to people on the one hand and to enhance their productivity and employability on the other. It is clear, that NREGA can play an important role in this context.

Appendix A-4.1

Village SAM for Village Nana Kotda-2006-07 (March 2008)

	Rice	Wheat	Jowar	Bajra	Maize	Tur	Pulses	Castor	Groundnut	Cotton	Fruits & Vegetables	Other Crop
Rice	0	0	0	0	0	0	0	0	0	0	0	0
Wheat	0	198450	0	0	0	0	0	0	0	0	0	0
Jowar	0	0	7580	0	0	0	0	0	0	0	0	0
Bajra	0	0	0	350	0	0	0	0	0	0	0	0
Maize	0	0	0	0	33510	0	0	0	0	0	0	0
Tur	0	0	0	0	0	4932	0	0	0	0	0	0
Pulses	0	0	0	0	0	0	850	0	0	0	0	0
Castor	0	0	0	0	0	0	0	4900	0	0	0	0
Groundnut	0	0	0	0	0	0	0	0	800	0	0	0
Cotton	0	0	0	0	0	0	0	0	0	233490	0	0
Fruits & vegetables	0	0	0	0	0	0	0	0	0	0	5720	0
Other crops	0	0	0	0	0	0	0	0	0	0	0	17828
Animal husbandry	0	91200	21872	4100	145200	36785	3450	5000	3200	260180	6250	17828
Wood	0	0	0	0	0	0	0	0	0	0	0	0
Kerosene	0	0	0	0	0	0	0	0	0	0	0	0
LPG	0	0	0	0	0	0	0	0	0	0	0	0
Cooking oil	0	0	0	0	0	0	0	0	0	0	0	0
Sugar	0	0	0	0	0	0	0	0	0	0	0	0
Tea & coffee	0	0	0	0	0	0	0	0	0	0	0	0
Tobacco products	0	0	0	0	0	0	0	0	0	0	0	0
Salt	0	0	0	0	0	0	0	0	0	0	0	0
Spices	0	0	0	0	0	0	0	0	0	0	0	0

contd...

...contd...

	Rice	*Wheat*	*Jowar*	*Bajra*	*Maize*	*Tur*	*Pulses*	*Castor*	*Groundnut*	*Cotton*	*Fruits & Vegetables*	*Other Crop*
Other food products	0	0	0	0	0	0	0	0	0	0	0	0
Cosmetics	0	0	0	0	0	0	0	0	0	0	0	0
Fertiliser	0	67900	19600	1500	84175	24115	1275	5500	1500	174840	4425	0
Pesticide	0	15600	2400	0	7250	0	0	1100	500	104250	2150	0
Textiles	0	0	0	0	0	0	0	0	0	0	0	0
Cotton ginning	0	0	0	0	0	0	0	0	0	0	0	0
Furniture	0	0	0	0	0	0	0	0	0	0	0	0
Bicycle	0	0	0	0	0	0	0	0	0	0	0	0
Fan	0	0	0	0	0	0	0	0	0	0	0	0
Two-wheeler	0	0	0	0	0	0	0	0	0	0	0	0
Four-wheeler	0	0	0	0	0	0	0	0	0	0	0	0
Electronics	0	0	0	0	0	0	0	0	0	0	0	0
Bricks	0	0	0	0	0	0	0	0	0	0	0	0
Cement	0	0	0	0	0	0	0	0	0	0	0	0
Sand	0	0	0	0	0	0	0	0	0	0	0	0
Roof metal sheet	0	0	0	0	0	0	0	0	0	0	0	0
Construction	0	0	0	0	0	0	0	0	0	0	0	0
Electricity	0	5179	0	0	5179	0	0	0	0	0	0	0
Medical & health	0	0	0	0	0	0	0	0	0	0	0	0
Education	0	0	0	0	0	0	0	0	0	0	0	0
Rent	0	0	0	0	0	0	0	0	0	0	0	0
Other exp.	0	5612	0	0	5612	0	0	0	0	0	0	0
Equipment & repair	0	1897	0	0	1897	0	0	0	0	0	0	0
Bangle vendor	0	0	0	0	0	0	0	0	0	0	0	0
Bangles	0	0	0	0	0	0	0	0	0	0	0	0

contd...

...contd...

	Rice	*Wheat*	*Jowar*	*Bajra*	*Maize*	*Tur*	*Pulses*	*Castor*	*Groundnut*	*Cotton*	*Fruits & Vegetables*	*Other Crop*
Fruit & vegetable vendor	0	0	0	0	0	0	0	0	0	0	0	0
Barber	0	0	0	0	0	0	0	0	0	0	0	0
Carpenter	0	0	0	0	0	0	0	0	0	0	0	0
Cloth shop	0	0	0	0	0	0	0	0	0	0	0	0
Paan shop	0	0	0	0	0	0	0	0	0	0	0	0
PDS shop	0	0	0	0	0	0	0	0	0	0	0	0
Transport	0	48675	10450	1200	61975	30518	0	4600	1600	126800	1500	0
Other services	0	48972	600	500	49381	1090	0	1200	500	500	1900	0
Labour M	0	301651	42908	3762	230454	39837	8404	17307	13200	531377	8077	71313
Labour F	0	224047	30936	3762	195796	39837	6876	17307	13200	507279	8077	71313
Labour income from outside	0	0	0	0	0	0	0	0	0	0	0	0
Labour from outside	0	0	0	0	0	0	0	0	0	0	0	0
Capital	0	1095425	98249	19476	642538	68360	51910	123982	97500	3055835	42673	534848
Marginal farmer	0	0	0	0	0	0	0	0	0	0	0	0
Small farmer	0	0	0	0	0	0	0	0	0	0	0	0
Large farmer	0	0	0	0	0	0	0	0	0	0	0	0
Self-employed in non-agriculture	0	0	0	0	0	0	0	0	0	0	0	0
Labour	0	0	0	0	0	0	0	0	0	0	0	0
Services	0	0	0	0	0	0	0	0	0	0	0	0
All other households	0	0	0	0	0	0	0	0	0	0	0	0
Village *panchayat*	0	0	0	0	0	0	0	0	0	0	0	0
Capital A/C	0	0	0	0	0	0	0	0	0	0	0	0
From outside the village	428203	0	0	58854	0	0	145319	0	0	145321035	336072	92228
Total	428203	2104608	234595	93504	1462967	245474	218084	180896	132000	150315586	416844	805358

contd...

...contd...

	Animal Husbandry	Wood	Kerosene	LPG	Cooking Oil	Sugar	Tea & Coffee	Tobacco Products	Salt	Spices	Other Food Products	Cosmetics
Rice	0	0	0	0	0	0	0	0	0	0	0	0
Wheat	82095	0	0	0	0	0	0	0	0	0	0	0
Jowar	82095	0	0	0	0	0	0	0	0	0	0	0
Bajra	82095	0	0	0	0	0	0	0	0	0	0	0
Maize	82095	0	0	0	0	0	0	0	0	0	0	0
Tur	0	0	0	0	0	0	0	0	0	0	0	0
Pulses	82095	0	0	0	0	0	0	0	0	0	0	0
Castor	0	0	0	0	0	0	0	0	0	0	0	0
Groundnut	0	0	0	0	0	0	0	0	0	0	0	0
Cotton	82095	0	0	0	0	0	0	0	0	0	0	0
Fruits & vegetables	0	0	0	0	0	0	0	0	0	0	0	0
Other crops	713130	0	0	0	0	0	0	0	0	0	0	0
Animal husbandry	0	0	0	0	0	0	0	0	0	0	0	0
Wood	0	0	0	0	0	0	0	0	0	0	0	0
Kerosene	0	0	0	0	0	0	0	0	0	0	0	0
LPG	0	0	0	0	0	0	0	0	0	0	0	0
Cooking oil	0	0	0	0	0	0	0	0	0	0	0	0
Sugar	0	0	0	0	0	0	0	0	0	0	0	0
Tea & coffee	0	0	0	0	0	0	0	0	0	0	0	0
Tobacco products	0	0	0	0	0	0	0	0	0	0	0	0
Salt	0	0	0	0	0	0	0	0	0	0	0	0
Spices	0	0	0	0	0	0	0	0	0	0	0	0
Other food products	138930	0	0	0	0	0	0	0	0	0	0	0
Cosmetics	0	0	0	0	0	0	0	0	0	0	0	0
Fertiliser	0	0	0	0	0	0	0	0	0	0	0	0

contd...

...contd...

	Animal Husbandry	*Wood*	*Kerosene*	*LPG*	*Cooking Oil*	*Sugar*	*Tea & Coffee*	*Tobacco Products*	*Salt*	*Spices*	*Other Food Products*	*Cosmetics*
Pesticide	0	0	0	0	0	0	0	0	0	0	0	0
Textiles	0	0	0	0	0	0	0	0	0	0	0	0
Cotton ginning	0	0	0	0	0	0	0	0	0	0	0	0
Furniture	0	0	0	0	0	0	0	0	0	0	0	0
Bicycle	0	0	0	0	0	0	0	0	0	0	0	0
Fan	0	0	0	0	0	0	0	0	0	0	0	0
Two-wheeler	0	0	0	0	0	0	0	0	0	0	0	0
Four-wheeler	0	0	0	0	0	0	0	0	0	0	0	0
Electronics	0	0	0	0	0	0	0	0	0	0	0	0
Bricks	0	0	0	0	0	0	0	0	0	0	0	0
Cement	0	0	0	0	0	0	0	0	0	0	0	0
Sand	0	0	0	0	0	0	0	0	0	0	0	0
Roof metal sheet	0	0	0	0	0	0	0	0	0	0	0	0
Construction	0	0	0	0	0	0	0	0	0	0	0	0
Electricity	0	0	0	0	0	0	0	0	0	0	0	0
Medical & health	5100	0	0	0	0	0	0	0	0	0	0	0
Education	0	0	0	0	0	0	0	0	0	0	0	0
Rent	0	0	0	0	0	0	0	0	0	0	0	0
Other exp.	0	0	0	0	0	0	0	0	0	0	0	0
Equipment & repair	0	0	0	0	0	0	0	0	0	0	0	0
Bangle vendor	0	0	0	0	0	0	0	0	0	0	0	0
Bangles	0	0	0	0	0	0	0	0	0	0	0	0
Fruit & vegetable vendor	0	0	0	0	0	0	0	0	0	0	0	0
Barber	0	0	0	0	0	0	0	0	0	0	0	0

contd...

...contd...

	Animal Husbandry	*Wood*	*Kerosene*	*LPG*	*Cooking Oil*	*Sugar*	*Tea & Coffee*	*Tobacco Products*	*Salt*	*Spices*	*Other Food Products*	*Cosmetics*
Carpenter	0	0	0	0	0	0	0	0	0	0	0	0
Cloth shop	0	0	0	0	0	0	0	0	0	0	0	0
Paan shop	0	0	0	0	0	0	0	0	0	0	0	0
PDS shop	0	0	0	0	0	0	0	0	0	0	0	0
Transport	0	0	0	0	0	0	0	0	0	0	0	0
Other services	0	0	0	0	0	0	0	0	0	0	0	0
Labour M	298981	0	0	0	0	0	0	0	0	0	0	0
Labour F	0	0	0	0	0	0	0	0	0	0	0	0
Labour income from outside	0	0	0	0	0	0	0	0	0	0	0	0
Labour from outside	0	0	0	0	0	0	0	0	0	0	0	0
Capital	1341101	0	0	0	0	0	0	0	0	0	0	0
Marginal farmer	0	0	0	0	0	0	0	0	0	0	0	0
Small farmer	0	0	0	0	0	0	0	0	0	0	0	0
Large farmer	0	0	0	0	0	0	0	0	0	0	0	0
Self-employed in non-agriculture	0	0	0	0	0	0	0	0	0	0	0	0
Labour	0	0	0	0	0	0	0	0	0	0	0	0
Services	0	0	0	0	0	0	0	0	0	0	0	0
All other households	0	0	0	0	0	0	0	0	0	0	0	0
Village *panchayat*	0	0	0	0	0	0	0	0	0	0	0	0
Capital A/C	0	0	0	0	0	0	0	0	0	0	0	0
From outside the village	0	729200	254630	58789	780095	285284	329257	415823	31487	157150	176130	172121
Total	2989812	729200	254630	58789	780095	285284	329257	415823	31487	157150	176130	172121

contd...

...contd...

	Fertiliser	*Pesticide*	*Textiles*	*Cotton Ginning*	*Furniture*	*Bicycle*	*Fan*	*Two-Wheeler*	*Four-Wheeler*	*Electronics*	*Bricks*	*Cement*
Rice	0	0	0	0	0	0	0	0	0	0	0	0
Wheat	0	0	0	0	0	0	0	0	0	0	0	0
Jowar	0	0	0	0	0	0	0	0	0	0	0	0
Bajra	0	0	0	0	0	0	0	0	0	0	0	0
Maize	0	0	0	0	0	0	0	0	0	0	0	0
Tur	0	0	0	0	0	0	0	0	0	0	0	0
Pulses	0	0	0	0	0	0	0	0	0	0	0	0
Castor	0	0	0	0	0	0	0	0	0	0	0	0
Groundnut	0	0	0	0	0	0	0	0	0	0	0	0
Cotton	0	0	0	150000001	0	0	0	0	0	0	0	0
Fruits & vegetables	0	0	0	0	0	0	0	0	0	0	0	0
Other crops	0	0	0	0	0	0	0	0	0	0	0	0
Animal husbandry	0	0	0	0	0	0	0	0	0	0	0	0
Wood	0	0	0	0	0	0	0	0	0	0	0	0
Kerosene	0	0	0	0	0	0	0	0	0	0	0	0
LPG	0	0	0	0	0	0	0	0	0	0	0	0
Cooking oil	0	0	0	0	0	0	0	0	0	0	0	0
Sugar	0	0	0	0	0	0	0	0	0	0	0	0
Tea & coffee	0	0	0	0	0	0	0	0	0	0	0	0
Tobacco products	0	0	0	0	0	0	0	0	0	0	0	0
Salt	0	0	0	0	0	0	0	0	0	0	0	0
Spices	0	0	0	0	0	0	0	0	0	0	0	0
Other food products	0	0	0	0	0	0	0	0	0	0	0	0
Cosmetics	0	0	0	0	0	0	0	0	0	0	0	0
Fertiliser	0	0	0	0	0	0	0	0	0	0	0	0

Contd...

...contd...

	Fertiliser	Pesticide	Textiles	Cotton Ginning	Furniture	Bicycle	Fan	Two-Wheeler	Four-Wheeler	Electronics	Bricks	Cement
Pesticide	0	0	0	0	0	0	0	0	0	0	0	0
Textiles	0	0	0	0	0	0	0	0	0	0	0	0
Cotton ginning	0	0	0	0	0	0	0	0	0	0	0	0
Furniture	0	0	0	0	0	0	0	0	0	0	0	0
Bicycle	0	0	0	0	0	0	0	0	0	0	0	0
Fan	0	0	0	0	0	0	0	0	0	0	0	0
Two-wheeler	0	0	0	0	0	0	0	0	0	0	0	0
Four-wheeler	0	0	0	0	0	0	0	0	0	0	0	0
Electronics	0	0	0	0	0	0	0	0	0	0	0	0
Bricks	0	0	0	0	0	0	0	0	0	0	0	0
Cement	0	0	0	0	0	0	0	0	0	0	0	0
Sand	0	0	0	0	0	0	0	0	0	0	0	0
Roof metal sheet	0	0	0	0	0	0	0	0	0	0	0	0
Construction	0	0	0	40000	0	0	0	0	0	0	0	0
Electricity	0	0	0	1600000	0	0	0	0	0	0	0	0
Medical & health	0	0	0	0	0	0	0	0	0	0	0	0
Education	0	0	0	0	0	0	0	0	0	0	0	0
Rent	0	0	0	0	0	0	0	0	0	0	0	0
Other exp.	0	0	0	800	0	0	0	0	0	0	0	0
Equipment & repair	0	0	0	149999	0	0	0	0	0	0	0	0
Bangle vendor	0	0	0	0	0	0	0	0	0	0	0	0
Bangles	0	0	0	0	0	0	0	0	0	0	0	0
Fruit & vegetable vendor	0	0	0	0	0	0	0	0	0	0	0	0
Barber	0	0	0	0	0	0	0	0	0	0	0	0

contd...

...contd...

	Fertiliser	Pesticide	Textiles	Cotton Ginning	Furniture	Bicycle	Fan	Two-Wheeler	Four-Wheeler	Electronics	Bricks	Cement
Carpenter	0	0	0	0	0	0	0	0	0	0	0	0
Cloth shop	0	0	0	0	0	0	0	0	0	0	0	0
Paan shop	0	0	0	0	0	0	0	0	0	0	0	0
PDS shop	0	0	0	0	0	0	0	0	0	0	0	0
Transport	0	0	0	0	0	0	0	0	0	0	0	0
Other services	0	0	0	0	0	0	0	0	0	0	0	0
Labour M	0	0	0	415099	0	0	0	0	0	0	0	0
Labour F	0	0	0	109863	0	0	0	0	0	0	0	0
Labour income from outside	0	0	0	0	0	0	0	0	0	0	0	0
Labour from outside	0	0	0	398438	0	0	0	0	0	0	0	0
Capital	0	0	0	15234238	0	0	0	0	0	0	0	0
Marginal farmer	0	0	0	0	0	0	0	0	0	0	0	0
Small farmer	0	0	0	0	0	0	0	0	0	0	0	0
Large farmer	0	0	0	0	0	0	0	0	0	0	0	0
Self-employed in non-agriculture	0	0	0	0	0	0	0	0	0	0	0	0
Labour	0	0	0	0	0	0	0	0	0	0	0	0
Services	0	0	0	0	0	0	0	0	0	0	0	0
All other households	0	0	0	0	0	0	0	0	0	0	0	0
Village *panchayat*	0	0	0	0	0	0	0	0	0	0	0	0
Capital A/C	0	0	0	0	0	0	0	0	0	0	0	0
From outside the village	384830	133250	812010	0	172591	206650	209250	784000	753000	607280	756000	155400
Total	384830	133250	812010	167948438	172591	206650	209250	784000	753000	607280	756000	155400

contd...

...contd...

	Sand	*Roof Metal Sheet*	*Construction*	*Electricity*	*Medical & Health*	*Education*	*Rent*	*Other Exp.*	*Equipment & Repair*	*Bangle Vendor*	*Bangles*	*Fruit & Vegetable Vendor*
Rice	0	0	0	0	0	1557	0	0	0	0	0	0
Wheat	0	0	0	0	0	8327	0	0	0	0	0	0
Jowar	0	0	0	0	0	11	0	0	0	0	0	0
Bajra	0	0	0	0	0	48	0	0	0	0	0	0
Maize	0	0	0	0	0	1157	0	0	0	0	0	0
Tur	0	0	0	0	0	0	0	0	0	0	0	0
Pulses	0	0	0	0	0	1927	0	0	0	0	0	0
Castor	0	0	0	0	0	0	0	0	0	0	0	0
Groundnut	0	0	0	0	0	0	0	0	0	0	0	0
Cotton	0	0	0	0	0	0	0	0	0	0	0	0
Fruits & vegetables	0	0	0	0	0	2974	0	0	0	0	0	110000
Other crops	0	0	0	0	0	0	0	0	0	0	0	0
Animal husbandry	0	0	0	0	0	7410	0	0	0	0	0	0
Wood	0	0	168000	0	0	0	0	0	0	0	0	0
Kerosene	0	0	0	0	0	2100	0	0	0	0	0	0
LPG	0	0	0	0	0	2200	0	0	0	0	0	0
Cooking oil	0	0	0	0	0	750	0	0	0	0	0	0
Sugar	0	0	0	0	0	160	0	0	0	0	0	0
Tea & coffee	0	0	0	0	0	0	0	0	0	0	0	0
Tobacco products	0	0	0	0	0	0	0	0	0	0	0	0
Salt	0	0	0	0	0	0	0	0	0	0	0	0
Spices	0	0	0	0	0	50	0	0	0	0	0	0
Other food products	0	0	0	0	0	0	0	0	0	0	0	0
Cosmetics	0	0	0	0	0	0	0	0	0	0	0	0

Contd...

...contd...

	Sand	*Roof Metal Sheet*	*Construction*	*Electricity*	*Medical & Health*	*Education*	*Rent*	*Other Exp.*	*Equipment & Repair*	*Bangle Vendor*	*Bangles*	*Fruit & Vegetable Vendor*
Fertiliser	0	0	0	0	0	0	0	0	0	0	0	0
Pesticide	0	0	0	0	0	0	0	0	0	0	0	0
Textiles	0	0	0	0	0	0	0	0	0	0	0	0
Cotton ginning	0	0	0	0	0	0	0	0	0	0	0	0
Furniture	0	0	0	0	0	0	0	0	0	0	0	0
Bicycle	0	0	0	0	0	0	0	0	0	0	0	0
Fan	0	0	0	0	0	0	0	0	0	0	0	0
Two-wheeler	0	0	0	0	0	0	0	0	0	0	0	0
Four-wheeler	0	0	0	0	0	0	0	0	0	0	0	0
Electronics	0	0	0	0	0	0	0	0	0	0	0	0
Bricks	0	0	756000	0	0	0	0	0	0	0	0	0
Cement	0	0	155400	0	0	0	0	0	0	0	0	0
Sand	0	0	96600	0	0	0	0	0	0	0	0	0
Roof metal sheet	0	0	168000	0	0	0	0	0	0	0	0	0
Construction	0	0	0	0	0	2227	0	0	0	0	0	0
Electricity	0	0	0	0	0	981	0	0	0	0	0	0
Medical & health	0	0	0	0	0	1204	0	0	0	0	0	0
Education	0	0	0	0	0	0	0	0	0	0	0	0
Rent	0	0	0	0	0	600	0	0	0		0	4800
Other exp.	0	0	0	0	0	9166	0	0	0	4400	0	16600
Equipment & repair	0	0	0	0	0	0	0	0	0	0	0	0
Bangle vendor	0	0	0	0	0	0	0	0	0	0	0	0
Bangles	0	0	0	0	0	0	0	0	0	75600	0	0
Fruit & vegetable vendor	0	0	0	0	0	0	0	0	0	0	0	0

contd...

...contd...

	Sand	*Roof Metal Sheet*	*Construction*	*Electricity*	*Medical & Health*	*Education*	*Rent*	*Other Exp.*	*Equipment & Repair*	*Bangle Vendor*	*Bangles*	*Fruit & Vegetable Vendor*
Barber	0	0	0	0	0	0	0	0	0	0	0	0
Carpenter	0	0	0	0	0	0	0	0	0	0	0	0
Cloth shop	0	0	0	0	0	0	0	0	0	0	0	0
Paan shop	0	0	0	0	0	0	0	0	0	0	0	0
PDS shop	0	0	0	0	0	0	0	0	0	0	0	0
Transport	0	0	0	0	0	800	0	0	0	0	0	0
Other services	0	0	0	0	0	0	0	0	0	0	0	0
Labour M	0	0	462000	0	0	55122	0	0	0	0	0	0
Labour F	0	0	0	0	0	0	0	0	0	0	0	0
Labour income from outside	0	0	0	0	0	0	0	0	0	0	0	0
Labour from outside	0	0	0	0	0	1228907	0	0	0	0	0	0
Capital	0	0	121027	0	0	0	0	0	0	32000	0	146600
Marginal farmer	0	0	0	0	0	0	0	0	0	0	0	0
Small farmer	0	0	0	0	0	0	0	0	0	0	0	0
Large farmer	0	0	0	0	0	0	0	0	0	0	0	0
Self-employed in non-agriculture	0	0	0	0	0	0	0	0	0	0	0	0
Labour	0	0	0	0	0	0	0	0	0	0	0	0
Services	0	0	0	0	0	0	0	0	0	0	0	0
All other households	0	0	0	0	0	0	0	0	0	0	0	0
Village *panchayat*	0	0	0	0	0	0	0	0	0	0	0	0
Capital A/C	0	0	0	0	0	0	0	0	0	0	0	0
From outside the village	96600	168000	0	2143761	970204	0	69200	128849	232633	0	75600	0
Total	96600	168000	1927027	2143761	970204	1327678	69200	128849	232633	112000	75600	278000

contd...

...contd...

	Barber	*Carpenter*	*Cloth Shop*	*Paan Shop*	*PDS Shop*	*Transport*	*Other Service*	*Labour M*	*Labour F*	*Labour Income from Outside*	*Labour from Outside*	*Capital*
Rice	0	0	0	0	72000	0	0	0	0	0	0	0
Wheat	0	0	0	0	144000	0	0	0	0	0	0	0
Jowar	0	0	0	0	36000	0	0	0	0	0	0	0
Bajra	0	0	0	0		0	0	0	0	0	0	0
Maize	0	0	0	0	36000	0	0	0	0	0	0	0
Tur	0	0	0	0		0	0	0	0	0	0	0
Pulses	0	0	0	0	36000	0	0	0	0	0	0	0
Castor	0	0	0	0	0	0	0	0	0	0	0	0
Groundnut	0	0	0	0	0	0	0	0	0	0	0	0
Cotton	0	0	0	0	0	0	0	0	0	0	0	0
Fruits & vegetables	0	0	0	0	0	0	0	0	0	0	0	0
Other crops	0	0	0	74400	0	0	0	0	0	0	0	0
Animal husbandry	0	0	0	0	0	0	0	0	0	0	0	0
Wood	0	380000	0	0	0	0	0	0	0	0	0	0
Kerosene	0	0	0	0	36000	0	0	0	0	0	0	0
LPG	0	0	0	0	0	0	0	0	0	0	0	0
Cooking oil	0	0	0	0	0	0	0	0	0	0	0	0
Sugar	0	0	0	0	0	0	0	0	0	0	0	0
Tea & coffee	0	0	0	0	0	0	0	0	0	0	0	0
Tobacco products	0	0	0	223200	0	0	0	0	0	0	0	0
Salt	0	0	0		0	0	0	0	0	0	0	0
Spices	0	0	0	37200	0	0	0	0	0	0	0	0
Other food products	0	0	0	37200	0	0	0	0	0	0	0	0
Cosmetics	4025	0	0	0	0	0	0	0	0	0	0	0
Fertiliser	0	0	0	0	0	0	0	0	0	0	0	0

contd...

...contd...

	Barber	*Carpenter*	*Cloth Shop*	*Paan Shop*	*PDS Shop*	*Transport*	*Other Service*	*Labour M*	*Labour F*	*Labour Income from Outside*	*Labour from Outside*	*Capital*
Pesticide	0	0	0	0	0	0	0	0	0	0	0	0
Textiles	0	0	400000	0	0	0	0	0	0	0	0	0
Cotton ginning	0	0	0	0	0	0	0	0	0	0	0	0
Furniture	0	0	0	0	0	0	41200	0	0	0	0	0
Bicycle	0	0	0	0	0	0	0	0	0	0	0	0
Fan	0	0	0	0	0	0	0	0	0	0	0	0
Two-wheeler	0	0	0	0	0	0	0	0	0	0	0	0
Four-wheeler	0	0	0	0	0	83000	0	0	0	0	0	0
Electronics	0	0	0	0	0	0	0	0	0	0	0	0
Bricks	0	0	0	0	0	0	0	0	0	0	0	0
Cement	0	0	0	0	0	0	0	0	0	0	0	0
Sand	0	0	0	0	0	0	0	0	0	0	0	0
Roof metal sheet	0	0	0	0	0	0	0	0	0	0	0	0
Construction	0	0	0	0	0	0	0	0	0	0	0	0
Electricity	0	31200	1500	1200	1800	0	5190	0	0	0	0	0
Medical & health	0	0	0	0	0	0	0	0	0	0	0	0
Education	0	0	0	0	0	0	0	0	0	0	0	0
Rent	0	1320	0	7200	480	0	8600	0	0	0	0	0
Other exp.	3600	499	4800	15600	19200	33160	3800	0	0	0	0	0
Equipment & repair	7500	32000	0	0	40	17200	7100	0	0	0	0	0
Bangle vendor	0	0	0	0	0	0	0	0	0	0	0	0
Bangles	0	0	0	0	0	0	0	0	0	0	0	0
Fruit & vegetable vendor	0	0	0	0	0	0	0	0	0	0	0	0
Barber	0	0	0	0	0	0	0	0	0	0	0	0

contd...

...contd...

	Barber	*Carpenter*	*Cloth Shop*	*Paan Shop*	*PDS Shop*	*Transport*	*Other Service*	*Labour M*	*Labour F*	*Labour Income from Outside*	*Labour from Outside*	*Capital*
Carpenter	0	0	0	0	0	0	0	0	0	0	0	0
Cloth shop	0	0	0	0	0	0	0	0	0	0	0	0
Paan shop	0	0	0	0	0	0	0	0	0	0	0	0
PDS shop	0	0	0	0	0	0	0	0	0	0	0	0
Transport	0	0	0	0	0	0	0	0	0	0	0	0
Other services	0	0	0	0	0	0	0	0	0	0	0	0
Labour M	0	80	16000	0	6000	0	3000	0	0	0	0	0
Labour F	0	0	0	0	0	0	0	0	0	0	0	0
Labour income from outside	0	0	0	0	0	0	0	0	0	0	0	0
Labour from outside	0	0	0	0	0	0	0	0	0	0	0	0
Capital	74875	276000	137700	84000	20480	485640	350520	0	0	0	0	0
Marginal farmer	0	0	0	0	0	0	0	0	0	0	0	3483429
Small farmer	0	0	0	0	0	0	0	0	0	0	0	2043283
Large farmer	0	0	0	0	0	0	0	0	0	0	0	2057010
Self-employed in non-agriculture	0	0	0	0	0	0	0	0	0	0	0	1243202
Labour	0	0	0	0	0	0	0	2538458	1197048	181018	0	0
Services	0	0	0	0	0	0	0	66259	31245	2001256	0	0
All other households	0	0	0	0	0	0	0	0	0	0	0	436098
Village *panchayat*	0	0	0	0	0	0	0	0	0	0	0	0
Capital A/C	0	0	0	0	0	0	0	0	0	0	0	0
From outside the village	0	0	0	108000	0	0	0	0	0	0	2182256	0
Total	90000	721099	560000	588000	408000	619000	419410	2604717	1228293	2182274	2182256	9263022

contd...

...contd...

	Marginal Farmer	*Small Farmer*	*Large Farmer*	*Self-employed in Non-agriculture*	*Labour*	*Services*	*All Other HH*	*Village Panchayat*	*Capital A/C*	*Going Outside the Village*	*Total*
Rice	67153	28482	14576	18749	193797	20842	11047	0	0	0	428203
Wheat	138006	67993	71241	26312	429923	33450	19526	0	0	885285	2104608
Jowar	0	2434	0	0	0	0	0	0	0	106475	234595
Bajra	3346	1217	0	0	5718	0	730	0	0	0	93504
Maize	42743	8342	8636	9663	118032	12984	4696	0	0	1105109	1462967
Tur	29949	23818	22518	13739	78174	13635	3936	0	0	54773	245474
Pulses	23494	12592	7921	6156	38021	7191	1837	0	0	0	218084
Castor	0	0	0	0	0	0	0	0	0	175996	180896
Groundnut	0	0	0	0	0	0	0	0	0	131200	132000
Cotton	0	0	0	0	0	0	0	0	0	0	150315586
Fruits & vegetables	79538	40500	21171	24896	81143	32741	18161	0	0	0	416844
Other crops	0	0	0	0	0	0	0	0	0	0	805358
Animal husbandry	272985	157899	127577	120260	256306	163221	51061	0	0	1238028	2989812
Wood	38080	13200	10060	12600	90380	9600	7280	0	0	0	729200
Kerosene	49200	16800	8400	12700	106330	14400	8700	0	0	0	254630
LPG	14702	4631	6768	6116	7448	14444	2480	0	0	0	58789
Cooking oil	190110	80726	54628	73243	285044	67586	28008	0	0	0	780095
Sugar	73757	28275	16048	20172	111649	21559	13664	0	0	0	285284
Tea & coffee	82831	32084	22508	26365	126244	26158	13067	0	0	0	329257
Tobacco products	53327	13128	5109	18007	88634	5293	9125	0	0	0	415823
Salt	6661	2324	1350	2287	15008	2318	1539	0	0	0	31487
Spices	25343	8439	4718	9155	59202	6996	6047	0	0	0	157150
Other food products	0	0	0	0	0	0	0	0	0	0	176130
Cosmetics	16698	5701	3296	5339	126621	5640	4801	0	0	0	172121
Fertiliser	0	0	0	0	0	0	0	0	0	0	384830

contd...

...contd...

	Marginal Farmer	*Small Farmer*	*Large Farmer*	*Self-employed in Non-agriculture*	*Labour*	*Services*	*All Other HH*	*Village Panchayat*	*Capital A/C*	*Going Outside the Village*	*Total*
Pesticide	0	0	0	0	0	0	0	0	0	0	133250
Textiles	101230	35618	23613	35469	164369	38552	13159	0	0	0	812010
Cotton ginning	0	0	0	0	0	0	0	0	0	167948438	167948438
Furniture	14443	27708	7636	12863	35411	25668	7662	0	0	0	172591
Bicycle	51100	19400	11400	10900	90350	13800	9700	0	0	0	206650
Fan	49950	24150	13900	14100	75750	23500	7900	0	0	0	209250
Two-wheeler	200000	147000	110000	32000	49000	206000	40000	0	0	0	784000
Four-wheeler	300000	0	370000	0	0	0	0	0	0	0	753000
Electronics	107300	98200	79400	50800	120300	124700	26580	0	0	0	607280
Bricks	0	0	0	0	0	0	0	0	0	0	756000
Cement	0	0	0	0	0	0	0	0	0	0	155400
Sand	0	0	0	0	0	0	0	0	0	0	96600
Roof metal sheet	0	0	0	0	0	0	0	0	0	0	168000
Construction	70950	33290	20600	19750	171635	37320	10730	80000	1440525	0	1927027
Eletricity	100420	45500	29107	25800	200605	40500	22000	27600	0	0	2143761
Medical & health	318140	124070	27390	45150	337320	80050	31780	0	0	0	970204
Education	185583	39750	45670	40114	202590	187046	12595	0	0	614330	1327678
Rent	9000	0	1200	0	33600	0	2400	0	0	0	69200
Other exp.	0	0	0	0	0	0	0	6000	0	0	128849
Equipment & repair	0	0	0	0	0	0	0	15000	0	0	232633
Bangle vendor	40262	13744	7947	12873	12000	13597	11577	0	0	0	112000
Bangles	0	0	0	0	0	0	0	0	0	0	75600
Fruit & vegetable vendor	55536	28278	14782	17383	126479	22861	12681	0	0	0	278000

contd...

...contd...

	Marginal Farmer	*Small Farmer*	*Large Farmer*	*Self-employed in Non-agriculture*	*Labour*	*Services*	*All Other HH*	*Village Panchayat*	*Capital A/C*	*Going Outside the Village*	*Total*
Barber	32210	10995	6357	10298	10000	10878	9262	0	0	0	90000
Carpenter	100617	21012	36014	20057	63869	35282	11588	0	0	432660	721099
Cloth shop	122700	43172	28622	42991	259836	46728	15951	0	0	0	560000
Paan shop	162784	40074	15599	54967	270565	16156	27855	0	0	0	588000
PDS shop	82725	32306	28292	20813	207891	23234	12739	0	0	0	408000
Transport	90169	66863	50033	14555	22288	68780	18194	0	0	0	619000
Other services	112969	38564	22297	36119	35073	38152	31593	0	0	0	419410
Labour M	0	0	0	0	0	0	0	80145	0	0	2604717
Labour F	0	0	0	0	0	0	0	0	0	0	1228293
Labour income from outside	0	0	0	0	0	0	0	0	0	2182274	2182274
Labour from outside	0	0	0	0	0	0	0	0	0	554911	2182256
Capital	0	0	0	0	0	0	0	0	0	-14871955	9263022
Marginal farmer	0	0	0	0	0	0	0	396000	0	0	3879429
Small farmer	0	0	0	0	0	0	0	0	0	0	2043283
Large farmer	0	0	0	0	0	0	0	0	0	0	2057010
Self-employed in non-agriculture	0	0	0	0	0	0	0	179999	0	0	1423201
Labour	0	0	0	0	0	0	0	828001	0	0	4744525
Services	0	0	0	0	0	0	0	72001	0	0	2170761
All other households	0	0	0	0	0	0	0	36000	0	0	472098
Village *panchayat*	70363	23122	15634	10531	0	9281	54069			0	183000
Capital A/C	293055	581882	684992	489909	37920	650618	-123622	-1537746	0	363517	1440525
From outside the village	0	0	0	0	0	0	0	0	0	0	160921041
Total	3879429	2043283	2057010	1423201	4744525	2170761	472098	183000	1440525	160921041	

5 Time Use Pattern in Nana Kotda and its Implications for NREGS

One of the objectives of the study is to examine the feasibility as well as the multiple impacts of reducing unpaid work of the poor and particularly of poor women through NREGS, on the village economy. It is expected that when the burden of the unpaid work, which usually has low productivity and low remuneration, and which is time consuming, is reduced, the unpaid worker enjoys less time stress and are in a position to participate in the productive and remunerative work in the labour market. Since, neither the NREGS works already undertaken in the village nor the design of NREGS focuses directly on reducing unpaid work, this discussion will be largely based on the potential of reducing this work in the village and its likely impacts on the village economy.

The database required for this analysis is the time use pattern of the village population. We are using two sources of time use data here, namely, the Indian time use survey conducted in 1998-99, which covered Sabarkantha district in which the village Nana Kotda is located; and the focus group 'discussions' organised in the village as a part of data collection. The former is the main source of the data and the latter is the supplementary source.

Time Use Survey 1998-99

The first national level time use survey (a pilot survey) was conducted in six major states in India in 1998-99 by the Department of Statistics, Government of India. The main objectives of the national survey included collection of comprehensive information on how people spend their time on different paid and unpaid activities.[1] In all, 18591 households (12750 rural and 5841 urban) were selected for the survey. All the members (above 6 years) of the households were selected for the purpose of collecting their time use. In all, 77593 persons were selected, of whom of 53981 were from rural areas and 23612 were from urban areas.

The Indian time use survey collected time use data through a well designed set of schedules/survey instruments.[2] The main questionnaire was divided into three blocks: Block One collected data on major household characteristics, Block Two collected particulars of each of the household members (6 years+) selected for the survey, while Block Three collected data on how the members of the selected households spent their time during the past 24 hours. The data were collected for a normal week day and a weekly variant day, and for an "abnormal" day if the selected day happened to be an "abnormal day". Weekly estimates on time use were prepared based on the data.

Keeping in mind the level of literacy of its population, the data collection was done by interviewers, who collected time use data for the previous day.[3] Women investigators were hired to collect information on women's time use particularly in rural areas where women are

---

1. The specific objectives of the survey were: (1) to collect and analyse data on the time use pattern of people in the selected states in India, (2) to use the data in generating more reliable estimates of workforce, and if possible national income as per the SNA 1993, and in computing the value of unpaid work, (3) to infer policy/ programme implications from the analysis of the data on distribution of paid and unpaid work among men and women, and nature of unpaid work and sharing of unpaid work by men and women, (4) to use the data to draw inference for employment and welfare programmes, particularly for women and children, and (5) to develop a conceptual framework and a suitable methodology for designing and conducting time use studies in India on a regular basis.
2. A Technical Advisory Committee, headed by Prof. Indira Hirway, was set up by the Government of India (Ministry of Statistics and Programme Implementation) to finalise the design of the survey, methods of data collection, classification of activities and data analysis.
3. The interviewer asked how the respondents spent the day before, and recorded chronologically the activities in one hour time slot in the 24 hour time diary, which was designed for entering the time use of respondents during the past 24 hours. No proxy was allowed for data collection. Investigators were instructed to visit the household more than once if any respondent was not available.

sometimes reluctant to speak freely to men. Two context variables were used for the collected information, namely whether the work was paid or unpaid, and whether the activity was performed within the home or outside home. Preparation of a detailed instruction manual in the local languages, intensive training workshops along with a follow-up training workshop as well as close monitoring were used to ensure good quality of data (Hirway, 2003).

The Technical Advisory Committee designed a suitable classification for time use activities. This classification had nine major groups:

1. Primary production activities.
2. Secondary sector activities.
3. Tertiary sector activities (trade, business and services).
4. Household maintenance, management and shopping for own household.
5. Care of children, elderly, disabled and sick of own household.
6. Community voluntary services.
7. Learning.
8. Social and cultural activities and mass media etc.
9. Personal care and self-maintenance.

The first three categories refer to SNA activities, the next three categories refer to non-SNA activities or unpaid domestic and community work, and the last three categories refer to personal activities. These broad categories are divided into sub-categories (two digits), and into three digit activities. In all, there are 154 three digit activities (Refer to Appendix A-5.1). Interviewers were instructed to record activities performed by respondents in their own language, and later on code and classify them as per the classification.

The following categories of unpaid work were identified for the purpose of this study:

- Non-market SNA activities, which involved free collection of basic necessities like fetching water, collecting fuel wood etc.

- Non-market SNA activities, which involved free collection of raw material for income generating activities, such as collection of fodder for animals, collection of wood/bamboo for crafts etc.
- Non-market production of goods for self-consumption: subsistence crop cultivation.
- Unpaid non-SNA work involving care of children, the sick, old, disabled in the household.
- Unpaid non-SNA work related to domestic work.
- Travelling.

Insights Gained through Focus Group Discussions (FGD) on Time Use

In addition to the national time use survey, focus group discussions were held to understand the specific time use pattern of the village population, and their major concerns with respect to unpaid SNA and non-SNA work. The discussions revealed the following:

- Women have to spend long hours in fetching drinking water, as there is only one outlet for drinking water under the group scheme from Dharoi dam. Women walk long distance (particularly those living in distant *falias*) and frequently wait for water supply, and their turn in the queue. As many women mentioned, fetching water is time consuming because: (1) water supply is not regular, and (2) there is only one outlet for water in the village. Women end up in quarreling with each other at the water works. They need better water facility, which is more dependable (preferably from a local source) and which brings water within homes.
- Another activity that consumes a lot of time of people is medical services. Since no reliable medical facility is available locally, villagers go all the way to Idar town if they fall sick. They go to private doctors, as government facilities are irregular and as doctors are frequently absent. There was a common demand from all sectors of the population for creating a local health facility.
- Many women observed that they are not able to take up any work/ job in the labour market because they have to take care of small

kids at home. They cannot work on NREGA sites because there is no child care facility provided on the NREGA work site. In fact, many more reported that they would like to participate in the labour market if a facility is made available to take care of their infants and children.

- And lastly, the FGDs revealed that easy access to fuel wood and fodder will make their life easy. Since collection of fuel wood and fodder from the depleted common land has become difficult, there was a strong demand for regeneration of common lands for fuel wood and fodder as well as for reclaiming encroached common lands from powerful/rich farmers.

Men in the village agreed with women in their demand for regeneration of common land for securing fodder and fuel wood for the village. They also agreed with the demand for constructing water harvesting structures for ensuring adequate potable water supply for the village.

Time Use Statistics for Nana Kotda

Gujarat state, in which Nana Kotda village is located, is one of the states selected for the national pilot survey. Out of the total 19 districts in the state (in 1998-99), 7 were selected, and of these 140 were rural centres/villages and 124 were urban centres. In all, 3168 households were selected of which 1680 were rural households and 1488 were urban households. Nana Kotda village is located in one of the districts, Sabarkantha district, selected for the survey in Gujarat State. We used the time use pattern of rural areas of this district for the study. The details of the methodology and the design of the survey are presented in the Appendix A-5.1 at the end of this chapter.

As mentioned above, it is assumed that the time use pattern of the rural Sabarkantha district is applicable to Nana Kotda village, which is located in the district.

Time Spent by Men and Women on Different Activities

As seen above, men and women distribute their time broadly in three types of activities, namely, SNA activities or the activities which are covered under the national income accounting; non-SNA activities which fall outside the purview of national income accounting but which contribute to human well-being (for example, cooking, washing, cleaning etc. and care of children, the old and sick etc. for own household); and personal activities which are related to personal care and well-being but are non-delegable (for example, sleeping, watching movies or listening to music, personal care etc.). Table 5.1 presents how men and women in Nana Kotda distribute their time between these activities.

The table shows that, on an average, men spend 44.83 hours in a week on SNA work as against 23.90 hours of women. However, women spend 37.55 hours on non-SNA work while men spend only 3.25 hours! The weekly average time spent by men and women on total work (SNA + non-SNA) is 48.08 hours and 61.45 hours respectively. That is, women spend 28 per cent more time on total work than what men spend. On an average, women spend almost 9 hours per day on work as against 6.8 hours by men. If we apply the ILO norm of 48 hours a week, women in Nana Kotda are highly time stressed, while men are within the limits of the norms. Women get much less personal time, 106.52 hours as against 120 hours of men. Women get less time to sleep and to rest.

To put it differently, the time use pattern of men and women in Sabarkantha district shows that: women work much harder than men, and women's work is predominantly unpaid in nature.

This highly unequal sharing of work and the consequent gender inequalities has multiple impacts on women's opportunities for development. Firstly, the burden of work which causes time stress affects women's health and well-being adversely. Secondly, it leaves less time for women including young girls to acquire capabilities like education and skills. The very low educational status of women in the village can be attributed to their excessive burden of work. It also leaves less time for productive work in the labour market. And thirdly, since the unpaid work does not receive any remuneration, it is not recognised, giving women low status inside as well as outside home.

Table 5.1

Weekly Average Time Spent by Men and Women on SNA, Non-SNA and Personal Activities (All)

	Men	%	*Women*	%	*Total*	%
SNA	44.83 (77.96)	26.68	23.90 (70.75)	14.23	34.74 (74.50)	20.68
Non-SNA	3.25 (37.52)	1.93	37.55 (92.50)	22.35	19.73 (63.88)	11.74
Personal services	119.93 (100)	71.39	106.52 (100)	63.40	113.69 (100)	67.67
Total	168.00 (100)		168.00 (100)		168.00 (100)	

Note: Figures in the brackets indicate participation rates, i.e. percentage of persons participating in the activities.

Source: Indian Time Use Survey 1998-99.

Time Spent on Unpaid SNA and Unpaid Non-SNA Work

As seen earlier, unpaid work essentially means the work that does not receive any direct remuneration. It includes unpaid SNA work, covered under the Production Boundary of the UN System of National Accounts[4] as well as unpaid non-SNA work covered under the General Production Boundary[5] of the UN System of National Accounts. Unpaid SNA work includes non-marketed work such as collection of free basic necessities like water, fuel wood etc. from common lands, forests and other sources (private land); free collection of raw materials for income generating activities like fodder for animal husbandry, leaves, bamboo or wood for crafts and other manufacturing; as well as other subsistence work, i.e. production for self-consumption, on farms, in forestry, fishery etc. Unpaid non-SNA work on the other hand, includes domestic work that consists of: (1) household upkeep and management (cleaning, washing, cooking, shopping for the household etc.), (2) care of children

4. This production boundary includes the activities that fall within the purview of national income accounts.
5. General production boundary includes those activities which fall outside the production boundary and are related to production of services by households for household members and community services.

Figure 5.1

Weekly Average Time Spent by Men and Women on SNA, Non-SNA and Personal Activities

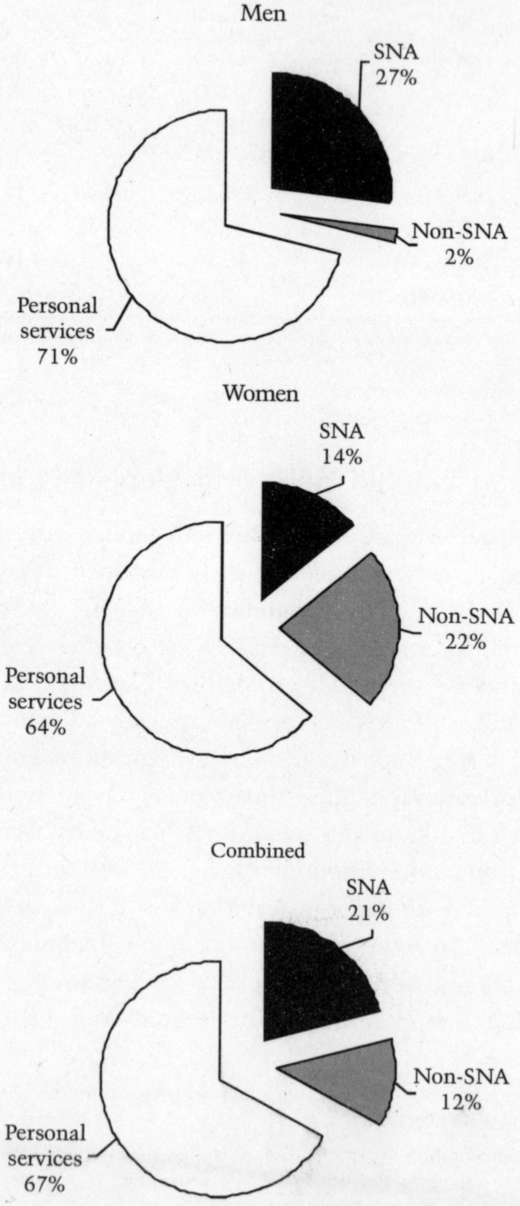

(active and passive care), (3) care of the sick, old, disabled in the household, and (4) community services. This work is also predominantly performed by women and sometimes by children.

Time Spent on Unpaid Non-Market SNA Work: Officially, Nana Kotda has 42.12 acres of common land and 3.66 acres of government wasteland. Due to legal and illegal encroachment, however, the actual common land has declined to around 12–15 acres. This land, which is degraded, is an important source of fuel wood, fodder, fruits, vegetables, leaves etc. as well as of small wood and grass for repairing and constructing shelter for rural population, and particularly for the poor and women. The common practice is that women, and sometimes men as well children go to common lands for collecting these items. Since common lands are degraded, they spend a lot of time in collecting these basic necessities.

Table 5.2

Weekly Average Time Spent by Men and Women in Collection of Free Goods (Participants)

	Activity	*Men*		*Women*	
		Time	*PR*	*Time*	*PR*
1	Fetching of water	3.2	1.69	5.54	36.83
2	Collection of fruits, vegetables, berries, mushrooms etc. edible goods	14.25	0.21	3.96	2.66
3	Collection of minor forest produce, leaves, bamboo etc.	1.33	0.03	8.33	0.04
4	Collection of fuel/fuel wood/twigs	3.23	0.65	4.19	16.90
5	Collection of raw material for crafts	1.32	0.10	4.44	0.58
6	Collection of building materials	0	0.00	4.67	0.08
7	Collection of fodder	8	9.30	13.25	25.42
8	Sale and purchase related activities	10	0.28	8.39	0.66
9	Collection of other items	13	0.10	16.81	0.15
	Total	7.15	11.64	13.41	65.92

Note: PR stands for participation rate of persons in the specified activity.
Source: Indian Time Use Survey 1998-99.

As Table 5.2 shows women spend 13.41 hours a week on free collection of goods as against 7.15 hours by men. Also, almost two-third of the women participate in these activities as against 11 per cent of men.

Fetching water for household use is the most common activity for women. This is a time consuming task, as there is only one stand post in the village for the water supply coming from the regional scheme from the Dharoi dam. 36.83 per cent of women spend more than 5.54 hours in a week on fetching water for the family. Similarly, 16.90 per cent women spend 4.19 hours a week on collection of fuel wood as against 3.23 hours by 0.65 per cent men.

The maximum time, however, is spent on collection of fodder, 13.25 hours by women and 8 hours by men. More than one-fourth of women and 9.30 per cent of men perform this activity. A careful look at the data indicates that many of these workers are children below 14 years.

Common lands/forests are also used for collecting wood, bamboo and other raw material for craft; material for construction, and repair of shelter (building material) etc. Though the participation rates are small in some of these activities, participant households seem to be spending more than 4 hours a week on the activities like collection of minor forest produce like bamboo, leaves and collection of other material for craft, collection of building material etc.

In all, as Table 5.2 indicates, about 520 women and 100 men spend about 13.41 hours and 7.15 hours each on collection of free goods. That is, men spend approximately 715 hours while women spend approximately 6973 hours on collection of free goods in a week. Clearly, a lot of time of this can be saved by appropriate assets/infrastructure generated under the NREGS.

Animal husbandry happens to be an important economic activity in the village. As indicated in Table 5.3, women and men (and particularly children) spend considerable time on these activities. About 13 per cent of men (mainly boys) and 8 per cent of women (girls) spend between 18-20 hours a week on animal grazing. Since the common grassland in the village is depleted and retarded, men and women have to spend a lot of time to allow animals to graze. Regeneration of common lands, with a special focus on growth of nutritious grasses, can reduce this time on the one hand and improve the production of milk on the other.

Table 5.3

Weekly Average Time Spent by Men and Women on Animal Husbandry (Participants)

Sr. No.	Activity	Men		Women	
		Time	PR	Time	PR
1	Grazing animals outside	18.75	12.72	19.42	8.24
2	Tending animals	7.47	24.79	8.88	63.07
3	Caring for animals—breeding, medical service etc.	4.08	1.79	3.5	6.44
4	Milking, processing of milk, storing	3.78	11.26	4.44	37.36
5	Making dung cakes	4.27	0.21	3.92	17.96
6	Poultry rearing	40.09	0.14	41.61	0.31
7	Other related activities	3.23	1.34	3.31	7.56
8	Sale and purchase related activities	9.45	0.79	2.19	1.93
9	Travel to work	4.85	3.79	4.07	8.91
	Total	11.5	28.51	15.8	71.78

Source: Indian Time Use Survey 1998-99.

Time Spent on Unpaid Non-SNA Work: Care of Children, the old and the sick: A major component of unpaid non-SNA work is care related work. As indicated by Table 5.4, about 25.33 per cent women in the district spend, on an average, 13.15 hours in a week on care activities. As against this, only 5.85 per cent men participate in care activities in a week.

Child care is the most important care activity, with 22 per cent women spending 12 hours in a week for physical care of children, 20 per cent women spending time on accompanying children to different places and 6-8 per cent women busy with supervising children and taking indirect care of children. These percentages are much smaller for men.

Women's participation is higher than men also in other care activities like taking care of adults, disabled, sick etc. in the family. About 2 per cent women spend up to 15 hours a week on this care. Men's participation is less than 0.50 per cent, and they spend up to 8 hours a week on this care.

In all, 202 women spend 13.15 hours a week on care related activities and 50 men spend about 6 hours a week on these activities.

Table 5.4

Weekly Average Time Spent in Care for Children, the Sick, Elderly and Disabled for Own House Holders (Participants)

Sr. No.	Activity	Men		Women	
		Time	PR	Time	PR
1	Physical care of children: washing, cleaning, feeding, dressing	4.48	2.27	11.58	21.70
2	Teaching, trainings, instructions	4.84	0.96	9.93	0.66
3	Accompanying children to school, sports, lessons etc.	5.72	0.34	3.75	20.39
4	Supervising children needing care	4.44	2.17	9.4	6.82
5	Physical care of sick, disabled, elderly members of the household	8.64	0.34	5.84	1.77
6	Accompanying adults to receive care etc.	1	0.03	4.31	0.08
7	Supervising adults needing care	5.25	0.14	9.43	0.15
8	Travel related to adult care	3.39	0.14	1.17	0.04
9	Any other related activity	2.31	0.34	3.51	0.46
	Total	6.17	5.85	13.15	25.33

Source: Indian Time Use Survey 1998-99.

Time Spent on Unpaid Non-SNA Work: Household Work: More than half of the women (52.66 per cent) in the district spend about 30 hours each on household work. This comes to more than four hours of work per day. As against this, 15 per cent men spend about five hours on household work in a week, which comes to 0.7 hours a day. Women spend maximum time on cooking (15.46 hours), followed by cleaning and washing (13 hours), and care of textiles (7.15 hours). In the case of men, the most important activity is "do it yourself work", followed by pet care, cooking and cleaning.

About 7 per cent women (56 women) spend 5.50 hours on hours do-it-yourself and about 1 per cent men (9 men) spend 6.38 hours do-it-yourself. Since houses in this region are semi-durable, they need constant repairs of floor, roof and walls. Construction of durable housing under the NREGS can reduce this work of men and women.

It needs to be underlined, that the burden of non-SNA work on women is a major cause for their lower participation and lower status in the labour market. To put it differently, women's engagement in unpaid domestic work deprives them of their equal opportunities in the labour market: (a) mothers with small children cannot participate in the labour market in the absence of adequate facilities of child care, (b) other women cannot work long hours due to their domestic responsibilities, (c) they do not get adequate time to acquire skills/human capital, and (d) they are not treated as equals with men due to their low status within and outside the household.

Table 5.5

Weekly Average Times Spent by Men and Women on Household Maintenance and Management (Participants)

Sr. No.	*Activity*	*Men*		*Women*	
		Time	*PR*	*Time*	*PR*
1	Cooking food items and serving	3.79	6.06	15.46	46.07
2	Cleaning and upkeep of dwelling	2.97	2.48	6.07	43.83
3	Cleaning utensils	3.25	2.07	6.74	41.94
4	Care of textiles: washing, mending, ironing etc.	2.36	2.13	7.15	32.00
5	Shopping of goods and household appliances etc.	3.18	5.68	2.99	4.20
6	Household management: planning, supervising etc.	3.21	0.59	5	0.27
7	Do it yourself/have improvement	6.38	0.90	5.49	6.94
8	Pet care	5.31	0.10	3.99	0.31
9	Travel related to household management	2.42	1.89	2.89	2.66
10	Other activities related to household maintenance and management	2	1.07	4.87	2.85
	Total	5.15	15.05	29.57	52.66

Source: Indian Time Use Survey 1998-99.

Personal Time Available: As a result of the higher burden of total work (SNA + non-SNA work), women get: (a) less time for sleeping (58.82 hours) than men (61.56 hours, (b) they get less time for eating, drinking etc. and for personal care, and (c) they get less time for relaxation and entertainment. If one adds up the total time for sleep, rest and relaxation, men spend 101.8 hours on these activities while women spend 96.8 hours on the same activities. That is, women get almost 5-6 hours less of relaxation and rest than men.

Table 5.6

Weekly Average Time Spent on Personal Care, Rest and Relaxation (Participants)

Sr. No.	Activity	Men		Women	
		Time	PR	Time	PR
1	Sleep and related activities	61.56	100	58.82	100
2	Eating and drinking	9.01	100	8.36	100
3	Smoking, drinking alcohol, intoxicants	7.49	13.95	5.84	0.69
4	Personal hygiene and health	6.29	100	5.42	100
5	Walking, exercise, jogging etc.	3.67	8.30	3.1	2.39
6	Receiving medical care and other care from professionals	3.38	0.69	1.94	0.39
7	Receiving medical care and other care from household members	3.55	0.21	23.01	0.12
8	Talking, gossiping	9.04	52.72	9.67	44.68
9	Doing nothing: rest, relaxation	14.52	63.98	13.04	58.64
10	Religious practices	6.38	4.06	5.09	3.01
11	Other related activities	5.65	7.64	6.26	6.05
12	Convalescing	46.64	0.48	37.87	0.23
13	Travel related to personal care	3.51	23.04	3.26	18.50
	Total	101.8	66.08	96.8	61.80

Source: Indian Time Use Survey 1998-99.

Unpaid Work and Poverty

In order to understand the relationship between the time use and the poverty levels, we divided the households into four categories based on the monthly per capita expenditure (MPCE) levels: ultra poor, poor, non-poor and rich.[6] Our careful analysis of the time use of the households has shown the following:

Time spent on collection of basic necessities and raw materials for household enterprise: The analysis shows that the ultra poor households spend a significant proportion of their productive time, on

6. This has been done with reference to the income poverty line determined by the Planning Commission, India. All the households are divided into four categories: (i) ultra poor (the poor below the half of the poverty line); (ii) poor (the poor above the ultra poverty line and below the poverty line); (iii) non-poor (non-poor above the poverty line and below the one and a half of the poverty line); and (iv) rich (the rest of the non-poor).

the subsistence work of collecting basic necessities of the household (collection of fuel wood, making dung cakes, fetching water, and collection of other free goods like vegetables, fruits, wood for construction and repair of shelter etc.) and raw materials for the household income generating activities (collection of fodder for animals and other raw materials for family enterprises). It is estimated that men from ultra poor households spend 1.24 hours per week on this work while women spend 4.20 hours. That is, women spend about 18 per cent of their productive time (i.e. time spent on SNA activities) on this unpaid work.

It is important to note that women from the non-poor and rich households are not excluded from this burden. They spend about three hours per week on this unpaid work as against less than one hour by their men.

Time spent on household management and care: Our analysis shows that ultra poor men and women spend 3.18 hours and 31.20 hours on unpaid domestic work per week. The corresponding percentages of the non-poor are 2.98 and 35.29 hours respectively. The longer hours are largely because there are almost no facilities for child care and poor infrastructural support for other household work. It is important to note here that this burden of unpaid work is experienced by women in ultra poor as well as non-poor households. Infrastructural support like child day care facility for children can help women in reducing this burden of work.

In short: (1) the burden of unpaid work is significant on the poor as compared to the non-poor, and (2) women from non-poor households are not excluded from this burden. Since the drudgery of unpaid work is a major obstacle for women's participation in the productive market oriented work, it is necessary to relieve these workers from this burden.

Addressing Unpaid Work through NREG Works

Table 1.1 (Chapter 1) shows how a scheme like NREGS can reduce this work by constructing appropriate assets. The table has been used while identifying the potential of NREGS works for the village.

Table 5.7 has been designed to indicate the time spent on unpaid work that can be reduced through NREGS works. As the table indicates, 15494 hours of women and 3315 hours of men are spent on unpaid work that can be reduced by NREGS works. Even if we assume that 80 per cent of the unpaid time can be saved by suitable NREGS works, 332 man-days and 1551 woman-days can be saved for other productive work, preferably on NREGS works. At the daily wage rate of Rs. 60, the additional direct income earned in the village will be Rs. 1.14 lakh. The indirect income will be additional to this. Also, some girls and boys will be released for attending the school.

Table 5.7

Time Spent on Unpaid Work that can be reduced through NREGS

Sr. No.	*Activity*	*Men*			*Women*		
		Number	*Total time*	*PR*	*Number*	*Total time*	*PR*
1	Fetching of water	15	46.4	1.7	295	1634.3	36.8
2	Collection of fuel/fuel wood/twigs	6	18.2	0.7	135	565.6	16.9
3	Collection of fodder	80	661.3	9.3	203	2689.8	25.4
4	Collection of other items	4	38.2	0.4	29	131.0	3.5
5	Grazing animals outside	109	2043.75	12.7	66	1281.7	8.24
6	Making dung cakes	2	7.6	0.2	144	563.4	18.0
7	Care of children-direct & indirect	53	253.4	6.1	243	2626.1	30.4
8	Cooking food items and serving	52	197.5	6.1	368	5697.7	46.1
9	Do it yourself/home improvement	8	49.1	0.9	56	304.8	6.9
	Total		3315.45			15494.40	

Note: PR stands for participation rate of persons in the specified activity.
Source: Indian Time Use Survey 1998-99.

Addressing unpaid SNA and unpaid non-SNA work through the right kind of asset/infrastructure creation will bring unpaid work into public domain, and this will have positive impact in multiple ways. It will reduce the time stress of men and particularly women workers to relieve them for leisure or for productive work; it will improve productivity in SNA work and thereby reduce poverty; it will also improve health and overall well-being of women and children; and it will expand long term employment as there will be a need to hire people to run/manage these new services. The additional time used for productive work will have multiplier impact on the village economy. This will be estimated later on using multiplier analysis.

To sum up, NREGS has the potential for empowering women, and engendering the mainstream development process. There is, therefore, a need to expand the purview of employment guarantee programmes to take up works that replace unpaid work, to the extent possible, by creating public assets/infrastructure.

Appendix A-5.1

Time Use Survey—Classification Used in the Indian Time Use Survey

I Primary Production Activities

Crop farming, kitchen gardening, etc.

111 Ploughing, preparing land, cleaning of land

112 Sowing, planting, transplanting

113 Application of manure, fertiliser, pesticides and watering, preparing organic manure, harvesting, threshing, picking, winnowing

114 Weeding

115 Supervision of work

116 Kitchen gardening—backyard cultivation

117 Stocking, transporting to home, guarding or protection of crops

118 Sale and purchase related activities

119 Travel to work

Animal husbandry

121 Grazing animal outside

122 Tending animals—cleaning, washing shed, feeding, watering, preparation of feed

123 Caring for animal: breading, shearing, medical treatment, grooming, shoeing, etc.

124 Milking and processing of milk collecting, storing of poultry products

125 Making dung cakes

126 Poultry rearing—feeding, cleaning

127 Other related activities

128 Sale and purchase related activities

129 Travel to work

Fishing, forestry, horticulture, gardening

131 Nursery—seedings

132 Planting, tending, processing of trees

133 Collecting, storing and stocking of fruits, etc.

134 Wood cutting, chopping and stocking firewood

135 Fish farming, cleaning seabed, feeding fish, catching fish, gathering other aquatic life

136 Care of house plants, indoor and outdoor garden work

137 Flower gardening—landscaping, maintenance, cutting, collecting, storing

138 Sale and purchase related activities

139 Travel to work

14 Fetching of fruits, water, plants etc. storing and hunting

141 Fetching of water

142 Fetching of fruits, vegetables, berries, mushrooms etc. edible goods

143 Fetching of minor forest produce, leaves, bamboo, etc.

144 Fetching of fuel/fuel wood/twigs

145 Fetching of raw material for crafts

146 Fetching of building materials

147 Fetching of fodder

148 Sale and purchase related activities

149 Collection of other items

15 Processing and storage

151 Milling, husking, pounding

152 Parboiling

153 Sorting, grading

154 Grinding, crushing

156 Any other related activity

157 Sale and purchase related activities

159 Travel to work

16 Mining quarrying, digging, cutting, etc.

161 Mining/extraction of salt

162 Mining/digging/quarrying of stone, slabs, breaking of stones for construction of building road, bridges, etc.

163 Digging out clay, gravel and sand

164 Digging out minerals—major and minor

165 Transporting in vehicles

166 Storing and stocking

167 Any other related activity

168 Sale and purchase related activities

169 Travel to work

II Secondary Activities

21 Construction Activities

211 Building and construction of dwelling (laying bricks, plastering, thatching, bamboo work, roofing) and maintenance and repairing of dwelling

212 Construction and repair of animal shed, shelter for poultry etc.

213 Construction of well, storage facilities, fencing, etc. for farms, irrigation work

214 Construction of public works/common infrastructure—roads, buildings, bridges, etc.

217 Any other activity related

218 Sale and purchase related activities

219 Travel to work

22 Manufacturing Activities

221 Food processing and cooking for sale—making pickles, spices and other products; canning fruits, jams and jellies; baking; beverage preparation; selling readymade food, etc.

222 Butchering, curing, processing, drying, storing, etc. of meat, fish, etc.

223 Manufacturing of textiles—spinning, weaving, processing of textiles; knitting, sewing, garment making of cotton, wool and other materials

224 Making handicrafts, pottery, printing and other crafts made primarily with hands (wood based, leather based crafts, embroidery work, etc.)

225 Fitting, installing, tool setting, tool and machinery—moulding, welding, tool making

226 Assembling machines, equipment and other products

227 Production related work in large and small factories in different industries—as production workers, maintenance workers paid trainees and apprentices, sales administration and management activities

228 Sale and purchase activity

229 Travel to work

III Trade, Business and Services

31 Trade and Business

311 Buying and selling goods—such as capital goods, intermediate goods, consumer durable, and consumer goods—in the organised and formal sectors

312 Petty trading, street and door to door vending, hawking shoe cleaning, etc.

313 Transporting goods in trucks, tempos and motor vehicles

314 Transporting in hand carts, animal carts, cycle *rickshaws*, etc. or manually

315 Transport of passengers by motorised and non-motorised vehicles

32 Services

321 Service in government and semi-government organisations (salaried)

322 Service in private organisations (salaried)

323 Petty services: domestic servants, sweepers, washers, priest, barber, cobbler, gardener, massaging, prostitution, (wages) watching and guarding

324 Professional services: medical and educational services (private tuition, non-formal teaching, etc.) financial services and management and technical consultancy services

325 Professional services: computer services, xerox/photocopying services, beauty parlours, hair cutting salons, etc.

326 Technical services: plumbing, electrical and electronic repair and maintenance and other related services

327 Others

328 Travel to work

IV Household Maintenance, Management and Shopping for Own Household

411 Cooking food items, beverages and serving

421 Cleaning and upkeep of dwelling and surroundings

422 Cleaning of utensils

431 Care of textiles: sorting, mending, washing, ironing and ordering clothes and linen

441 Shopping for goods and non-personal services; capital goods, household appliances, equipment, food and various household supplies

451 Household management: planning, supervising, paying bills, etc.

461 Do-it-yourself home improvements and maintenance, installation, servicing and repair of personal and household goods

471 Pet care

481 Travel related to household maintenance, management and shopping

491 Household maintenance, management and shopping not elsewhere classified

V Care for Children, the Sick, Elderly and Disabled for Own Household

511 Physical care of children: washing, dressing, feeding

521 Teaching, training and instruction of own children

531 Accompanying children to places: school, sports, lessons, etc. /PHC/ doctor

541 Physical care of sick, disabled, elderly household members; washing, dressing, feeding, helping

551 Accompanying adults to receive personal care services such as hairdresser's therapy sessions, temple, religious places, etc.

561 Supervising children needing care with or without other activity

562 Supervising adults needing care with or without other activity

571 Travel related to care of children

572 Travel related to care of adults and others

581 Taking care of guests/visitors

591 Any other activity not mentioned above

VI Community Services and Help to Other Households

611 Community organised constructions and repairs; buildings, roads, dams, wells, ponds, etc. community assets

621 Community organised work: cooking for collective celebration, etc.

631 Volunteering with/for an organisation (which does not involve working directly for individuals)

641 Volunteering work through organisations extended directly to individuals and groups

651 Participation in meetings of local and informal groups/castes, tribes, professional associations, union, fraternal and political organisations

661 Involvement in civic and related responsibilities; voting, rallies, attending meetings, *panchayat*

671 Informal help to other households

681 Community services not elsewhere classified

691 Travel related to community services

VII Learning

711 General education: school/university/other educational institutions attendance

721 Studies, homework and course review related to general education

731 Additional study, non-formal education under adult education programmes

741 Non-formal education for children

751 Work-related training

761 Training under government programme such as TRYSEM, DWCRA and others

771 Other training/education

781 Learning not elsewhere classified

791 Travel related to learning

VIII Social and Cultural Activities, Mass Media, etc.

811 Participating in social events: wedding, funerals, births and other celebrations

812 Participating in religious activities: Church services, religious ceremonies, practices, *kirtans*, singing, etc.

813 Participating in community functions in music, dance, etc.

814 Socialising at home and outside the home

821 Arts, making music hobbies and related courses

822 Indoor and outdoor sports participation and related courses

831 Games and other past-time activities

832 Spectator to sports, exhibitions/museums, cinemas/theatre/concerts and other performances and events

841 Other related activities

851 Reading other than newspaper and magazines

852 Watching television and video

853 Listening to music/radio

861 Accessing information by computing

862 Visiting library

863 Reading newspaper and magazines

871 Mass media use and entertainment not classified elsewhere

891 Travel related to social, cultural and recreational activities, social cultural and recreational activities not elsewhere classified, mass media use and entertainment

892 Travel related to search of job

IX Personal Care and Self-Maintenance

911 Sleep and related activities

921 Eating and drinking

922 Smoking, drinking, alcohol and other intoxicants

931 Personal hygiene and health

932 Walking, exercise, running, jogging, yoga, etc

941 Receiving medical and personal care from professional

942 Receiving medical and personal care from household members

951 Talking, gossiping and quarrelling

961 Doing nothing, rest and relaxation

971 Individual religious practices and meditation

981 Other activities

982 Resting/convalescing due to physical illness and physical unwell persons

992 Travel related to personal care and self-maintenance

6 NREGA in Nana Kotda

Launching of NREGA in Nana Kotda

The National Rural Employment Guarantee Act (NREGA), under which every rural household has been guaranteed at least 100 days of wage employment at the state minimum wage rate was passed by the Indian Parliament in 2005, and has been implemented since February 2006. The Act, which was implemented in the most backward 200 districts in the first year, is now (since 2008-09) expanded to cover all the districts in the country. Since Sabarkantha district, was included in the most 200 backward districts in India, NREGA was introduced in the district in February 2006. Though all state governments were expected to design a state level scheme based on the national guidelines, the Government of Gujarat could not design such a scheme for more than one year after the official launching of the NREGA, with the result that the state followed the national guidelines and the act while implementing the NREGA in the initial years.

As far as the implementation of NREGA in Nana Kotda is concerned, it started on 30th March 2006, when a village assembly[1] was organised to inform people about the Act and the underlying scheme. Out of the more than 2000 people in the village, 151 persons participated in the meeting. The village *talati* (revenue collector cum the secretary of the village *panchayat*) and the *sarpanch* addressed the assembly to inform them about the scheme. Another meeting was held after a month when the local MLA (Member of the State Legislative Assembly) visited the village. After this meeting, a few posters were put up in the village to inform people about the NREGP.

---

1. A village assembly consists of all adults in the village. They meet to take major decisions about village affairs.

Distribution of forms for registration under the NREGS had started on 21st February 2006, but people started applying for registration mainly after the meeting held on 30th March. About 300 forms were distributed. Households were asked to get themselves photographed for getting registered. The village *panchayat* arranged this through a photographer who charged Rs. 15 per household (group) photograph. After registration, job cards were distributed to households. So far about 264 job cards have been issued. That is, about 63 per cent households have a job card.

Households were expected to demand work under the NREGA only after receiving the job cards. Most of them demanded work orally, as there was no form left to be filled in to demand work. The first work under NREGS started on 10th April 2006, 2 months and 8 days after the Act came in to being.

NREG Works Undertaken

So far (April 2008), six works have been taken up under the scheme. All the works are for de-silting the check dams in the village.

Six check dams were constructed in Nana Kotda during the period 2001-2003, under the check dam programme of the Government of Gujarat (Sardar Patel Participatory Programme for Construction of Check Dams) on the small river, Debhol, flowing by the village to harvest water. Since check dams need de-silting after every 4-5 years, this work was taken up under the NREGS. The work continued for 91 days spread over the period from 10th April to 5th July 2006. The work stopped after the rains started.

Table 6.1 provides the details of the work sites. It shows that NREGA works continued for 91 days during the first six months of the NREGS, i.e. from February 2006 to July 2006. Rs. 586131 was spent on the works. The entire cost is reported as labour cost, as the money was spent on wages. In addition, 5 per cent of the total amount was spent on contingency, i.e. maintenance of implements and administration.

Employment Generated under NREGS

In all, 161 households, and 238 persons (127 women and 111 men) participated in NREGS. The total 9812 person days of

Table 6.1

NREGA Works in Nana Kotda (2006-07)

Sr. No.	Description of Work	From	To	Duration in Days	Labour Cost (INR)	Material Cost (INR)	Other Cost (INR)	Total Cost (INR)
		Duration			Total Cost			
1	De-silting check dam near Raval *falia*	10/4/06	30/4/06	21	1,73,481			1,73,481
2	De-silting check dam near Uparvas *falia*	1/5/06	14/5/06	14	1,73,481			1,73,481
3	De-silting check dam near Vanjara *falia*	15/5/06	20/5/06	6	60,327			60,327
4	De-silting check dam near Amthavada *falia*	20/5/06	27/5/06	8	22,799			22799
5	De-silting check dam near farm of Divchand *falia*	29/5/06	18/6/06	21	87676			87,676
6	De-silting check dam Uparvas near the tank	19/6/06	9/7/06	21	68367			68367
	Total			91 days	5,86,131			5,86,131

employment was generated: 5492 women-days and 4320 man-days (Table 6.2). That is, from February 2006 to August 2007 (almost 18 months), 9812 person days of work has been undertaken in the village.[2] Of which, 56 per cent has been for women and the rest for men. Women have also shared 56 per cent of the total NREGA earnings. The daily wage rate under the programme has varied between Rs. 55.00 to Rs. 74.00. The average wage rate has been Rs. 60.00.

A careful study of the nature of participation in NREGA works by people in Nana Kotda shows that the entitlements under the act were not guaranteed:

- Of the total 264 job card holders, only 161 households participated in NREGS. That is, about 60 per cent of job card holders have participated.
- The 127 women and 111 men who participated in the NREGS (from 161 households) got employment for 36.13 and 38.25 days respectively, with the average employment per person being 36.27 days during the one and a half years of the NREGS in the village (from February 2006 to July 2007).

2. The system of generating small scattered employment under NREGA has continued in the village. The works taken up later on have been that of deepening of a tank and repairing of the check dams.

Table 6.2

Employment Generated under NREGS Works

	Person Days			*Wage Incomes Earned (Rs.)*			*Average Wage Rate (Daily) Rs.*
	Men	*Women*	*Total*	*Men*	*Women*	*Total*	
Work No. 1	1655	2104	3759	74475	94680	169155	45
Work No. 2	1074	1287	2361	78402	93951	172353	73
Work No. 3	463	467	930	29632	29632	59264	64
Work No. 4	236	269	505	12980	14795	27775	55
Work No. 5	493	708	1201	36482	52392	88874	74
Work No. 6	399	657	1056	25935	42705	68640	65
Total	4320	5492	9812	257906	328155	586061	60

Source: Village Records at Nana Kotda and Records at Block Office at Idar.

- At the household level, the participating households got employment of 53.62 person days during the first 18 months, against the target of 100 days per 12 months.

In short, the right of "work on demand" was not really fulfilled. The works were undertaken in a scattered manner without any intention of providing any guarantee of work.

As regards payment of the minimum wage rate and other entitlements, the following was observed:

- The average daily wage rate on the works was Rs. 60.00. Since the SORs, on the basis of which the wage rate is calculated, were revised late, the wage rate was low on the first work. The variations in the wage rates thereafter, also reflect the variations in the hours of work put in by workers. In most cases workers worked for more than 8 hours a day.
- There are no separate wage rates for women, as wages were paid to the gang leaders (a gang is a group of 4-5 workers who work together), who were usually male heads of the households.
- Drinking water was provided on the work sites. However the other facilities like a shed, first-aid kit, crèche etc. were found missing.

On an average, 1.47 persons participated, from each participating household. In 88 families, i.e. in more than half the participating households, only 1 person each participated, while in 68 families, i.e. in 42 per cent households, 2 persons each participated. In the case of 2 households, 3 persons each participated and in 2 households, 4 persons each participated in NREGP. The participants came mainly from labour households and farming households.

Table 6.3

Person Days of Employment Generated for Participating Households in NREGS

Main Occupation	*No. of HH Participating*	*No. of Persons Participating*			*No. of Persons Days Generated*			*Person Days per Person*			*No. of Days per HH*
		M	*F*	*T*	*M*	*F*	*T*	*M*	*F*	*T*	
Agriculture	150	103	119	222	3672	4349	8021	35.65	36.54	36.13	53.47
Labour	11	8	8	16	282	330	612	35.25	41.25	38.25	55.64
Total	161	111	127	238	3954	4679	8633	35.62	36.84	36.27	53.62

Person Days of Participation: It is interesting to note that 13.71 per cent of the participating households got employment for less than 20 days, and 27.62 per cent households got employment between 21 and 40 days, implying, more than 40 per cent of the participating households got employment of less than 40 days under the NREGP. Only six households got work for more than 100 days during the period from February 2006 to July 2007, i.e. during 18 months (Table 6.4).

Table 6.4

Average Employment Generated during February 2006-July 2007

No. of Days of Work	*No. of Households*	*Person Days of Work*	*Person Days per Household*
0-20	14	192	13.71
21-40	42	1160	27.62
41-60	44	2177	49.48
61-80	31	2104	70.13
81-100	24	2270	94.58
100+	6	634	105.67
Total	161	8537	53.36

Profile of Participant Households

The highest participation is of landless households (90 households participated), followed by marginal farmers, i.e. farmers with less than 2.5 acres of land (64 households participated). The participation from medium and large farmers is small.

However, when we view this participation in the context of the total households in these categories, the data show that 43.24 per cent of the total marginal farmers, and 38.8 per cent of the total landless households participated in these works. Also, the percentages were significant for other land size categories: 28 per cent of the small farm households and 33 per cent of the medium farm households participated in the NREGP.

Table 6.5

Participation in NREGP by Land Holding

Land Holding (acres)	*Total No. of HHs*	*No. of HHs Participating in NREGS*	*% of the HHs Participating*	*% Share in Participation*
No land	232	90	38.79	55.90
0-2.5	148	64	43.24	39.75
2.5-5.0	18	5	27.77	3.10
5-10	6	2	33.33	1.24
10+ acres	0	0	0	0

An important implication of this is that: (1) NREGS is attractive to non-poor households also and (2) a relatively small proportion of the poorest, the landless, participated in the programme.

Similar observations can be made about the participation in NREGS by income groups (Table 6.6). The participation from the poorest income groups, up to Rs. 10,000 is much less than the participation in higher income groups. The highest participation is from the income groups Rs. 10000-25000 and Rs. 25000-50,000, i.e. the groups just below the poverty line and just above the poverty line respectively. About 50 per cent households participated in NREGS from these groups. The participation is also high (42.86 per cent) from the highest income group with an annual income above Rs. 125000. On the other hand, less than one-fourth households participate from the poorest income groups.

The table once again indicates that the poorest strata do not participate fully in the NREGP and that the poorest households constitute only 2.48 per cent of the total participating households.

Table 6.6

Participation in NREGS by Household Income

HH Income (Rs)	*Total No. of HHs*	*HHs Participating in NREGS*	*% of HHs Participating*	*% Share in Participation*
-5000	17	4	23.53	2.48
5000-10000	61	13	21.31	8.07
10000-25000	194	94	48.45	58.38
25000-50000	95	43	45.26	26.70
50000-75000	17	1	5.88	0.62
75000-100000	13	2	15.38	1.24
100000-125000	7	1	14.29	0.62
125000+	7	3	42.86	1.86
Total	401	161	39.85	100

There are several reasons for the poorest to participate less in NREGP. To start with, many of the poorest commute to neighbouring villages to work on farm and non-farm activities as manual labourers. They have a long term contract, formal or informal, with the employers according to which the workers get continuous employment for several days. As against this, the work on NREGA is short term, and scattered without any employment guarantee component. Even though many of the workers who commute reported that they prefer to work in their own village, they cannot do so as the NREGA work is not dependable. Secondly, the wage rates on NREG works, and outside are fairly comparable, around Rs. 50-60 per day. There is, therefore, a general preference for local work as: (1) it saves their travel cost and (2) spares them from the inconvenience of commuting. However, NREG work is just not available on any significant scale. The guarantee component of the scheme is missing in practice. The poorest households who are mobile to migrate (as many of them are landless), therefore, prefer to migrate rather than participate in NREGA work.

As regards the sex and age of the participants, the data in Table 6.7 show that except for one, no children participated in the NREGS. The highest participation is from the age group 15-35 years, followed by the 35-50 age groups. The participation is low in the age groups 50-60 years and 60+ years. It is to be noted that persons above 60 years, also do participate in the programme.

Table 6.7

Participation in NREGS by Age and Sex

Age Group	*Total Persons*			*No. of Persons Participating in NREGP*			*% Participation in NREGP*		
	M	F	T	M	F	T	M	F	T
0-14	264	250	514	0	1	1	0	0.4	0.019
15-35	391	351	742	68	68	136	17.43	20.79	18.96
36-50	171	189	360	41	50	91	24.11	26.45	25.35
51-60	65	63	128	6	1	7	9.23	1.58	5.46
60+	55	53	108	0	2	2	0	3.77	1.85
Total	946	906	1852	115	122	237	12.19	13.87	13

Why Don't People Participate in NREGA?

The above discussion has shown that the level of participation in NREGA has been very low—in terms of number as well as days. This raises a question: Why is the level so low? On the one hand it is argued (mainly by government officials) that there is no demand for this kind of strenuous manual work, while on the other hand it is argued that the administration has not been able to disseminate information about the NREGA, and is not able to identify and cater to the needs of the people who want work. Our investigation showed that the reasons why people are not able to access NREGS work are multiple (Table 6.8):

- About 46 per cent of the households wanted to work but could not work on NREGS due to some or other reasons. Some of them did not know about the scope of NREGS or did not know when the works started, as there is no system of informing them about this. No boards are put up or no notice is circulated among the people. Some others could not work because they were not registered or because they did not have a job card, while some others could not work because work was made available only to selected people in the village, as the works were undertaken on a small scale. In other words, half of the households who could not work on NREGA did not know about the works or could not get the registration or the job card.

- Small and scattered work under the NREGA did not meet the demand for work of those who migrate outside the village to work. Our study showed that about 300 persons commute to neighbouring villages/Idar to work everyday, as work is not available locally. They earn about Rs. 50–60 per day, which is not more than the NREGA wage rate. They prefer to work at home also because it will save their transport cost as well as time. However they prefer to migrate for assured work.
- Many have demanded work, but the *talati* and sarpanch are not able to start work, as "they do not have power to start work." They also said that the decisions about the works are taken by the *taluka* office.
- About 30 households (mainly women) could not work because there were small children at home and there was no arrangement for child care at the work site or because they had household work, mainly collection of water and fuel wood, to attend to. Some of these households also found NREGS wages to be low.
- About 118 (29 per cent) households did not work on NREGA because they were not available when the works started. They were either busy with social functions, were sick or were tied up with their farm work when the works were undertaken. Some of them did not have a person in the family who could work.

Only 20 per cent households are not interested in NREGA work because they find the work too strenuous or because they do not need extra employment. In other words, about 20 per cent households in the village are not really interested in participating in NREGS. To put it differently, 80 per cent of the households in the village are interested in participating in NREGP—some of them are interested in working during the lean season or for limited number of days while some are interested in working whenever work is available.

To sum up, there is no guarantee of work given under the NREGS in the village. The works are taken up in a scattered manner, and its availability still depends on the sweet will of the local bodies or government administration. Neither are the implementers interested in ensuring guarantee of work nor are people capable of demanding work as their right.

The argument that there is not much scope for NREGA kind of works in the village also did not prove correct. This kind of thinking had come up largely because there was no long-term view or long-term planning under NREGA. The village does not have a perspective on NREGA works, decisions are taken on purely ad hoc basis. However, when we sat with village leaders and helped them in building a long term view, a long list of works emerged from their suggestions. In other words, there is a need to develop a long term perspective for the NREGA, to make it more useful.

Do People Want More NREGA Work?

When we asked the NREGA workers whether they are interested in getting more NREGA work, the response was positive. Almost 80 per cent of the workers replied that they want more work on the programme. The demand came from men as well as women.

It is important to note, however, that women want more work, but not necessarily on NREGA. This is partly because the available work does not always suit women (no efforts are made to design works that suit women) and partly because they do not get adequate support for child care or for reducing the drudgery of collecting fuel wood, water, fodder etc. Considering the fact that in spite of these constraints, women's participation is significant in NREGA, it is clear that there is a need to pay attention to women's unpaid work under the programme.

Table 6.8

Reasons for not Working in NREGA

Reasons	*Caste of Households*				
	SC	*ST*	*OBC*	*Others*	*Total*
We do not know about NREGA	3	0	5	5	13
We do not know when/where NREGA work started	0	0	3	1	4
Absent from the village when the programme came	1	3	1	0	5
Not allowed to work	0	0	1	1	2
Work stopped because of rains	35	2	54	9	100
Could not form a gang	0	0	4	0	4
Could not get registration	8	2	24	8	42
Could not get a job card	3	0	13	2	18
Sub-total (i)	50	7	105	26	188
Small children at home	1	0	3	0	4
Engaged in HH work	1	1	1		3
Busy with outside village work	5	3	9	13	30
Wages are low	0	0	4	1	5
Sub-total (ii)	7	4	17	14	42
Social functions	16	5	16	0	37
Sickness	19	16	13	0	48
Caste does not allow (Rajput)	0	0	13	0	13
Working as crop sharer	1	0	1	0	2
No worker in the HH	2	3	10	3	18
Sub-total (iii)	38	24	53	3	118
We do not need any extra work	9	2	19	11	41
We do not like the hard work involved/too old	5	0	20	12	37
NR	10	4	6	3	23
Sub-total (iv)	24	6	45	26	101
Grand total (i+ii+iii+iv)	119	41	220	69	452

Suggestions for Improving NREGS

When households were asked about their suggestions for improving the working of NREGA, they came out with several important suggestions. The most important suggestion was that they should get more employment under NREGA, as the present employment is very low.

Table 6.9

Persons Who Want More NREGA Employment

Total Employment during the Last Year (Man-days)	Do you Want More Work?		How Many Days (per person)		Type of Work					
					NREGA		Other Labour		Other Work	
	Male	Female	Male	Female	Male	Female	Male	Female	Male	Female
0–30	47	52	102	109	47	40	0	12	0	0
30–60	60	62	99	98	60	40	0	22	0	0
60–90	6	10	107	104	6	4	0	6	0	0
90–120	1	0	150	0	1	0	0	0	0	0
120–150	0	0	0	0	0	0	0	0	0	0
150–200	0	0	0	0	0	0	0	0	0	0
200–250	0	0	0	0	0	0	0	0	0	0
250–300	0	0	0	0	0	0	0	0	0	0
300+	0	0	0	0	0	0	0	0	0	0
Total	114	124			114	84	0	40	0	0

The demand for additional NREGA work comes primarily from labour households (agricultural and other labour), agriculture and self-employed households. Households engaged in private service also want that the village should have more NREGA works. More than half the suggestions are for removing the limit of 100 days of work per household. This is perhaps because the households which are migrating/commuting want local employment to avoid migration. In short, there does not seem to be any dearth of demand for NREGA work.

Potential NREGA Works for Nana Kotda: Suggestions about Works

There does not seem to be a dearth of works in the village, if we go by what the villagers want for the village under the programme. In fact, households have useful suggestions on what kind of works should be taken up under NREGA in the village.

It is interesting to note that during our first meeting, the *sarpanch*, the *talati* and other village leaders stated that there was not much scope for NREGA kind of works in the village. They could not

Table 6.10

Suggestions for Improving NREGP by Household Occupation

Sr.No.	*Main Occupation of HH*	*1*	*2*	*3*	*4*	*5*	*Total*
1	Agriculture	50	2	0	1	45	98
2	Self-employed non-professional in non-agriculture	5	0	0	0	4	9
3	Agricultural labour	74	1	21	0	74	170
4	Other labour	1	0	0	0	25	26
5	Service (govt.)	1	0	0	0	1	2
6	Service (pvt.)	6	0	0	0	1	7
7	Animal husbandry	2	0	0	0	5	7
8	Interest/royalty	1	0	0	0	0	1
9	Pension income	0	0	0	0	0	0
10	Beggar	0	0	0	0	2	2
11	Misc.	0	0	0	0	0	0
	Total	140	3	21	1	157	322

Note: 1: We need (more) NREGS employment, 2: More NREGS employment needed in non-agricultural seasons, 3: Local employment needed to avoid migration, 4: Food grains should be distributed as part wages, 5: The limit of 100 days per household should be removed.

think of many works which can be undertaken under the NREGA. Our subsequent visits to the village and discussions with them, however, did make a difference. They realised that a lot can be done for the village by using NREGA if a long-term view is taken for the development of the village. In fact, villagers made concrete suggestions on what their village needs for promoting growth of the village economy and how NREGA can help in this.

Focus group discussions (FGDs) on the time use in the village (to draw attention to the time spent on unpaid work and to show how this can be saved), and on the needs of the village based on our study of the village also helped a lot. They helped in the identification of potential works for the village: (1) these helped people to view NREGS in the long term perspective in the sense that it made them realise how NREGS works in the coming 5-7 years can contribute to the development of the village, (2) they also helped them to realise that NREGS is not a 'one more' government programme or a programme that creates and supports a permanent army of manual workers, but is a transitional programme that can help the economy to participate in the mainstream development process. That is, NREGS can promote long term development of the village economy, to start with, in agriculture, animal husbandry etc. and then help in diversification in to other sectors to participate in the overall development process in the state. These discussions helped villagers to make concrete suggestions for NREGA.

The most important demand from the village is for constructing a water harvesting structure, i.e. deepening of the village tank for ensuring potable water. This is to address the inadequacy of the present facility of drinking water. The other important demands namely, plantation on common lands; deepening of the small river that passes by the village; creating other irrigation facilities for the village etc. are all related to improved natural resource management in the village in agriculture, animal husbandry including dairying. Improved management of land and water resources is expected to stabilise and improve the existing livelihoods in the village. The recommendation of growing fodder on common lands also falls into this category.

The villagers also want cleanliness in the village, their major recommendations here being construction of drainage, paving of internal roads, construction of latrines etc.

Table 6.11

Suggestions for NREGS Works by Household Occupation

Main Occupation of HH	*No. of HHs Suggesting*	*1*	*2*	*3*	*4*	*5*	*6*	*7*	*8*	*9*	*10*	*11*
Agriculture	32	9	3	12	0	3	21	1	31	12	20	5
Self-employed non-professional in non-agriculture	0	4	2	0	0	1	0	0	0	2	0	0
Agricultural labour	117	11	8	12	1	4	23	1	10	30	10	6
Other labour	1	0	0	0	0	0	1	0	0	1	0	0
Service (govt.)	1	0	1	1	0	0	1	0	0	1	0	0
Service (pvt.)	2	1	0	0	0	1	0	1	0	2	0	0
Animal husbandry	7	1	2	3	0	0	0	0	0	5	0	0
Interest/royalty income	0	0	0	0	0	0	0	0	1	0	0	0
Pension income	0	0	0	0	0	0	0	1	0	0	0	0
Beggar	0	0	2	0	0	0	0	0	0	0	0	0
Servant	0	1	0	0	0	0	0	0	0	0	0	0
Total	160	27	18	28	1	9	46	4	42	53	30	11

Note: 1: House construction, 2: Latrines and bathrooms for households, 3: Drainage, 4: Construction, 5: Growing fodder for animals, 6: Irrigation works and digging a new tank, 7: Basic needs/infrastructure, 8: Forestation and plantation on common lands, and nursery, 9: Drinking water/water harvesting, 10: Deepening of tanks and the river, 11: Construction of road/paving internal roads.

When asked, in focus group discussions, why they did not make these suggestions in the village assembly that was called for NREGA, we were told that: (1) they did not know about the meeting of the assembly, (2) they did not know about the details of the NREGA, and (3) nobody asked them for their suggestions. In other words, the role of participatory planning in NREGA is not known or appreciated by the implementers of the scheme.

Not all the works suggested are labour-intensive. However, with good planning, it may be possible to manage the overall labour material ratio for all these works put together for the village. The gender dimension is somehow missing from the suggestions in the sense that the specific needs of women, such as child care facilities, plantation for fodder, energy security through energy plantation etc. are missing from the suggestions. Even women did not come out with any of these suggestions until we pointed these out.

In short, our experience in the village indicates that villagers do make their suggestions for NREGA works if helped. Also, if helped, they do develop a long-term view of development of the village and do incorporate women's concerns in to NREGA planning.

The details of the potential works for the village are produced below:

Works that reduce drudgery of unpaid/non-market SNA work: The first category of potential works for Nana Kotda are the works that reduce the drudgery of non-market SNA work. The time use statistics show that women and children, spend long hours in collecting water and fuel wood in the village. This time work can be reduced by undertaking assets that provide water supply at the doorstep and fuel/ energy within the easy access of people.

1. Drinking Water in Nana Kotda: As seen in chapter 3, Nana Kotda gets water for drinking and cooking purposes from a multi-village scheme (i.e. Dharoi Group Scheme that covers 15 villages) under which water is brought to the village from the Dharoi dam which is about 50 km away from the village. Women of the village go to the one stand post for fetching water, with some of them walking up to 1 km distance to the stand post.

Since the long distance pipelines under this multi-village scheme are not maintained well, there are one or two breakages every month, resulting in the lack of water supply for 4–6 days at a stretch.

Nana Kotda therefore, needs the following to reduce the drudgery of fetching water and to ensure adequate water supply:

- Deepening of the tank located in the village to augment local water resources,
- Water works to treat the harvested water, and
- Pipelines in the wards with a stand post to reduce the time spent on fetching water.

All these woks can be taken up under the NREGA.

2. Regeneration of Common Lands for Energy Security: Another major drudgery in Nana Kotda is collecting fuel wood. As seen before, women spend long hours in collecting fuel wood for family.

Energy needed at the household level is primarily for cooking, lighting and for other uses like using electric equipments. The cooking energy is most important component of the energy particularly in poor households. The most important source of this energy in Nana Kotda is fuel wood and cow dung. However, both this sources have several problems: (a) collection of fuel wood or making cow dung is time consuming and it is a drudgery which involves hard work and low productivity. With the environmental degradation and declining common lands, the problem has acquired serious dimensions in the village, (b) collecting fuel wood is also a danger to the safety of collectors, mainly women, (c) it does not allow them to participate in other productive activities, (d) use of this energy creates indoor pollution which has several serious health hazards, and (e) this method of acquiring energy is also responsible, to a considerable extent, for children's lack of education as children are engaged in this activity in a big way.

There are several alternative solutions to these problems, such as, plantation of fuel wood and use of fuel efficient stoves, use of kerosene or gas, use of natural gas or use of non-conventional energy sources etc. Considering the fact that more than 85 per cent households in Nana

Kotda use fuel wood (the village does not use cow dung for fuel), the immediate need is to promote fuel wood plantation, supported by fuel efficient stoves and by charcoal manufacturing.

Nana Kotda has, officially 42 acres of common land. Of this, about 14 acres is available (the rest of the land is either encroached by villagers or is under ponds), but is badly degraded. A part of this land can be regenerated for fuel wood plantation and fodder for animals. Since about 42 per cent households in the village have milch animals that need fodder, it will be a good idea to develop common lands for fuel and fodder.

Systematic and scientific regeneration of common land will ensure good quality highly productive fodder on the one hand and good quality fuel wood supported by fuel efficient stoves on the other. This will also enable the landless to buy milch animals and participate in the fast developing dairy industry in the state. According to the official scheme, a plot of 5 acres is taken up for regeneration of common lands. Of this, 3 acres is meant for fodder or good quality grasses and 2 acres is used for plantation of trees that provide fuel wood and fodder. The work is highly labour-intensive, as the major tasks involved are fencing (with vegetation), land development and plantation. We propose that about 15 acres of common land (i.e. 3 plots of 5 acres each) should be regenerated in the village.

Works that reduce burden of unpaid domestic work: According to the time use statistics, women in Nana Kotda spend considerable time in household work, including care of children and other household members, with the result that they are not able to take part in economic activities, including NREGA. That is, the burden of child care restricts their entry in to the labour market and prevents them from taking part in productive employment.

NREGA works can reduce their burden of care work: Child care centres that run for full hours (8 hours a day) and well run pre-schools can help considerably here. We propose both as potential works for the village. Nana Kotda has 2 pre-schools (*anganvadi*). However, one of them sits in a private home and the other one sits in a hired room, which is not adequate. Also, they run only for 3 hours. There is a need to construct buildings for the pre-schools and organise full day care for children.

Works that improve the quality of life of people: While discussing the amenities and facilities in the village, we have identified the gaps that need to be filled in to ensure a minimum quality of life of people. We list these facilities as potential NREGS works for the village.

1. Paving of Internal Roads: Paving of internal roads is important as: (a) it improves access to the village level services like schools, bus stop, PDS shop, school, temple, cremation ground, flour mill etc. (b) reduces the time spent on accessing these services, (c) improves cleanliness, reduces breeding places for mosquitoes (particularly in the rainy season) and other germs. As seen earlier, half the wards do not have paved roads. The village needs paving of internal roads of the length of 2500 metres, with 3.5 m width and 0.30 m thickness. The first phase of this work will be of earth work, which will be highly labour-intensive, with more than 85–90 per cent of the costs being labour cost. The second phase will use materials as well as skilled labour for making roads durable.

2. Construction of Toilets (Under Total Sanitation Campaign Programme): The number of households with their own toilet is 156 in Nana Kotda. That is, 248 households do not have a toilet. Construction of toilet will improve the quality of life in multiple ways: (a) it will improve cleanliness in the village, (b) improve women's health, as it is women who suffer maximum when there is no toilet facility available, and (c) help in producing manure. NREGA can take up this work without much problem. We propose construction of at least 200 toilets under the programme. Since the Total Sanitation Campaign Programme requires that the beneficiaries also contribute to the total cost, the cost of labour (covered under NREGA) can be treated as the contribution of the beneficiaries.

3. Construction of Drainage: Nana Kotda does not have any drainage system to dispose off domestic waste water and rainwater. Construction of a drainage system will: (a) improve cleanliness in the village, reduce breeding places for mosquitoes and other germs, and (b) help in reusing the water for irrigation and other purposes. The village needs drainage of about 2500 metres.

Productive assets for income generation: NREGS can contribute to the village economy by constructing productive assets to enhance productivity in the existing economic activities as well as in new economic activities.

Agriculture is a major economic activity in the village. However, as seen earlier, it suffers from uncertainty and consequent fluctuations, and low productivity. Lack of ensured water supply is a major problem, which can be addressed effectively by NREGS. De-silting of check dams has already contributed to improvement in agriculture, as seen earlier. The village has a good potential for further water harvesting, as there is good rainfall and good geo-hydrological conditions for water harvesting in the village. In this context, the following can be suggested:

1. Digging Two More Tanks: Our consultation with the village leaders and farmers indicated that two more tanks can be dug in the village area to harvest rainwater. This will further improve the groundwater levels, which will allow ensured water supply to many more farmers. The first phase of the digging will involve manual work, while later on the material component will be used for pitching to make the assets durable.

2. Deepening of the River/Stream: Another possibility for water harvesting is through deepening of the river.

Table 6.12 presents the details of the potential NREGA works for Nana Kotda.

The table indicates that the village can have 10 NREGA works to start with. These works, as seen above, are related to water harvesting, improving connectivity and natural resource management—all of which are "admissible" according to the NREG Act. In addition, we have proposed some works that improve the quality of life, i.e. the sanitation and public hygiene in the village. While the ratio of labour cost and material cost is 100:00 for the earlier works, the ratio is slightly tilting towards the material component in the latter works. The overall ratio of labour and material component therefore is 36:64 rather than 60:40.

We propose, as the village has agreed, that the additional funds required for the works will come from the other sources, such as the grants from the State Finance Commission, the special funds of the local and the MLA, or the funds from the district planning board, or any other ongoing programme. It needs to be underlined here that: (1) it is important to ensure durability of NREGS assets, and (2) it is important to follow the priorities as laid down by the local population, i.e. local needs.

It needs to be underlined that the list of the potential NREGS works is not exhaustive, in the sense that many more works are needed in the village to enhance the capital formation in the village to improve productivity in agriculture and allied activities (like construction of farm ponds, deepening of the small river, and massive watershed development works) as well as in other activities in the secondary and tertiary sectors.

Summing Up

One major observation coming out of the discussion in the chapter is that though the NREGP has a good potential in the village, the potential is far from being tapped.

The programme has been implemented in a most ad hoc manner with a few scattered works undertaken under the programme. The size of the programme is very small, as the six works undertaken during 91 days on the first year have created an employment of only 8537 person days so far. Only six households got employment of 100 days.

The small and scattered work created under the NREGA could reach only a selected number of households, and the poorest at the bottom could not enter the programme. The total absence of the guarantee of work has not made any impact on the migration.

In fact, almost no attention has been paid to the entitlements of the workers. That is, no systems have been set up to guarantee work on demand (or for payment of unemployment allowance); no arrangements have been made to see that minimum wages are paid within the stipulated time; no adequate efforts are made to ensure all the worksite facilities; and no serious attempts have been made to ensure transparency and accountability of the implementers.

Table 6.12

Potential NREGS Works for Nana Kotda

Works	*Skilled Labour*	*Material Cost*	*Unskilled Labour*	*Total*	*Skilled Labour %*	*Material Cost %*	*Unskilled Labour %*	*Total*
Deepening of the tank	0	0	36000	36000	0	0	100	100
Laying pipelines to distribute water in the wards	0	1695200	423800	2119000	0	80	20	100
Regeneration of common lands	0	60000	45000	105000	0	57.14	42.86	100
Construction of child care centres	50000	300000	150000	500000	10	60	30	100
Paving of internal roads								
First phase: Only earth work	0	0	156750	156750	0	0.00	100.00	100
Second phase: Surfacing the roads	100000	600000	300000	1000000	10	60	30	100
Construction of toilets (under Total Sanitation Campaign Programme)	80000	480000	240000	800000	10	60	30	100
Construction of drainage	45000	270000	135000	450000	10	60	30	100
Digging two more tanks								
First phase: Digging	0	0	400000	400000	0	0	100	100
Second phase: Pitching	50000	300000	150000	500000	10	60	30	100
Total cost	325000	3705200	2036550	6066750	2.36	61.07	35.57	100.00

What is important to note, however, is that people *are* willing to work on NREGA works. In fact, 80 per cent of the households in the village reported that they would like to work on these works either during the lean season or to avoid migration or to work throughout the year to fill in the periods of unemployment.

It is also worth noting that if helped, villagers do see the role of a programme like this to improve the quality of life as well as to improve productivity and production in the sectors where they are working. It is clear that by involving local people it is feasible to tap the potential of the programme at the village level.

There is a need to re-orient the programme towards it goals.

7 Multiplier Impacts of NREGA

This chapter examines the multiple impacts of an employment guarantee programme (NREGA) on the village economy of Nana Kotda. This has been done through multiplier analysis in which NREGS works are treated as external shocks on the village SAM (social accounting matrix). The study also examines how portions of unpaid SNA and non-SNA work can be substituted by NREGA works and what impact it can make on the incomes and employment of households and on the economy. This has been done by estimating the multiplier impacts of the substitution of unpaid work by NREGA assets/infrastructure on the village economy.

Social Accounting Matrix (SAM) for the Village

As seen earlier, a SAM is a comprehensive accounting framework within which, the full circular flow of income from production to factor incomes, household income to household consumption and back to production is captured. The village SAM for Nana Kotda has four components: (1) production activities: crop husbandry, animal husbandry, construction, service providers and self-employed, manufacturing, services (government and private), (2) factors of production: labour and capital, (3) institutions: households, government, village *panchayat* etc. and (4) outside the village, consisting of values of sectors and labour going out of the village and coming into the village.

In all, there are 55 producing sectors. First 13 sectors from rice to animal husbandry correspond to agriculture where many of the items are produced in the village. For the construction of SAM, the normal yield for the crops (as averages of the last two years) has been taken for last two years, because 2006-07 happened to be a drought year. Sectors 14 to 38 are manufacturing sectors where all the items are brought from outside the village except for cotton ginning (for which there is only one factory), which produces cotton inside the village and sends the entire production, including that of cotton seed outside the village. The other remaining sectors are the service providing sectors in the village. The activities could not be separated from commodities because the data available was directly on commodity basis both for inputs as well as outputs. Hence, the SAM is directly in the commodity X commodity form. Again, as seen earlier, the commodity X commodity matrix is derived from use and supply matrices. In addition, detailed information was collected from all institutions/organisations like schools, cooperative societies and *panchayats* about their activities, costs and revenues as well as on the working of NREGA in the village.

MULTIPLIER ANALYSIS

The NREGA works undertaken in the village will have multiplier impact on the total output, income and employment of the village economy. This impact has been estimated using multiplier analysis treating NREGA works as external shocks to the village SAM. This section analyses the multiplier impacts and presents them. It also goes beyond the multiplier analysis, and discusses the other impacts of the works.

The village SAM has been used for estimating the direct and indirect impact of various external shocks on the economy. With the help of multiplier models, questions related to the nature of linkages between the structure of production and distribution of income have been addressed.

Let us write SAM model as

$$Y = W + X,$$

Where W consists of endogenous accounts and X is the exogenous account.

$$A_{ij} = W_{ij} / y_j,$$

Where A_{ij} gives the requirement of account i for one unit account j.

The above equation can be written as

$$Y = AY + X$$

$$(I-A)\,Y = X$$

$$Y = (I - A)^{-1}\,X = (mij)X = MX,$$

Where M is SAM multiplier matrix, mij is the total impact on account i, because of a unit shock in account j. Different multipliers can be output, income and employment.

The multipliers measure the responses of the economy to a change in demand of a sector. When total output of a sector increases or decreases, it impacts the economy due to this sector's direct as well as indirect effect. Direct effects are the immediate effects associated with the change in the final demand for a particular sector or industry. In addition to the direct effects, the indirect effects or the secondary effects are due to backward linkages of sectors. The following paragraphs present the results of our multiplier analysis.

The Output, Income and Employment Multipliers

The output multiplier for a sector is defined as the total value of production by all the sectors of the economy required to satisfy one unit of final demand for that sector's output. For example, if one unit of final demand is increased in animal husbandry sector (say milk), this will require inputs in terms of feed of live stock (different crops), which, in turn, will increase the demand for the output of these crops. To increase the output of these crops will require the inputs needed to increase the inputs (seed, fertilisers, labour etc.). The increased employment of labour will result in their higher incomes, which will increase in their expenditure. The increased expenditure will need more output and so on. These are called indirect requirements. These direct and indirect requirements are estimated by the SAM multiplier matrix, given in Table 7.1.

The income or value added (labour + capital) multiplier gives an estimate of the direct and indirect income changes resulting from the one unit change in output. These are also obtained from the labour and capital rows of the SAM multiplier matrix. Table 7.2 gives the total output, income and HH income multipliers.

The employment multiplier gives an estimate of the direct and indirect employment changes resulting from a change in unit output. These multipliers are obtained by multiplying the output multiplier of each sector with the relevant employment coefficient. The employment coefficient of each sector presents the number of person days generated per unit of output (say for per thousand rupees).

The inverse of the SAM (only those sectors are taken for the inverse for which there is production in village) is given in Table 7.1. Each column of this inverse (from rows 1 to 24) gives the increase in output of different sectors because of one unit increase in the final demand of that sector. Rows 25 to 27 of the sectors gives the corresponding income multiplier. Rows from 28 to 34 give the impact on the incomes of various sections of the households. For example, one unit of increase in the demand for labour will increase 0.338 units of income from wheat, 0.305 units of income from *jowar* and so on. The rows from 28-34 present the impact of the increased purchasing power on the incomes of various sections of the population. Again, one unit increase in demand for wheat will increase income of marginal farmers by 0.320 units, of small farmers by 0.188 units, of large farmers by 0.189 units and of all households (which also includes labour households, households self-employed in non-agriculture, households in services) by 0.040 units. The differences in the values of multipliers arise from the output and income structures in the village economy. Rows 1 to 24 will indicate output multiplier, the rows 25 to 27 will give the values of corresponding income multiplier and the totals of the rows 28 to 34 will give household income multipliers.

Table 7.2 presents these totals in terms of output, income and household income multipliers. The output multipliers indicate the coefficients by which the outputs will increase if there is an increase in the expenditure due to an external stock (here NREGA works). For example, if the expenditure on the consumption of wheat increases by Rs. 1000 due to some NREGA works, its impact in terms of increase in total production of wheat will be Rs.1793 (1000 X 1.793). In other words, the table shows that one unit increase in the demand for wheat will increase the total output by 1.793 units, one unit increase in the demand for *jowar* will increase the total output by 1.671 units and so

Table 7.1

Per Unit Change in Output and *Income due to Change in Final Demand from Different Sectors*

	Wheat	*Jowar*	*Bajra*	*Maize*	*Tur*	*Pulses*	*Castor*	*Groundnut*	*Cotton*	*Fruits & Vegetables*	*Other Crops*	*Animal Husbandry*
Wheat	1.184	0.067	0.029	0.082	0.015	0.026	0.074	0.076	0.002	0.014	0.068	0.095
Jowar	0.007	1.040	0.003	0.008	0.002	0.002	0.006	0.006	0.000	0.001	0.006	0.033
Bajra	0.005	0.005	1.006	0.006	0.001	0.002	0.004	0.004	0.000	0.001	0.004	0.030
Maize	0.021	0.019	0.008	1.047	0.004	0.007	0.019	0.020	0.001	0.004	0.018	0.044
Tur	0.014	0.011	0.005	0.014	1.006	0.005	0.013	0.014	0.000	0.002	0.012	0.012
Pulses	0.013	0.012	0.006	0.015	0.003	1.009	0.013	0.013	0.000	0.003	0.012	0.038
Castor	0.000	0.000	0.000	0.000	0.000	0.000	1.028	0.000	0.000	0.000	0.000	0.000
Groundnut	0.000	0.000	0.000	0.000	0.000	0.000	0.000	1.006	0.000	0.000	0.000	0.000
Cotton	0.004	0.004	0.002	0.005	0.001	0.001	0.003	0.003	1.002	0.001	0.003	0.030
Fruits & vegetables	0.030	0.023	0.011	0.029	0.005	0.010	0.030	0.031	0.001	1.019	0.028	0.027
Other crops	0.039	0.045	0.021	0.052	0.011	0.013	0.035	0.035	0.001	0.009	1.054	0.273
Animal husbandry	0.137	0.166	0.077	0.188	0.042	0.047	0.121	0.118	0.005	0.031	0.107	1.095
Cotton ginning	0.000	0.000	0.000	0.000	0.000	0.000	0.000	0.000	0.000	0.000	0.000	0.000
Construction	0.025	0.020	0.009	0.025	0.005	0.008	0.024	0.024	0.001	0.004	0.022	0.021
Education	0.042	0.033	0.015	0.041	0.007	0.014	0.042	0.043	0.001	0.007	0.039	0.037
Bangle vendor	0.008	0.006	0.003	0.008	0.001	0.003	0.009	0.009	0.000	0.002	0.008	0.008
Fruit & vegetable vendor	0.020	0.016	0.007	0.020	0.004	0.006	0.019	0.019	0.001	0.003	0.017	0.017
Barber	0.006	0.005	0.002	0.006	0.001	0.002	0.007	0.007	0.000	0.001	0.006	0.006
Carpenter	0.021	0.016	0.008	0.020	0.003	0.007	0.021	0.022	0.001	0.004	0.020	0.019
Cloth shop	0.040	0.032	0.014	0.040	0.007	0.013	0.038	0.039	0.001	0.007	0.035	0.034

Contd...

...contd...

	Wheat	*Jowar*	*Bajra*	*Maize*	*Tur*	*Pulses*	*Castor*	*Groundnut*	*Cotton*	*Fruits & Vegetables*	*Other Crops*	*Animal Husbandry*
Paan shop	0.044	0.036	0.016	0.044	0.008	0.015	0.043	0.044	0.001	0.008	0.039	0.038
PDS shop	0.030	0.024	0.010	0.030	0.005	0.010	0.028	0.029	0.001	0.005	0.026	0.025
Transport	0.052	0.066	0.023	0.068	0.027	0.010	0.054	0.041	0.002	0.009	0.026	0.029
Other services	0.051	0.023	0.015	0.059	0.005	0.009	0.035	0.032	0.001	0.010	0.025	0.026
Labour total	0.338	0.305	0.107	0.368	0.074	0.091	0.253	0.258	0.009	0.051	0.232	0.218
Labour income from outside	0.000	0.000	0.000	0.000	0.000	0.000	0.000	0.000	0.000	0.000	0.000	0.000
Labour from outside	0.039	0.031	0.014	0.038	0.007	0.013	0.039	0.040	0.001	0.007	0.036	0.034
Capital	0.852	0.617	0.327	0.779	0.123	0.320	0.954	0.983	0.029	0.157	0.883	0.857
Marginal farmer	0.320	0.232	0.123	0.293	0.046	0.120	0.359	0.370	0.011	0.059	0.332	0.322
Small farmer	0.188	0.136	0.072	0.172	0.027	0.071	0.211	0.217	0.006	0.035	0.195	0.189
Large farmer	0.189	0.137	0.073	0.173	0.027	0.071	0.212	0.218	0.006	0.035	0.196	0.190
Self-employed in non-agriculture	0.114	0.083	0.044	0.104	0.016	0.043	0.128	0.132	0.004	0.021	0.118	0.115
Labour	0.329	0.297	0.104	0.359	0.072	0.088	0.246	0.252	0.009	0.050	0.226	0.212
Services	0.008	0.008	0.003	0.009	0.002	0.002	0.006	0.006	0.000	0.001	0.006	0.005
All other households	0.040	0.029	0.015	0.037	0.006	0.015	0.045	0.046	0.001	0.007	0.042	0.040

	Cotton Ginning	*Construction*	*Education*	*Bangle Vendor*	*Fruit & Vegetable Vendor*	*Barber*	*Carpenter*	*Cloth Shop*	*Paan Shop*	*PDS Shop*	*Transport*	*Other Services*
Wheat	0.008	0.037	0.014	0.017	0.037	0.051	0.023	0.019	0.017	0.438	0.048	0.052
Jowar	0.001	0.002	0.001	0.001	0.003	0.004	0.002	0.001	0.001	0.095	0.004	0.004
Bajra	0.000	0.001	0.000	0.001	0.002	0.003	0.001	0.001	0.001	0.003	0.003	0.003
Maize	0.002	0.010	0.003	0.004	0.009	0.013	0.006	0.005	0.004	0.103	0.012	0.013
Tur	0.002	0.005	0.001	0.004	0.008	0.011	0.005	0.004	0.003	0.008	0.010	0.011
Pulses	0.001	0.005	0.002	0.003	0.007	0.010	0.004	0.003	0.003	0.097	0.009	0.010
Castor	0.000	0.000	0.000	0.000	0.000	0.000	0.000	0.000	0.000	0.000	0.000	0.000
Groundnut	0.000	0.000	0.000	0.000	0.000	0.000	0.000	0.000	0.000	0.000	0.000	0.000
Cotton	0.895	0.001	0.000	0.001	0.002	0.002	0.001	0.001	0.001	0.002	0.002	0.002
Fruits & vegetables	0.004	0.011	0.004	0.009	0.420	0.025	0.012	0.009	0.008	0.018	0.024	0.026
Other crops	0.004	0.009	0.003	0.008	0.019	0.024	0.011	0.008	0.138	0.025	0.023	0.024
Animal husbandry	0.014	0.028	0.012	0.028	0.064	0.081	0.037	0.027	0.028	0.090	0.077	0.082
Cotton ginning	1.000	0.000	0.000	0.000	0.000	0.000	0.000	0.000	0.000	0.000	0.000	0.000
Construction	0.003	1.011	0.004	0.006	0.012	0.017	0.008	0.006	0.006	0.015	0.016	0.017
Education	0.005	0.016	1.003	0.012	0.024	0.034	0.016	0.012	0.011	0.026	0.032	0.035
Bangle vendor	0.001	0.002	0.000	1.003	0.006	0.009	0.004	0.003	0.003	0.005	0.008	0.009
Fruit & vegetable vendor	0.002	0.009	0.002	0.005	1.010	0.014	0.006	0.005	0.005	0.012	0.013	0.014
Barber	0.001	0.001	0.000	0.002	0.005	1.007	0.003	0.002	0.002	0.004	0.006	0.007
Carpenter	0.003	0.006	0.001	0.007	0.014	0.020	1.009	0.006	0.006	0.012	0.018	0.020
Cloth shop	0.004	0.018	0.003	0.009	0.020	0.028	0.013	1.010	0.009	0.024	0.026	0.028
Paan shop	0.005	0.019	0.003	0.011	0.023	0.032	0.015	0.012	1.011	0.027	0.030	0.033

Contd...

...contd...

	Cotton Ginning	*Construction*	*Education*	*Bangle Vendor*	*Fruit & Vegetable Vendor*	*Barber*	*Carpenter*	*Cloth Shop*	*Paan Shop*	*PDS Shop*	*Transport*	*Other Services*
PDS Shop	0.003	0.014	0.003	0.007	0.014	0.020	0.009	0.007	0.007	1.018	0.018	0.020
Transport	0.005	0.006	0.002	0.009	0.021	0.027	0.012	0.009	0.008	0.033	1.026	0.027
Other services	0.004	0.006	0.001	0.009	0.020	0.026	0.012	0.008	0.008	0.028	0.025	1.027
Labour total	0.016	0.262	0.050	0.013	0.045	0.039	0.018	0.043	0.036	0.205	0.037	0.047
Labour income from outside	0.000	0.000	0.000	0.000	0.000	0.000	0.000	0.000	0.000	0.000	0.000	0.000
Labour from outside	0.007	0.015	0.929	0.011	0.023	0.031	0.014	0.011	0.010	0.024	0.030	0.032
Capital	0.136	0.136	0.023	0.345	0.698	1.003	0.462	0.304	0.285	0.516	0.947	1.010
Small farmer	0.051	0.051	0.009	0.130	0.262	0.377	0.174	0.114	0.107	0.194	0.356	0.380
Marginal farmer	0.030	0.030	0.005	0.076	0.154	0.222	0.102	0.067	0.063	0.114	0.209	0.223
Large farmer	0.030	0.030	0.005	0.077	0.155	0.223	0.103	0.067	0.063	0.114	0.210	0.224
Self-employed in non-agriculture	0.018	0.018	0.003	0.046	0.093	0.134	0.062	0.041	0.038	0.069	0.127	0.135
Labour	0.015	0.256	0.049	0.013	0.044	0.038	0.018	0.042	0.035	0.200	0.036	0.046
Services	0.000	0.007	0.001	0.000	0.001	0.001	0.000	0.001	0.001	0.005	0.001	0.001
All other households	0.006	0.006	0.001	0.016	0.033	0.047	0.022	0.014	0.013	0.024	0.044	0.047

on. Similarly, one unit increase in demand for wheat will increase total income by 1.228 units, one unit increase in demand for *jowar* will increase total income by 0.953 units and so on.

The multipliers are small because more than half of the impact is on the commodities obtained from outside the village. Multiplier impact will increase when some manufacturing (even at small scale) activity like processing of food grains and oilseeds takes place in the village.

Table 7.2

Total Output, Income and HH Income Multipliers

Sr. No.	*Sector*	*Output Multipliers*	*Income Multipliers*	*HH Income Multipliers*
1	Wheat	1.793	1.228	1.189
2	*Jowar*	1.671	0.953	0.922
3	*Bajra*	1.291	0.448	0.434
4	Maize	1.805	1.185	1.147
5	*Tur*	1.165	0.204	0.197
6	Pulses	1.219	0.423	0.410
7	Castor	1.666	1.246	1.207
8	Groundnut	1.636	1.281	1.241
9	Cotton	1.024	0.039	0.038
10	Fruits & vegetables	1.144	0.215	0.208
11	Other crops	1.576	1.151	1.116
12	Animal husbandry	1.936	1.108	1.074
13	Cotton ginning	1.966	0.158	0.152
14	Construction	1.217	0.413	0.398
15	Education	1.063	1.002	0.073
16	Bangle vendor	1.157	0.369	0.358
17	Fruit & vegetable vendor	1.742	0.765	0.743
18	Barber	1.456	1.074	1.042
19	Carpenter	1.210	0.494	0.480
20	Cloth shop	1.157	0.358	0.347
21	*Paan* shop	1.278	0.331	0.321
22	PDS shop	2.085	0.744	0.721
23	Transport	1.430	1.013	0.983
24	Other services	1.463	1.089	1.057

The education sector has a forward linkage with the wheat sector as wheat is used for preparing mid-day meals in village schools. Similarly, per unit change can be studied for all the sectors in which change is instituted. The maximum impact on the increased output generated in the economy is due to increase in the consumption of PDS services with multiplier of 2.08 followed by maize with value 1.80 and wheat sector with multiplier of 1.79. Within the economy the sectors which have maximum impact in absolute value terms due to the increased expenditure are wheat, animal husbandry, *paan* shop, cloth shop and education as these sectors have the maximum consumption within the village and more demand for these items would be generated.

Impact of NREGA Works on the Village Economy

Six check dams were de-silted in the village during the year 2006-2007. The total cost of the works was Rs. 586131, all of which was the labour cost (there was no material cost incurred). The effect of this cost on the economy is worked out by assuming its distribution as that of the total income of labour. Out of this, the labour households spends Rs. 297579 (approximately 50 per cent of Rs. 586131) on items which are produced inside the village (such as, wheat, *jowar*, *bajra* etc.) and the rest of the expenditure is incurred on items which are imported or bought from outside the village (rice, pesticides etc.). By distributing the amount Rs. 297579 among the sectors in the ratio of household expenditure, we get a column. This column is multiplied with the inverse matrix, and by adding these, we get an additional output of Rs. 452219, additional value added of Rs. 226577 and additional household income of Rs. 196823 in the village economy. In other words, the effect will be in terms of increase in expenditure on items produced in the village and also the items brought from outside the village. The effect of the increase in output of sectors having production in the village will increase the income of the hired workers as well as those of the capital. This will again have an impact on the expenditure structure of different occupational households.

Of the additional GVA generated in the village, 34 per cent is contributed by labour from inside and outside the village, and 66 per cent is contributed in the form of capital. Of the 34 per cent contribution, 15 per cent is contributed by internal male labour, 6 per cent is contributed by internal female labour, and the rest 13 per cent is contributed by labour from outside. Similarly in the increased income of the households, the share of marginal farmers is 28 per cent, followed by labour households (24 per cent). In all, the cultivator households will share 62 per cent of the increase in the household incomes.

The impact of this expenditure on the output as well as occupation wise household income is given in Tables 7.3 and 7.4.

Table 7.3, which presents data on the increase in the village output due to the NREGA works, shows that the absolute increase is the highest in agriculture (Rs.1.74 lakh), followed by self-employed in non-agriculture (Rs.1.67 lakh) and animal husbandry (Rs.53,077). In all, the total increase is Rs.4.20 lakh, which is 2.23 per cent of the base output. In terms of percentage growth, self-employed in non-agriculture has experienced the highest rate, 4.53 per cent. The highest increase in the output of self-employed in non-agriculture is likely to be due to the increased demand for these products in the village economy.

Table 7.3

Increased Output Due to De-silting of the Six Check Dams

Output	*Base Rs.*	*Increased Rs.*	*Growth Per cent*
Agriculture	10256406	174535	1.70
Animal husbandry	2989812	53077	1.78
Construction	1927027	25451	1.32
Self-employed in non-agriculture	3687510	167023	4.53
Total	18860755	420086	2.23

Table 7.4 presents data on the increased household incomes arising from the NREGA works. The increase in the household incomes is smaller than that in output because all output does not go to income. The table shows that the overall increase has been Rs. 1.97 lakh, which is 1.17 per cent of the base income. The maximum increase in income has gone to farmers, as the demand for food has increased from NREGA incomes. Small and large farmers have, therefore, benefited maximum in terms of increase in income. The labour households have experienced

the lowest increase, though they have experienced high direct impact from NREGS in terms of wage incomes. It needs to be added that when we add the direct incomes generated under the NREGS works, the total increase in household incomes will be Rs.7.82 lakh (Rs.5.56 lakh + Rs.1.96 lakh).

Table 7.4

Increased HH Income due to De-silting of the Six Check Dams

HH Income	*Base*	*Increased*	*Growth*
Marginal farmer	3879411	55891	1.44
Small farmer	2043283	32851	1.61
Large farmer	2057010	32999	1.60
Self-employed in non-agriculture	1423202	19918	1.40
Labour	4744524	46973	0.99
Services	2170760	1204	0.06
All other HH	472098	6986	1.48
Total	16790288	196822	1.17

Impact of Additional Works on the Village

The above effects are of the NREGS works (construction of six check dams), which have already taken place in the village. Now let us have a look at the effects of the proposed works, which can be carried out in the village. As mentioned in the earlier chapter, these works have come as suggestions from the village during our discussions with the leaders and people in focus group discussions. There will be an additional expenditure of Rs. 1559882 in the village when these works are implemented. This will raise the output generated in the village, GVA, to the tune of Rs. 781554 and household income amounting to Rs. 678920 (Tables 7.5 and 7.6).

Table 7.5 presents data on the increased output in the sectors of the village economy achieved through increased expenditure of the households from NREGS incomes. This includes both, the works already undertaken (effect 1) as well as the proposed works (effects 2 to 8). The sector-wise impacts reflect the pattern of consumption of the items provided within the village.

If these works are taken up, the highest increase in output will be in the food grains (the increase being the highest in wheat, followed by maize), the demand for which will increase due to the increase in incomes from NREGA works. The output of wheat will increase by Rs. 3.69 lakh, of maize by Rs.0.96 lakh and of pulses including *tur* by 0.98 lakh. The output of fruits and vegetables will increase by Rs. 0.96 lakh. Since castor and groundnut are not important in the local consumption, there will not be any input on their output. The next important sector will be animal husbandry, the output of which will increase by Rs.2.36 lakh, followed by the construction sector (Rs.1.13 lakh). The output of self-employed in non-agriculture (shops and business) will also increase significantly. The total impact in terms of the increase in output will be Rs.20.12 lakh, as against the total NREGs expenditure of Rs.15.59 lakh. It needs to be noted that the per unit change in wheat is maximum with value 1.184, followed by animal husbandry and transport sector as these sectors have better linkages with the wheat sector as cow dung manure forms part of the animal husbandry sector, and goes as substantial input in the wheat production, similarly wheat sector gets inputs from transport sector in form of tractor and bullocks.

The differences in the size of the impacts arise from the differences in the size of the labour costs of the different proposed works. (The labour costs are presented at the end of the table.) The implications are that: (a) labour-intensive works (with higher labour costs) have higher impacts in terms of output, and (b) the initial impacts will be higher on agriculture, as it will raise food consumption in the initial stages.

We have not taken material costs into consideration because most of it comes from outside the village and, therefore, it will not have much multiplier impact on the village economy. However, when the village economy starts producing some materials locally, the values of the multiplier will go up.

It also is to be noted that the impact will be much more than what it appears in the table, i.e. the second round impact. Though this second round impact cannot be captured in this table (as the values of the multiplier coefficients are fixed in this SAM), there will be considerable second round impact that may raise the values of the multipliers. This aspect of the impact will be discussed at length later.

Table 7.5

Increased Output in Sectors Achieved through Increased Expenditure of Labour Households under NREGA Works—Past and Proposed Works (Rs.)

Sector	*Effect1*	*Effect2*	*Effect3*	*Effect4*	*Effect5*	*Effect6*	*Effect7*	*Effect8*	*Total*
Wheat	82961	59985	5662	28308	23354	56616	34394	77847	369127
Jowar	4298	3108	293	1467	1210	2933	1782	4033	19124
Bajra	2304	1666	157	786	649	1572	955	2162	10251
Maize	21625	15636	1476	7379	6088	14758	8965	20292	96219
Tur	12001	8678	819	4095	3378	8190	4976	11262	53399
Pulses	10086	7293	688	3442	2839	6883	4182	9465	44878
Castor	0	0	0	0	0	0	0	0	0
Groundnut	0	0	0	0	0	0	0	0	0
Cotton	1436	1038	98	490	404	980	595	1347	6388
Fruits & vegetables	21550	15582	1471	7353	6066	14707	8934	20222	95885
Other crops	18274	13213	1247	6235	5144	12471	7576	17147	81307
Animal husbandry	53077	38377	3622	18111	14941	36222	22005	49805	236160
Cotton ginning	0	0	0	0	0	0	0	0	0
Construction	25451	18402	1737	8685	7165	17369	10552	23882	113243
Education	32132	23233	2193	10964	9045	21928	13321	30151	142967
Bangle vendor	2917	2109	199	995	821	1991	1209	2737	12978
Fruit & vegetable vendor	18933	13690	1292	6460	5330	12921	7849	17766	84241
Barber	2335	1688	159	797	657	1593	968	2191	10388
Carpenter	11413	8252	779	3894	3213	7789	4732	10709	50781
Cloth shop	38744	28014	2644	13220	10907	26440	16063	36355	172387
Paan shop	40838	29528	2787	13935	11496	27869	16931	38320	181704
PDS shop	30618	22138	2090	10448	8619	20895	12694	28731	136233
Transport	10131	7325	691	3457	2852	6914	4200	9506	45076
Other services	11094	8021	757	3785	3123	7571	4599	10410	49360
Total	452218	326976	30861	154306	127301	308612	187482	424340	2012096

Note: The effects imply the following:

Effect 1= Desilting of six check dams, Labour cost: Rs. 586131

Effect 2= Laying pipelines to distribute water in the wards, Labour cost: Rs. 423800

Effect 3= Deepening of the tank, Labour cost: Rs. 40000

Effect 4= Construction of child care centres, Labour cost: Rs. 200000

Effect 5= Paving of internal roads-Phase I, Labour cost: Rs. 165000

Effect 6= Paving of internal roads-Phase II, Labour cost: Rs. 400000

Effect 7= Construction of toilets, Labour cost: Rs. 243000

Effect 8= Digging two more tanks (Digging+Pitching), Labour cost: Rs. 550000

Table 7.6 presents the increase in the incomes arising from the works already undertaken (i.e. effect 1) as well as the proposed works under the NREGS in the village. The total increase in the village income will be Rs.14.6 lakh, of which the highest increase will be in capital (Rs.5.13 lakh), followed by income to farmers (Rs.1.93 lakh to marginal farmers, Rs.1.13 lakh to small farmers and Rs.1.14 lakh to large farmers). Male labour will get Rs.1.21 lakh while female labour will each Rs.0.46 lakh, and labour from outside will earn Rs.1.03 lakh. Once again, the second round impacts will be significant, but not included in the multiplier analysis.

Table 7.6

Increase in Income of Labour, Capital and Households Arising from Increase in Expenditure of Labour Households under NREGA Works—Past and Proposed Works (Rs.)

	Effect1	*Effect2*	*Effect3*	*Effect4*	*Effect5*	*Effect6*	*Effect7*	*Effect8*	*Total (Effect2 to Effect8)*
Labour M	34976	25289	2387	11934	9846	23869	14500	32820	120645
Labour F	13202	9545	901	4505	3716	9009	5473	12388	45537
Labour from outside	29754	21514	2031	10153	8376	20305	12336	27920	102635
Capital	148645	107477	10144	50721	41845	101442	61626	139482	512737
Marginal farmer	55891	40412	3814	19071	15734	38142	23171	52445	192789
Small farmer	32851	23753	2242	11209	9248	22419	13619	30826	113316
Large farmer	32999	23860	2252	11260	9290	22520	13681	30965	113828
Self-employed in non-agriculture	19918	14402	1359	6797	5607	13593	8258	18691	68707
Labour	46973	33964	3206	16028	13223	32056	19474	44077	162028
Services	1204	871	82	411	339	822	499	1130	4154
All other households	6986	5051	477	2384	1967	4768	2896	6556	24099
Total	423399	306138	28895	144473	119191	288945	175533	397300	1460475

To put it differently, the change in the expenditure level of labour households will have maximum impact on the household incomes of small farmers followed by large farmers, marginal farmers and labour households. The marginal cultivators will get maximum benefits because they cultivate their small farms and also work as agricultural workers in others' farms. The least affected by this change are services households.

Employment Generation through NREGS

Employment multiplier for different sectors can be interpreted as the number of person days generated in the economy due to an increase in the output in a sector, caused by an increased consumption of that product arising from an external shock in the form of an increase in income of labour. For example, if there is an additional expenditure on wheat, due to the increase of expenditure by labour, the final demand for wheat increases, and the employment in terms of person days generated in the whole of the economy due to this sector will also increase as per the value of the multiplier. Similarly, multipliers of all the sectors are multiplied by the additional expenditure incurred by the labour in respective sectors. This will give us estimates of the employment generated in the economy due to the changes in the different sectors.

To get the detailed employment generated in each sector, we have multiplied the employment coefficients of each sector by the sector-wise effect of the NREGS works (already undertaken) on output. The additional employment generated is given in Table 7.7. The table also shows that the employment multiplier for sectors like barber, other services, fruits and vegetable vendor, carpenter are higher than the production sector except for *jowar* and *tur*, which would generate more number of person days in the economy due to increase in the output. More number of person days has been put into these two sectors but the return in terms of output have been very less. Also, the multipliers of the non-agriculture sectors are higher than the producing sectors like wheat, *jowar* etc. When there is an increase in the income of the labour households due to NREGA wages, they spend more on personal care, "other services", fruits and vegetables, education and all other service providing sectors. Due to this spending, the output of these sectors rises and therefore requires more people and creates more number of person days in the economy.

Table 7.7

Present and Indirect Employment Generated by NREGS Works Already Undertaken, by Sectors and Sex (Person Days)

	Base				*Increase*		*Growth (Per cent)*	
	Present Employment Total	*M*	*F*	*Indirect Employment*	*M*	*F*	*M*	*F*
Wheat	2041	1085	956	80	46	34	4.25	3.59
Jowar	1312	727	585	28	17	12	2.30	1.99
Bajra	44	22	22	3	1	1	6.65	6.65
Maize	4473	2500	1973	66	36	30	1.43	1.54
Tur	384	200	184	102	51	51	25.58	27.80
Pulses	144	73	71	20	11	9	15.04	12.65
Castor	114	65	49	0	0	0	0.00	0.00
Groundnut	76	59	17	0	0	0	0.00	0.00
Cotton	8834	6861	1973	3	1	1	0.02	0.06
Fruits & vegetables	216	101	115	58	29	29	28.53	25.06
Other crops	0	0	0	0	0	0	0.00	0.00
Animal husbandry	1291	426	865	23	23	0	5.36	0.00
Cotton ginning	16320	12720	3600	0	0	0	0.00	0.00
Construction	2925	1637	1288	39	39	0	2.36	0.00
Education	7300	7300	0	177	177	0	2.42	0.00
Bangle vendor	400	400	0	10	10	0	2.60	0.00
Fruit & vegetable vendor	1540	720	820	102	102	0	14.19	0.00
Barber	1025	1025	0	27	27	0	2.59	0.00
Carpenter	3491	3491	0	55	55	0	1.58	0.00
Cloth shop	640	640	0	8	8	0	1.30	0.00
Paan shop	730	730	0	62	62	0	8.51	0.00
PDS shop	480	480	0	36	36	0	7.50	0.00
Transport	1195	1045	150	20	20	0	1.87	0.00
Other services	2655	2555	100	75	75	0	2.95	0.00
Total	57630	44862	12768	994	826	167	1.84	1.30

The above table shows that the present employment in the village economy is 57630 person days. The indirect employment generated in the economy due to NREG interventions (de-siltation of the six check dams) is 994 person days, an increase in 1.67 per cent in the person days generated. Of this indirect employment, 826 are man days and 168 are women days.

If this indirect increase of 994 person days of employment is compared to the direct increase in employment of 9812 person days under the NREGA workers (already undertaken in the village), the former turns out to be more than 10 per cent of the latter. This is significant. It is interesting to note that the increase is less for women than, for men. In fact, the increase of 167 person days for women is about 17 per cent of the total increase (994 person days), though under the NREGA works, women's share in the total person days generated is much more, i.e. 56 per cent (5492 person days for women in the total of 9812 person days generated under NREGS). This indicates the tiny share of women in the mainstream employment in the village, though they are willing to work much more in the economy.

Table 7.8

Employment Multiplier

Wheat	2.639
Jowar	8.024
Bajra	1.834
Maize	4.796
Tur	8.844
Pulses	2.440
Castor	2.084
Groundnut	1.999
Cotton	1.811
Fruits & vegetables	2.989
Other crops	1.229
Animal husbandry	1.695
Cotton ginning	2.868
Construction	1.987
Education	5.609
Bangle vendor	3.950
Fruit & vegetable vendor	7.277
Barber	12.501
Carpenter	5.348
Cloth shop	0.588
Paan shop	1.870
PDS shop	3.538
Transport	2.966
Other services	7.925

It needs to be noted that the indirect employment would have been much larger if a large part of the additional income (from NREGS) was spent on goods and services produced in the village. However, since the village is less developed, about half of the goods and services consumed in the village come from outside, with the result that the multiplier impact is reduced.

Table 7.9 presents data on indirect impact of potential NREGS works. That is, it presents the number of additional days of employment generated due to increased output of the sectors arising from all NREGS works, including potential works. Part A refers to the additional man-days generated while Part B refers to the additional woman-days generated through the employment multiplier effects.

Table 7.9

Number of Additional Person Days Generated due to Increased Output of Sectors

Sector	*Effect1*	*Effect2*	*Effect3*	*Effect4*	*Effect5*	*Effect6*	*Effect7*	*Effect8*	*Total (Effect2 to Effect8)*
Part A. Man-days									
Wheat	46	33	3	16	13	32	19	43	159
Jowar	17	12	1	6	5	11	7	16	58
Bajra	1	1	0	0	0	1	1	1	4
Maize	36	26	2	12	10	24	15	34	123
Tur	51	37	3	17	14	35	21	48	175
Pulses	11	8	1	4	3	7	5	10	38
Castor	0	0	0	0	0	0	0	0	0
Groundnut	0	0	0	0	0	0	0	0	0
Cotton	1	1	0	0	0	1	1	1	4
Fruits & vegetables	29	21	2	10	8	20	12	27	100
Other crops	0	0	0	0	0	0	0	0	0
Animal husbandry	20	2	0	1	1	2	1	3	10
Cotton ginning	0	0	0	0	0	0	0	0	0
Construction	39	28	3	13	11	26	16	36	133
Education	177	128	12	60	50	121	73	166	610
Bangle vendor	10	8	1	4	3	7	4	10	37

Contd...

...*contd*...

Sector	*Effect1*	*Effect2*	*Effect3*	*Effect4*	*Effect5*	*Effect6*	*Effect7*	*Effect8*	*Total (Effect2 to Effect8)*
Fruit & vegetable vendor	102	74	7	35	29	70	42	96	353
Barber	27	19	2	9	7	18	11	25	91
Carpenter	55	40	4	19	16	38	23	52	192
Cloth shop	8	6	1	3	2	6	3	8	29
Paan shop	62	45	4	21	17	42	26	58	213
PDS shop	36	26	2	12	10	25	15	34	124
Transport	20	14	1	7	6	13	8	18	67
Other services	75	55	5	26	21	51	31	71	260
Total	826	584	54	275	226	550	334	757	2780
Part B Days for Women									
Wheat	34	25	2	12	10	23	14	32	118
Jowar	12	8	1	4	3	8	5	11	40
Bajra	1	1	0	0	0	1	1	1	4
Maize	30	22	2	10	9	21	13	28	105
Tur	51	37	3	17	14	35	21	48	175
Pulses	9	6	1	3	3	6	4	8	31
Castor	0	0	0	0	0	0	0	0	0
Groundnut	0	0	0	0	0	0	0	0	0
Cotton	1	1	0	0	0	1	1	1	4
Fruits & vegetables	29	21	2	10	8	20	12	27	100
Other crops	0	0	0	0	0	0	0	0	0
Animal husbandry	0	0	0	0	0	0	0	0	0
Cotton ginning	0	0	0	0	0	0	0	0	0
Construction	0	0	0	0	0	0	0	0	0
Education	0	0	0	0	0	0	0	0	0
Bangle vendor	0	0	0	0	0	0	0	0	0
Fruit & vegetable vendor	0	0	0	0	0	0	0	0	0
Barber	0	0	0	0	0	0	0	0	0
Carpenter	0	0	0	0	0	0	0	0	0
Cloth shop	0	0	0	0	0	0	0	0	0
Paan shop	0	0	0	0	0	0	0	0	0
PDS shop	0	0	0	0	0	0	0	0	0
Transport	0	0	0	0	0	0	0	0	0
Other services	0	0	0	0	0	0	0	0	0
Total	167	121	11	56	47	115	71	156	577

The above table shows the number of man-days and woman-days that will be generated in the village economy when the potential NREGA works are taken up in the village. The works will generate 2780 man-days and 577 woman-days. As seen above, the smaller number of woman-days generated in most sectors as well as in the total economy reflects the low participation of women in the village economy. The table shows that for men, the highest employment generated will be in agriculture (661 days), followed by non-agricultural employment. In the case of women, however, almost the entire increase in employment will be in agriculture.

The employment multipliers are expressed in person days, because if we measure employment in persons, there would be duplication in estimation as persons would work in more than one sector/crop production.

Impact of Reduction in Unpaid Work

As seen in Table 5.7 (chapter 5), women and men spend 18810 person days (3315 man-days and 15494 woman-days) in the village on unpaid work that can be reduced through NREGS works. The potential NREGS works are likely to reduce this unpaid work considerably. If we assume that 80 per cent of the unpaid work is likely to be reduced through the works, 15048 person days will be released for NREGS works in the village. At the wage rate of Rs. 60 per day, this will generate Rs. 9.03 lakh in the economy.

Out of Rs. 9.03 lakh, the households will spend Rs. 437688 (approximately 50 per cent of the amount) on items which are produced inside the village (such as, wheat, *jowar*, *bajra* etc.) and the rest of the expenditure is incurred on items which are imported or bought from outside the village (rice, pesticides etc.). By distributing the amount Rs. 437688 among the sectors in the ratio of household expenditure of all the households put together, we get a column. This column is multiplied with the inverse matrix, and by adding these, we get an additional output of Rs. 656846, additional value added of Rs. 346385 and additional household income of Rs. 294329 in the village economy.

The increased output in the different sectors, achieved through reduction in unpaid work is presented in Table 7.10.

As in the case of the other multipliers, the maximum output gains will be for agriculture, as the increased wage income of women will be largely spent on food items. The maximum increase is observed in wheat (Rs.86831), fruits and vegetables (Rs. 34129), pulses (Rs. 29082) and maize (Rs.22719). The increase in the output of animal husbandry is of the order of Rs.103525. In short, bringing unpaid work of men and mainly women into the public domain will increase the mainstream output significantly.

Table 7.10

Increased Output in Sectors Achieved Through Reduction in Unpaid Work of Men and Women

Sectors	*Rs.*
Wheat	86831
Jowar	6113
Bajra	3741
Maize	22719
Tur	15298
Pulses	29082
Castor	0
Groundnut	0
Cotton	2801
Fruits & vegetables	34129
Other crops	31575
Animal husbandry	103525
Cotton ginning	0
Construction	29390
Education	56216
Bangle vendor	9417
Fruit & vegetable vendor	22540
Barber	7489
Carpenter	23852
Cloth shop	45356
Paan shop	48331
PDS shop	33110
Transport	31245
Other services	29384
Total	656846

The increase in the household incomes emanating from the reduction in unpaid work through NREGA works is presented in Table 7.11. The table shows that the total increase in income will be of the order of Rs.640712, of which the major share of income will go to farming households, a little less than one-third of the total will be these households. The largest share of this will go to marginal farmers and then to large and small farmers. Labour households also will experience an increase in their income though of a smaller size. As expected, capital and labour from outside will get a much larger share. The lowest gain will be of services households.

Table 7.11

Increase in Income of Labour, Capital and Households Achieved Through Reduction in Unpaid Work of Men and Women

	Rs.
Labour total	60680
Labour from outside	52056
Capital	233648
Marginal farmer	87852
Small farmer	51636
Large farmer	51870
Self-employed in non-agriculture	31309
Labour	59163
Services	1517
All other households	10981
Total	640712

The multiplier impact of the reduction in unpaid work on the employment in the village economy is presented in Table 7.12. This has been computed using the employment multipliers of the SAM. The table shows that in all, there will be an increase of 1589 person days of work in the economy. This will be in addition to the direct employment generated in the construction of the assets which would reduce unpaid work of women and men. Once again, maximum employment is generated in agriculture, followed by education and then by employment in the non-agricultural sectors. In short, the reduction in the unpaid work of women in the economy will have considerable impact on the income output and employment in the village economy.

Table 7.12

Number of Additional Person Days Generated due to Reduction in Unpaid Work of Men and Women

Sector	*Person Days*
Wheat	84
Jowar	40
Bajra	5
Maize	69
Tur	130
Pulses	27
Castor	0
Groundnut	0
Cotton	5
Fruits & vegetables	91
Other crops	0
Animal husbandry	45
Cotton ginning	0
Construction	45
Education	309
Bangle vendor	34
Fruit & vegetable vendor	122
Barber	85
Carpenter	115
Cloth shop	10
Paan shop	74
PDS shop	39
Transport	60
Other services	200
Total	1589

To sum up, the above discussion shows that a small investment of Rs 5.86 lakh in the form of de-silting six check dams in a poor tribal village can have multiple impacts on the village economy in terms of increase in output, income and employment in the mainstream economy of the village. Though the NREGS works continued for 91 days and generated less than 10000 person days of employment for 161 households, it could trigger a process that generated some positive impacts on the economy.

Our simulation exercise for potential NREGA works also produces optimistic results in terms of income, output and employment increase in the villages. Our analysis also shows that there is a good scope for NREGA works for reducing unpaid work of men and women in the economy. If the unpaid workers are released from the drudgery of this work by appropriate NREGA works that shift the unpaid work in the public domain, they will be able to work (if not anywhere else, on NREGA works), and this will generate direct and indirect employment and incomes in the village economy.

Multipliers Underestimate the Impact

A striking feature of the above analysis is that, the values of the multipliers are low. The main reason for the low value is the fact that about half the products consumed in the village come from outside the village. That is, a considerable part of the impact has gone outside the village, which is not really a loss to the total economy.

It is important to note that the values of the multipliers are likely to increase if the right kind of works is selected. For example, availability of water supply will encourage farmers to introduce changes in agriculture that may increase the values of the multipliers. Let us examine the case of Nana Kotda. Each of the check dams in Nana Kotda is, on an average, 30 m. long, 1.5 m. deep and has the capacity of storing 45,000 cubic metre (1 cubic metre feet: M^3 = 1000 litres) water. That is, the village had created a storage capacity of 2,70,000 cubic metre water in the village by constructing six check dams. Since the storage of water gives 2.5 times additional water supply through seepage, the village had created a capacity of providing 625000 cubic metre water in the village. However, this capacity had declined due to the siltation of the check dams over time. When the check dams were de-silted under the NREGS (all check dams need de-silting after every 4-5 years), it de-silted 8268.22 cubic metre of soil through digging. This de-silting increased the storage capacity by 8268.22 cubic metres to reach the original capacity of the check dams. The de-silting had the following impact on the village economy:

- The groundwater level in the village increased with the result that groundwater is now available at 80 feet, even in the summer, instead of at 150 feet. The wells, which had dried up earlier, now have water. All the 200 wells now have good water supply.

- The area under irrigated crops has increased, particularly for those crops that are grown only under irrigation. The village has 461 ha. (1188 acres) net area under cultivation. Before the de-silting of the check dams, the gross cropped area in the village was 561 ha, implying 80 ha area was cropped more than once. (Cotton, a major crop in the village, being a long-term crop that takes 8 months to grow tends to reduce the area under multiple crops in the village). After the de-silting of the check dams, there has been an increase of 225 ha in the gross cropped area, implying the gross cropped area is now about 786 ha. The main increase has taken place in (irrigated) wheat by 100 ha and in the area under summer crops, namely black millet, *jowar* (a cereal) and *mung* (a pulse) by 60 ha. This has improved the productivity coefficients as well as the employment coefficients of agriculture.
- The area under cotton has not increased, but its productivity has increased due to improved water supply, also resulting in its labour intensity. Similarly, there has not been much increase in the area under castor, but there has been an increase in its productivity and labour intensity.
- In addition, a new crop, *variyali*, which is a highly profitable cash crop is now grown in the village on 25 acres by some farmers after the first year of NREGA. This area is likely to increase further with irrigation. It is also observed by the *talati* that people will grow more vegetables around their homes once the surety of water supply increases.
- The consumption of electricity per unit of water had declined, as water is now available at higher level in wells. There has been a decline in the cost of electricity by 50 per cent. This has reduced the cost of irrigation per acre.
- In addition, fodder (i.e. crop residues) on farms has increased due to increased gross cropped area. This has helped animal husbandry and dairying in the village.

In short, the farmers in the village have already shifted to more productive, more remunerative and more labour-intensive crops, changing the production and employment multipliers. Again, availability of nutritious grass also has contributed to improved productivity of animals considerably.

The present multiplier analysis has not been able to capture these changes as it has assumed that the values of the multipliers are constant. This is because SAM is a static model, and it assumes that all multiplying coefficients are static. This dynamics can be captured only after a new SAM is constructed for the village for the second year.

It is also assumed in our analysis that the share of the goods coming from outside the village remains the same. This situation is also likely to change gradually due to several reasons. According to local farmers, this share has slightly changed as local people consumed more of local crops this year (particularly wheat, *bajra*) and supplied more of local cotton to the ginning factory. It is also observed that with assured irrigation, farmers may grow more vegetables which are now imported to the village from outside.

In the long run, particularly with more water availability and its assured supply, many more changes are likely to occur in the village economy: (1) the surplus generation in the village may lead local production of other consumption goods, (2) an improvement may take place in health, nutrition, education and skills of people; it may take place as a consequence of NREGS works (as we shall see later). This will tend to increase skills and productivity of labour, (3) again, reduction in unpaid work of men and women, brought about by NREGA works will improve their productivity, which in turn will have an impact on the value of multipliers.

In short, the above factors are likely to increase the value of multiplier considerably. Well-planned right kind of NREGA works will increase the values of the multiplier coefficients gradually.

According to the *talati* and local farmers, it is possible to harvest enough water to irrigate the entire cultivated land in the village. However, this region (i.e. Idar *taluka*/block) is declared a dark zone, i.e. the area where digging of new wells is not permitted and the government does not provide electricity for new connection for drilling wells and bore wells. Once water harvesting is undertaken on a large scale and water availability is stabilised, these restrictions may be removed. In this context, deepening the existing ponds, and deepening of the local river are suggested by local farmers. The total cost of this is expected to be Rs. 10.00 lakh, of which 85 per cent will be labour cost. It has been estimated that 700 workers will get work for 6 months, if these works are taken up under the NREGA. In addition, digging of two more ponds also is seen as feasible and desirable to store more water. According to the *talati,* all these works will raise the level of irrigation to almost 100 per cent in the village.

The values of the multipliers can thus increase continuously, raising the impact of NREGS works over the years.

Maximising Values of Multipliers

It is seen above that the values of multipliers are likely to increase, if the right kind of NREGS works are planned systematically. How to increase the values of the multipliers should be a major question to be addressed under the planning and implementation of NREGA.

Basically, the strategy should aim at increasing the production of goods and services that are consumed in the village. The larger the share of the consumption of the goods and services produced in the village, the larger will be the values of the multipliers. Similarly, larger the export of the goods and services from the village (produced in the village), the larger will be the values of the multipliers. The value of the multiplier for the village economy will also depend, in addition to the extent to which people consume local goods and services, on: (1) the distribution of income in the village (the higher is the share of the poorer sections, the higher will be the value of the multiplier, and (2) the labour intensity of the production (for the employment multiplier) in the village. It must be noted that with the expansion of NREGA works, both these factors will move in the favourable direction to raise the value of the multiplier. In other words, there will be acceleration in the value of the multiplier as NREGA progresses. We propose the following strategy in this context:

Labour-Intensive NREGA Works For Labour-Intensive Growth: To start with, the value of the multipliers will be high if the works are labour-intensive and are likely to promote labour-intensive sectors in the economy. Labour-intensive NREGA works will increase the incomes of those workers—largely poor—whose marginal propensity to consume is very high. They will consume more food in the initial years resulting in higher demand for food grains. This, in turn, will push local agriculture upwards. In other words, labour-intensive NREGA works will increase the income of the poor directly and subsequently, promote the sectors (i.e. agriculture) where the poor are located. The increased productivity in agriculture will increase incomes of agricultural and rural labour.

Agriculture growth, including diversification of crops and increased production, will gradually generate surplus that will lift agriculture from subsistence levels to surplus generation level. This will not only increase the proportion of the goods consumed locally in the village, but also encourage farmers to sell their products outside village and/or promote agro-processing units within the village. Both of these will raise the values of multipliers, though the second option will be a more positive impact. This will encourage the badly needed gradual shift of agricultural workers, to non-agricultural sectors.

NREGA Works to Promote Quality of Life: NREGA works such as water harvesting and provision of potable water to people, drainages and waste disposal, sanitation and public hygiene facilities will improve the quality of life of people. The improved health of people, brought about by ensuring potable water and clean environment, will: (1) improve health and thereby reduce health related debts and vulnerability arising from health related expenditure, (2) reduce the loss of person days of work for workers and improve labour productivity arising from good health. These will have a highly favourable impact on the values of the multipliers.

NREGA for Health, Education and Other Basic Infrastructure: NREGS works that fill in the gaps in the education and health related infrastructure also can have a positive impact on the value of the multipliers, though these assets may not be very labour-intensive when constructed. This can happen in two ways: Firstly, easy access to these facilities and improved quality of these services will improve education levels and health status of the local population, improving their productivity and enabling them to participate in skilled work. Secondly, this infrastructure will create a number of jobs/services in the local economy in the form of teachers and staff to man these facilities such as child care centres, health centres, cooking for children etc.

Construction of basic infrastructure including connectivity will create an enabling condition for economic growth in the village. It will attract private investments in small and large enterprises, which in turn, will raise local production and thereby the values of the multipliers.

NREGA Works for Reducing Unpaid Work: NREGA works that reduce unpaid work of men and particularly women will also raise the values of the multipliers. To start with, such works will release women (and children) engaged in drudgery to undertake productive work in the labour market, including NREGA work. That is, apart from generating employment in the process of construction of the assets that reduce unpaid work, the works will promote employment of women in the market. Secondly, the NREGA works that reduce unpaid work will generate employment opportunities in the mainstream economy in several sectors. Regeneration of common lands that will improve access of fodder to women, will promote animal husbandry and dairying, which is a highly labour-intensive activity. Also, child care centres (day care included) will not only reduce women's work in child care, but will also ensure healthy development of children in their early childhood. This is because it will be possible to provide professional care of children for their healthy intellectual and physical growth. In the process, there will be an increase in the employment in the economy to operate child care centres and crèches. And thirdly, and more importantly, the increase in wage incomes of women will have multiplier impact in terms of income, output and employment multipliers in the village economy. As seen earlier, the values of the multipliers will be larger if the works are planned well.

Size of NREGA Funds for Significant Impact: And finally, the NREGA works will have a significant impact when the size of the programme is large enough to generate large scale employment, to meet the demand for such work. Scattered and intermittent implementation of NREGA, undertaken by the sweet will of administration or *panchayats* (as in the case of Nana Kotda) will not have the desired impact on the economy. The experience of Nana Kotda has shown that there is no concept of right to work incorporated in the way NREGA is implemented in Gujarat state and many other states in India at present. Neither there is any attempt to provide continuous employment to workers nor is there any strong demand coming from workers to start NREGA works. Consequently, the works are at a low level, not making any systematic attempt to maximise multiplier impacts of the works. Unless the size of the programme is upscaled significantly, NREGS is not likely to achieve much in terms of its long-term impact on the economy.

Going Beyond Multiplier Analysis

NREGA works are likely to have impact on the village economy in several other areas which cannot be estimated through a multiplier analysis. This multiple impact that goes beyond the multiplier analysis is discussed in the following paragraphs:

1. *Impact on Health Status in the Village*: The NREGS works that reduce unpaid SNA and non-SNA work of women and the poor is likely to improve the health status of the village population:

- Regular availability of clean potable drinking water is likely to protect the population from water-borne diseases, and improve the general health of the population.
- Construction of drainage will improve the cleanliness in the village, and thereby reduce the chances of occurrence of diseases through undisposed waste water.
- Construction of toilets will also improve the level of cleanliness in the village, and also improve public health status.
- Reduction in unpaid drudgery of women will reduce their time stress, and provide them more time to relax or to work.
- Construction of child care centre will improve general health of children, who will receive nutritious food and clean environment. It will help in their healthy physical and intellectual development.

In short, the kind of NREGA works proposed here, will improve the health status of the population in multiple ways. This will reduce their expenditure on health (which is usually private expenditure) and improve their productivity at work. Considering the fact, that ill health is one of the major risks that throws people in poverty, the improved status of health will go a long way in reducing vulnerability and poverty of people.

2. *Impact on Education Status in the Village*: As seen earlier, the level of literacy in the village is less than satisfactory. Many children in the school-going age are frequently engaged in collection of fodder, fuel wood, water etc. or in animal grazing. Assuring water supply at the doorstep, regeneration of common lands for fuel and fodder as well as child care centres will reduce unpaid work of children. This will enable them to attend school regularly. This will particularly be beneficial to girl children, who stay back at home either to take care of their younger siblings, or to help in collection of water, fodder etc. and other household work.

In addition, construction of two pre-school rooms will ensure healthy intellectual development of pre-school children in the village.

3. *Improved Access of Women to Productive Work:* As seen above, the burden of unpaid work restricts women's entry into the labour market. Since NREGA can address this burden, it can release women for more productive work in the labour market. NREGS will provide productive employment to women immediately, as well as in the long run through promoting development of labour-intensive sectors in the economy.

Contributing Towards Diversification of the Village Economy

As regards the impact of the potential NREGA works, one can say that the increased productivity in agriculture and animal husbandry will improve income levels of the households, and reduce poverty in the village. This will also help in turning subsistence farming into profitable farming. Diversification of crops, increased area under more productive crops like wheat, *bajra*, *jowar* and under new crops as well as increased productivity in agriculture are bound to lead the village economy to diversification: (a) the increased agricultural income and surplus will lead to increased savings and investment in agri-business or agro-processing, and in non-farm economic enterprises, (b) the increased demand for non-food products will encourage local enterprises to undertake new enterprises, and (c) there will be an overall increase in trading in the village.

This diversification is likely to be labour-intensive, as it will promote labour-intensive agriculture, diversification in the primary sector and labour-intensive processing as well as trading. Clearly, all these developments, if achieved in many villages/regions will contribute towards labour-intensive sustainable economic development of the regional economy.

NREGA: A Component in Full Employment Strategy

It needs to be underlined that NREGA can only be a component of a full employment strategy in an economy. It can be a first step, an essential, and critical step, towards full employment, but by itself (alone) it cannot lead the economy to full employment.

It will be an essential first step, because: (1) it will generate massive employment for people, particularly for the poor at the bottom, at the prevailing minimum wages to construct labour-intensive assets, (2) it will generate assets, which in turn, will generate large scale employment in the second, and subsequent rounds, (3) it will generate minimum incomes for people, who will raise the aggregate effective demand in the economy (which in turn will give a push to economic growth), and (4) it will construct/ensure basic infrastructure and ecological regeneration—both of which will provide a sound foundation for economic growth in the concerned regions.

However, the process towards full employment will continue only if it is supported by supplementary policies:

- Construction of durable assets will require skill training (to start with, on the job training or short training) in the areas of masonry, carpentry etc. Assets/infrastructure like durable approach roads and internal roads, water harvesting structures, watershed development, forestation will need training. The NREGS will have to incorporate this aspect in the scheme.

- Ensuring productive use of the assets/infrastructure constructed under NREGS will need support in terms of credit, technical guidance, marketing support etc. It will be necessary to link NREGS with ongoing programmes as well as additional programmes like entrepreneurship development training etc. to ensure that the assets generated, are used. For example, if an irrigation facility is created, farmers will need support in terms of access to inputs, technical guidance, credit etc.
- In order to see that NREGS does not promote development at low productivity/incomes, it will be necessary to link it with the mainstream development, if necessary through diversification, promoted through well-designed projects.

Summing Up

While concluding this chapter, it will be important to note that NREGA works will have, in the subsequent rounds, multiplier impacts on the output, income and employment levels in the village. Also, substituting unpaid work by NREGA works, will also have multiplier impacts on the economy. It will be highly desirable to increase the value of these multipliers by selecting the assets well. Assets that promote equitable and labour-intensive growth, will raise the values of the multipliers. Systematic planning of works, keeping in mind the features of the village economy will give maximum results in terms of: (1) economic growth of the economy, (2) reduction in unpaid work/drudgery, and (3) engenderment of the development.

8 Reorienting NREGA and NREGS

The present study has drawn attention to the potential of an employment guarantee programme like the NREGS in a developing economy like the Indian economy. The multiplier analysis has shown that even in a poor village located in one of the most 200 backward districts in India, NREGS can make significant positive impact on the economy. It has also shown that if undertaken on a scale and implemented well, in the short run, the NREGS can reduce poverty at the bottom and empower the poor. And if planned well, it can have highly positive output, income and employment multiplier effects on the local economy in the medium and long run. These works can also raise the multiplier coefficients and accelerate the process of development subsequently. The NREGS has a good potential for transferring unpaid work of women, both SNA and non-SNA, into productive work in the mainstream economy. NREGS can also relieve women from spending long hours on collection of water, fuel wood, fodder etc. and on child care by strengthening local infrastructure like drinking water, fuel wood and energy security, fodder security, child care facilities etc. The availability of extra time can help women to access better opportunities in the labour market. The reduction in unpaid work can also have multiplier impact on the economy that will give another push to the income, output and employment in the economy.

The study has also identified an approach to maximise the values of the multipliers in the short and long run. It has been shown that the value of the multipliers can be raised by selecting works that promote the production of the goods that are consumed in the economy as well as exported outside; works that are labour intensive in the construction phase and promote labour-intensive sectors in the post construction phase; works that improve quality of life of people and productivity of workers; works that improve infrastructure related to health, education and quality of life; and works that reduce unpaid work of women. Clearly, this calls for systematic planning of works, keeping in mind the needs of the local economy and its growth potential.

The positive impacts of NREGS go beyond the multiplier analysis: NREGS works can have positive impact on overall health and education status of the population; it can lead to gender equality and in the long run it can contribute towards pro-poor and engendered development of the economy.

Another important finding of the study is that NREGS does not yet give any guarantee of work. In fact, its performance in terms of guaranteeing the entitlements to workers is very poor. Since the guarantee of work and the related entitlements are at the core of NREGS, it is necessary to give them the highest priority. The entitlements also will mean multifold expansion of the programme, which will enable it to play its developmental role in the economy.

In order to create a significant impact of NREGS at the macro level, it is important that NREGS is treated as a major programme that can have multiple macroeconomic impacts. Now that NREGS is spread over the entire country (rural areas), and in 2009-10 covered 52.57 million rural households, generated 2830 million person days and spent about Rs.38,000 crore, it cannot be treated as a small programme. There is therefore a need to plan for NREGS keeping in mind this developmental role of the programme. We have made some recommendations keeping in mind this role of NREGS. It needs to be underlined, however, that NREGS needs supplementary interventions to ensure construction of the right kind of assets and productive use of the assets generated under the scheme. Unless this is organised the scheme may not yield optimum benefits.

Implications for Modifying NREGS Design

The above discussion implies that there is a need to reorient NREGS and to modify its design. Reorientation refers to changes in the emphasis while redesigning refers to addition of new features into NREGS.

Reorientation in NREGS: There is a need to enforce the following existing features with renewed focus:

- *Strong commitment to the basic entitlements to workers:* the first important reorientation required for NREGS to focus on guaranteeing the basic entitlements of NREGS, as this is at the core of the programme. As seen earlier, this focus will enable multipliers to work in the economy.
- *Long-term perspective:* NREGS will have to be viewed in terms of its medium- and long-term impact on the economy, and its planning will have to facilitate this long-term role. The provision of preparing a systematic perspective plan under the scheme needs to be enforced strictly. Such a plan will have to be prepared in a multi-level framework when necessary.
- *Strong planning component:* organising horizontal coordination and ensuring convergence of NREGS with ongoing programmes and processes will have to be an essential element of planning. Convergence will enable construction of durable assets along with the maintenance of the 60:40 labour-material ratio.
- *Decentralised planning and implementation:* decentralisation under NREGS will help in incorporating local needs and local potentials on the one hand and ensuring local participation, bringing transparency and accountability and in systematic monitoring on the other. It is essential therefore that this usually neglected component of NREGS is enforced seriously.
- *Social mobilisation:* the role of social mobilisation is critical in the enforcement of NREGS. Putting in place the different committees at state, district, block and village levels will go a long way in encouraging mobilisation of local people. Supporting NGOs as implementers and as social auditors will also help a lot.

Modifications in the design of NREGS: In addition to the above, the scheme needs some modifications in its designing. We strongly recommend the following:

- *Skill training:* it will have to be an important component of NREGS. It needs to be recognised that construction of quality infrastructure, systematic management of natural resources etc.

definitely requires skilled labour. Skill acquisition will help in improving productivity as well as employability of workers. NREGS should allow for skill formation on the job or through specially designed short-term courses.

- *Additional assets in list:* there is a need to include some infrastructural assets related to quality of life of the poor in the list of permitted assets. These assets could be drinking water, sanitation, public hygiene, child care centres, and critical and basic infrastructure for health and education. The required material component should come from other programmes.
- *Maintenance of public assets*: considering the fact that lack of proper maintenance of roads and other public infrastructure is a serious problem in India and this results in serious losses in the economy, inclusion of maintenance of public infrastructure will go a long way in maintaining the infrastructure on the one hand and generating regular wage employment for masses on the other hand. The successful case of the maintenance of public roads programmes in Bangladesh has shown that it keeps roads in good condition, reduces the cost of frequent repairs and creates surplus for further construction of roads (Rabbani, 2006). The other examples of countries which have included road maintenance in their employment programmes include Indonesia (*Padata Karya*) and South Africa (Expanded Public Works Programme, EPWP).
- *Inclusion of services*: this brings us to the question of including certain services under NREGS. There are several critical services which are important for women, children and the poor but which have not been provided by the government due to lack of funds and other reasons. These services include child care particularly day care for children; maintenance of public hygiene, water supply and roads, care of the disabled etc. NREGS can include these services by providing employment to beneficiaries for 3 to 4 months or so. The rationale behind the inclusion of services is that: (1) the persons performing these services are trained on the job so that their employability improves, (2) these services, which are very important, are provided to the community on rotation basis but continuously, and (3) in the long run these services can

be converted into permanent services available to communities. Several countries have included services, such as child care, care of the old and the sick (particularly HIV/AIDS patients), cooking for community, and other social services as a part of employment guarantee. *Jefes de Hogar* of Argentina, *Padata Karya* of Indonesia and EPWP of South Africa are again some of the examples of this.

- *Labour-based infrastructural development*: ILO has initiated a very useful programme on labour-based infrastructural development in many African countries (Miller, 2006; Islam, 2006). The EPWP of South Africa is a good success story in this context. The rationale of this programme is to maximise employment in the construction of infrastructure like roads, buildings, bridges, airports etc. The programme uses light equipments in the place of heavy machines whenever feasible. This reduces cost of construction of infrastructure on the one hand and expands employment avenues on the other. This approach emphasises that the quality of infrastructure is up to the mark, i.e. the quality of infrastructure is not compromised to generate employment. The issue of the ratio of labour cost and material cost is important here. However, this can be worked out by selecting the right kind of infrastructure and the labour-intensive component of infrastructure for NREGS. Convergence of infrastructure development programmes like Bharat Nirman, PM's rural road programme (Pradhan Mantri Gram Sadak Yojana) etc. with NREGS could be very important here.
- *Focus on unpaid work*: subsistence (unpaid) work in the labour market and unpaid domestic services including care are serious obstacles to the participation of women (and poor) in productive employment. The paradox of simultaneous existence of unpaid work and high level of un/under-employment indicates that there is good potential of bringing unpaid work out in the public domain to release unpaid workers for productive work in the labour market. It is believed that NREGS, through construction of the required infrastructure, can perform this task. Though there are some scattered programmes in the areas of child care, rural energy, water supply etc. they are far from adequate. There is

a need to develop a focused and effective strategy to reduce unpaid work, which is a big root cause and a major hurdle in gender equality. Since a lot of this work can be planned at the local level, we believe that reduction in unpaid work should be a major focus of NREGS.

To sum up, NREGS needs a new orientation to serve as a scheme that generates productive assets in the economy. It needs a medium/long-term perspective and goals, strong planning and some additional features that can enable it to perform well as a scheme (along with being a scheme that empowers the poor) that contributes towards the shift of the economy to a full employment path.

Some Additional Recommendations

Based on our field study, we make some additional recommendations: (1) the limit of 100 days should be raised to 200, at least in selected backward areas and for ST and SC population, (2) stress should be laid on dissemination of NREGS to villagers (ICE—information, communication and education) so that people know their entitlements clearly under the programme, (3) social audit should be organised to ensure public participation on the one hand and the accountability of administration to people on the other, (4) supervision and monitoring should be strengthened to see whether employment guarantee and other entitlements are enforced.

While concluding this study it can be observed that an employment guarantee scheme (under a legal act) can address the national concerns of developing countries in multiple ways: (1) it can empower people, particularly the poor, by ensuring them the legal entitlements and strengthening the decentralised democracy, (2) it can address the present employment challenge in these countries directly and indirectly by guaranteeing work at the lowest level on the one hand and by expanding the labour absorbing capacity of the mainstream economy on the other, (3) it can develop infrastructure that contribute towards creating an enabling condition for growth, and (4) it can reduce unpaid work by shifting it into the mainstream economy to relieve unpaid workers to access better opportunities in the labour market. The challenge is to maximise these benefits as well as maximise the values of multipliers—employment, output and income multipliers—by selecting the right kind of assets and by ensuring the use of productive assets.

References

Acharya, Sarathi (1990). *The Maharashtra Employment Guarantee Scheme: A Study on Labour Market Intervention*. New Delhi: ILO.

Altman, M. (2007). *Employment Scenario to 2014*. Zambia: HSRC (Human Sciences Research Council).

Antonopoulos, Rania (2007). "Impact of Employment Guarantee Programmes on Gender Equality and Pro-Poor Economic Development", *Background Paper* No-1, *A Review of Employment Guarantee Policies and Related Gender Dimensions*, Research Project No-34, supported by Gender Team, Bureau of Development Policy and UNDP, New York.

Antonopoulos, Rania and Marzia Fontana (2006). "Hidden Vacancies? From Unpaid Work to Gender-Aware Public Job Creation: Toward a Path of Gender Equality and Pro-Poor Development", Paper Prepared for Levy Economics Institute Conference on *Public Employment Guarantee*, October 13-14.

Bhaduri, Amit (2007). "Alternatives in Industrialization", *Economic and Political Weekly* 42(18). May 5-11.

Bhalla, G.S. (2007). "Globalization and Employment Trends in India", *Presidential Address*. Hyderabad: Indian Society of Labour Economics, CESS.

Bhalla, Sheila (2007). "Inclusive Growth? Focus on Employment", Paper presented at seminar on *Making Growth Inclusive with Special Reference to Employment Generation*, June 28-29, Delhi.

Central Statistical Organisation (2008). *Input Output Transactions Table (2003-04)*. Government of India.

Dandekar, Kumudini (1983). *EGS of Maharashtra: An Employment Opportunity for Women*. Pune, India: Gokhale Institute of Economics and Politics.

Datar, Chhaya (2007). "Failure of National Employment Guarantee Scheme in Maharashtra", *Economic and Political Weekly*, August 25.

De Janvry, A. and K. Subbarao (1986). *Agricultural Price Policy and Income Distribution in India*. New Delhi: Oxford University Press.

Dev, Mahendra (1995). "India's (Maharashtra's) Employment Guarantee Scheme", *Economic and Political Weekly* XXX (41-42), October.

Developing Support Centre (2000). *The Bopal Principles: The Non-negotiable Principles for Natural Resource Management*. Bopal, Ahmedabad District.

Devereux, Stephen and Colette Solomon (2006). "Employment Creation Programmes: The International Experience", *Issues in Employment and Policy Discussion Paper*-24, August. Geneva: Economic and Labour Market Analysis Department, ILO.

Farrington, John and Rachel Slater (2006). "Introduction: Cash Transfer – Panacea for Poverty Reduction or Money in Drain?", *Development Policy Review* 24 (5).

Fullwiler, Scott T. (2005). "Macro-economic Stabilization through an Employer at Last Resort", *Working Paper* No. 44. Centre for Full Employment and Price Stability, USA: University of Missouri Kansas City.

Government of India (2005). *The National Rural Employment Guarantee Act 2005*. New Delhi: Ministry of Law and Justice.

Gupta, Smita (2008). "Performance of the Rights-based NREGS: Initial Experiences and Possible Causes", Paper presented at the International Seminar on *NREGS in India*. New Delhi: IHD and Centre de Science Humaines.

Hirschman, A.O. (1958). *The Strategy of Economic Development*. New Haven, USA: Yale University Press.

Hirway, Indira (2003). "Indian Experience in Time Use Survey", in Government of India (ed.), *Applications of Time Use Statistics*. New Delhi: Central Statistical Organization, Government of India.

———. (2005). "Enhancing Livelihood Security through National Employment Guarantee Act: Towards Effective Opertionalisation of the Act", *Indian Journal of Labour Economics* 48, November 4. Ahmedabad: Centre For Development Alternatives.

———. (2007). "Stock Taking Paper: Implications of Time Use Patterns for Public Employment Guarantee Programmes in Global South", *Background Paper* 2 to Research Project No. 34 on *Impact of Employment Guarantee Policies on Gender Equality and Pro-poor Economic Development*. USA: Levy Economics Institute.

———. (2008). *Restructuring of Production and Labour under Globalization: Study in Textile and Garment Industry in India*. New Delhi: ILO.

Hirway, Indira and P. Terhal (1994). *Towards Employment Guarantee in India: Indian and International Experiences in Rural Public Works Programme*. New Delhi: Sage Publications India Pvt. Ltd.

Hirway, Indira and Subhrangsu Goswami (2007). *Valuation of Coastal Resources: The Case of Mangroves in Gujarat*. New Delhi: Academic Foundation.

Hirway, Indira, M.R. Saluja and Bhupesh Yadav (2008). *Employment Guarantee Programme and Pro-poor Economic Development: Construction of Village SAM for Nana Kotda, Gujarat State (India)*. Ahmedabad: Centre for Development Alternatives and Gurgaon: India Development Foundation.

ILO (International Labour Organization) (2004). *Economic Security For a Better World*. Geneva, Switzerland.

———. (2009). *Global Employment Trends*. Geneva: ILO.

Islam, Rizwanual (2006). *Decent Employment through Labour-based Infrastructure*. Geneva: ILO.

Kakwani, Nanak and Fabio Veras Soares (2005). "Conditional Cash Transfers in African Countries", *Working Paper* No. 9. Brazil: International Policy Centre.

Krishnaraj, Maitreyi, Divya Pandey and Aruna Kanchi (2006). *Employment Guarantee Scheme*. New Delhi: United Nations Development Fund for Women.

Miller, Steven (2006). *Employment Intensive Investment Strategies: Linking Sustainable Infrastructural Development and Social Transfers*. Geneva: ILO.

Mitchell, William (2007). "Why Public Sector Job Creation should be Fashionable", *WP* No. 07-03. Australia: Center for Full Employment and Equity, The University of New Castle.

Mitra, Arup (2006). "Labour Market Mobility of Low Income Households", *Economic and Political Weekly*, May 27.

Nurkse, Ragnar (1957). *Problems of Capital Formation in Underdeveloped Countries*. Oxford, UK: Oxford University Press.

Papola, T.S. (2008). *Employment Challenge and Strategies in India*. New Delhi: ILO, Sub-Regional Office for South Asia.

Patnaik, Prabhat (2003). "On the Need for Providing Employment Guarantee", Paper presented at National Institute of Rural Development, Hyderabad. November 4.

Planning Commission, Government of India (2008). "Eleventh Five Year Plan (2007-2012)", *Inclusive Growth: Volume-1*. New Delhi: Oxford University Press.

Pradhan, Basanta K. and Amarendra Sahoo (1996). "Social Accounting Matrix and its Multipliers for India", *Margin* 28(2), January-May.

Pradhan, Basanta K., M.R. Saluja and Shalabh K. Singh (2006). *Social Accounting Matrix for India, Concepts, Construction and Applications*. CA, USA: Sage Publications.

Rabbani, Mehnaz (2006). "Employment for Poverty Reduction in Bangladesh: A Review of the Rural Maintenance Program, Research and Evaluation Division", Bangladesh: BRAC.

Rodgers, Gerry (2007). *Decent Work, Social Inclusion and Development*. Geneva: International Institute of Labour Studies, ILO.

Sarkar, H. and M.K. Panda (1986). "Quantity-Price Money Interaction in a CGE Model", *Margin* 18(3): 31-47.

Sarkar, H. and S.V. Subbarao (1981). "A Short Term Macro-forecasting Model for India: Structure and Use", *Indian Economic Review* XVI (1-2).

Saluja, M.R. and Bhupesh Yadav (2006). *Social Accounting Matrix for India 2003-04*. Planning Commission. June.

Sathe, S.P. (2001). "Restructuring the EGS", Paper presented at the Workshop on *Maharashtra's Employment Guarantee Scheme*. Mumbai. May 22.

Sharma, Rita (2008). "NREGA: Impacts and Implementation Experiences: Poverty, Food Security and Environment", Government of India, Ministry of Rural Development, September.

Standing, Guy (2004). *Economic Security for a Better World*. Geneva: International Labour Organization.

Subramabian, S. and E. Sadoulet (1990). "The Transmission of Production Fluctuation and Technical Change in a Village Economy: A Social Accounting Matrix Approach", *Economic Development and Cultural Change* 39 (1):131-73.

Subramanian, Shankar (1993). *Agricultural Trade Liberalisation and India*. Paris: Development Center Studies, OECD.

Tcherneva, Pavlina and L. Randall Wray (2005). "Is Argentina's Job Creation Project Jefes de Hogar a True Employer of Last Resort Programme?", *Working Paper* 34, Kansas City, USA: Centre for Full Employment and Price Stability, University of Missouri.

Tinbergen, Jan (1994). "Foreword" to *Towards Employment Guarantee in India* by Indira Hirway and P. Terhal. New Delhi: Sage Publications.